# Lecture Notes
# in Business Information Processing    312

More information about this series at http://www.springer.com/series/7911

Marcela Ruiz

# TraceME: A Traceability-Based Method for Conceptual Model Evolution

## Model-Driven Techniques, Tools, Guidelines, and Open Challenges in Conceptual Model Evolution

 Springer

Marcela Ruiz 🆔
Utrecht University
Utrecht, The Netherlands

ISSN 1865-1348        ISSN 1865-1356   (electronic)
Lecture Notes in Business Information Processing
ISBN 978-3-319-89715-8        ISBN 978-3-319-89716-5   (eBook)
https://doi.org/10.1007/978-3-319-89716-5

Library of Congress Control Number: 2018940916

Cover illustration: This book is a revised version of the PhD dissertation written by the author at: Universitat Politècnica de València, Spain DOI: 10.4995/Thesis/10251/64553

Printed on acid-free paper

This Springer imprint is published by the registered company Springer International Publishing AG part of Springer Nature
The registered company address is: Gewerbestrasse 11, 6330 Cham, Switzerland

*This book is dedicated to my parents, Jairo and Patricia, and to my sister, Verónica.*

*To Sandro, for designing and instantiating together the best adventures in this beautiful world*

# Preface

This book encompasses a revised version of the PhD dissertation written by the author, at the department of Computer Science of the Universitat Politècnica de València (Spain).

In 2017, the PhD dissertation won the "CAiSE PhD Award," granted to outstanding PhD theses in the field of information systems engineering discussed in 2016.

This book presents various research endeavors for the development of methods and techniques to automate the evolution of software systems. The current book explores the requirements engineering field as a stepping-stone to successful software development processes. The main research objective is to contribute to the computer science field with well-funded requirements engineering solutions for automated software development.

Previous work on rules to generate the conceptual schemas of the OO-method from preconceptual schemas posed the challenge to design a full-fledged environment from requirements to code. As a result, the model-driven architecture, model-based engineering, and traceability-based paradigms have led to the integration of requirement models into software development processes.

As a proof of concept, the development of "A Model-Driven Framework to Integrate Communication Analysis and OO-Method" presents the use of model-based engineering to support information systems. It opened a new landscape where ontologies are used as a main tool to facilitate most of the activities for integrating information systems perspectives. Regarding to the use of model-driven architecture, as the saying goes "the tailor's wife is the worst clad," the book describes the importance to put in to practice model-driven architecture for the development of modelling and transformation tools. The requirements engineering community lacks implementation tools as a mean to facilitate industrial transference. In this book, the application of model-driven architecture is reflected in the development of requirements engineering tools.

Together with my research colleagues Óscar Pastor and Sergio España, we are curious to extend our solutions from requirements to code by introducing solutions for evolving information systems. In practice, information system development seldom starts from scratch. Thus, by enriching from requirements to code solutions with evolution support it is possible to be closer to meeting the needs of the real world. With this objective in mind, we provide "TraceME: Traceability-Based Method for Conceptual Model Evolution."

TraceME covers the spectrum of activities from requirements to code focusing on organizational evolution. This spectrum involves various information system perspectives of analysis that need to be integrated. In this complex setting, traceability and conceptual models are key concepts. Mechanisms to trace software specifications from requirements to code are provided to justify evolution processes, by supporting the connection between old and new specifications. Moreover, it involves guidelines and techniques to facilitate change, measurement, and interpretation of model changes.

This book reflects a research adventure depicted in the shape of different design and empirical cycles of the design science by Roel Wieringa. TraceME is built by making a method engineering effort, which shapes its fragmented nature in chunks. The architecture of TraceME opens a wide window of opportunities for its application in real-world situations. To facilitate industrial adoption, we develop open source tools to support the implementation of the TraceME chunks. For example, one case study and one action-research protocol have been executed in two different organizations in Spain.

The validation of TraceME has taken place in laboratory demonstrations, controlled experiments, action research, and case study experiences in industry. The results of the evaluations have influenced the maturity of the method. We discovered the importance of considering end users' perceptions for discovering needs to mitigate, and the significance of getting knowledge from the application of TraceME in different contexts. The evidence from the evaluations demonstrate that TraceME is feasible for application in evolution projects.

The TraceME method is not finished yet and further research needs to be done in order to achieve a stable version. It will continue evolving, and new evaluations in industry will raise new challenges to be overcome, but in a changing world, this is a typical situation. Information systems development is also changing to be closer to industry. The steps to bring academia out of its "ivory tower" are always vital. For this, the research around TraceME exemplifies opportunities to incorporate implementation partners and real-world use cases.

This book reports on the research experience of the design and evaluation of TraceME. This contribution motivates us to tackle future challenges so as to support evolution projects in the era of big data and IoT.

March 2018                                                                      Marcela Ruiz

# Acknowledgements

During the development of this research project, I have been very happy to meet and share my life with great people. To all of them, I gratefully acknowledge their support and company. In the following, I am going to use a mix of English and Spanish languages to express my feelings.

My PhD advisors have been very important during my research road. Oscar and Sergio have empowered me and created a great work environment for the development of my career. I deeply acknowledge their advice and support. I could not have done this research without them.

Sergio, gracias a ti he descubierto que es posible amar lo que uno hace. Gracias por fundamentar con tu alegría mis bases de investigadora, es un orgullo para mi tenerte como consejero, compañero y amigo. Nuestros proyectos de investigación me han tenido fascinada durante varios años. Gracias por tantas horas diseñando y creando soluciones para modelado organizacional. Tu sonrisa y energía me han motivado a querer siempre ir más lejos y alcanzar grandes metas. La libertad que siento trabajando contigo me llena de confianza y fuerza. Gracias a ti hoy puedo decir que amo lo que hago, ¡Gracias por nuestro futuro como investigadores!

Óscar, trabajar contigo es un privilegio. El desarrollo dirigido por modelos es una línea que me apasiona, y cada día que pasa en el PROS, más me gusta lo que hacemos y todos nuestros desarrollos. Gracias por guiarme, aconsejarme, e iluminarme con tu sabiduría. Gracias por las oportunidades que me das para crecer. Gracias por tu paciencia cuando no comprendo tus decisiones. Gracias por permitirme estar en tu grupo construyendo contigo. Gracias a ti el día de hoy soy una evolución Paisa-Valenciana muy feliz. Gracias por transmitirme tu alegría y vitalidad, eres un ejemplo para mí de que es posible vivir la vida muy feliz ejerciendo una profesión tan bonita como la nuestra. Gracias por correr esta carrera conmigo, por darme tu mano y llenarme de fuerza.

I spent many hours in the lab 1L04 of the DSIC, UPV. My lab mates are vital for my mental and physical health. They are my colleagues and friends:

Gracias Mariajo por ser mi compañera de PhD. Por motivarme y estar conmigo en las buenas y en las no tan buenas. Gracias por salir a correr, tocar la flauta y compartir cenas cenicientiles con vino de la casa. Tu amistad es muy especial para mí.

Paco, gracias por tu sensibilidad y estar siempre dispuesto a ayudar. Gracias por tus consejos y buscar las mejores estrategias para sacar un PhD adelante. Gracias por tus chistes que han alegrado nuestros momentos de descanso. Has hecho feliz mi estancia en Valencia.

Ignacio, gracias por tus sabios consejos y toda la ayuda que me has brindado durante el PhD. Admiro tu practicidad y madurez para enfrentar problemas. Espero que muy pronto podamos hacer trabajos juntos para ponerte como autor.

Agradezco especialmente a JLu por sus consejos, alegría y complicidad; a Nathalie por su cariño; a Urko por los desarrollos en GREAT; a Diego por dibujar una sonrisa en mí; a Vero por ser mi amiga de aventuras; a Nelly por su actitud positiva y entusiasmo; a Fátima, Caro y Diane, gracias por celebrar conmigo tantos logros durante estos años.

Agradezco a Bea, Giovanni y sus niñitas por tantos momentos en los que me dieron su consejo, fuerza y cariño. Gracias Fani por tu amistad, cariño y buenas energías. Gracias por todos los consejos que me has dado durante la realización de mi PhD, gracias por tus ánimos y positivismo, por el futuro que tenemos por delante. Gracias Clara por las conversaciones en las cuales me has hecho reflexionar, gracias por planear conmigo estrategias para asumir los retos de la vida con una sonrisa. Gracias Mario por compartir tantos buenos momentos en el lab y la salsa. Gracias José Reyes por tu actitud positiva y alegre. Gracias Ana por ayudarme con las tareas burocráticas, por tu creatividad y consejos de vida. Agradezco a Arturo González por todas por sus ideas que han sido parte de mi PhD.

I want to acknowledge to the reviewers that gave me feedback in conferences, journals, and meetings. All of you have helped me to improve my work.

I deeply acknowledge to Jolita Ralyté, Raúl Mazo and Renata Guizzardi, for the time they have dedicated reviewing my PhD thesis. Your valuable feedback has helped me to consolidate a very good manuscript.

Thanks to Antoni Olivé, Renata Guizzardi, and Vicente Pelechano for being part of my PhD jury. It is an honour to have your advice and support.

My PhD thesis would not be the same without the collaboration of my colleagues around the world. I have learnt a lot during our interaction, thank you for let me share my expertise with you. Thank you for all the good moments.

Gracias Dolors por nuestro *i*\*+CA, disfruto mucho trabajar contigo. Gracias por todo lo que he aprendido de ti y contigo, por tu entusiasmo y por el camino que tenemos por delante. Gracias Xavi por tus valiosos comentarios, consejos y ejemplo. Gracias por tu actitud positiva y entusiasta por nuestros proyectos.

Thank you Camille for sharing with me your experience and thoughts. Thank you for all the time that you have dedicated to our Delta Analysis, for your valuable feedback and positive attitude. Thank you for receiving me during my stay in Paris, and for all the future projects that we will accomplish together. Gracias Raúl por tu entusiasmo y compromiso, por las oportunidades que me has dado para ser parte de tu equipo.

I want to acknowledge specially to Raian Alí, Iyad Zikra, and Hasan Koç for the nice projects we have developed together. Also, I want to acknowledge to Roel Wieringa for his advices about design science and valuable feedback. Jean Vanderdonkt for being always positive and give me tricks in order to overcome challenges during the PhD. Stefan Bifl for giving me good advices to start my PhD. Giancarlo and Renata Guizzardi for their thoughts and feedback on our research. Thank you for sharing with me your passion and love for research.

I acknowledge very much to Camille for my stay in Paris, it was great to be part of the CRI. Thank you to Elena, Benedicte, Charlotte, Rebecca and Daniel for sharing with me the lunchtime, Christmas parties, and teatime. You let me feel part of your group in very short time.

I acknowledge to my master students Julio Sandobalín and Manuel Ogando. Especially I want to acknowledge Julio for his developments in the line of Delta Analysis. Thank you Viktor and Galina Manweiler for the nice projects we are performing as a team.

Agradezco especialmente a mis profesores Carlos Mario Zapata, Demetrio Ovalle y María Teresa Berdugo; ustedes han contribuido a que hoy sea una gran profesional.

I deeply acknowledge the advice and support of my mentor Sjaak Brinkkemper. Thank you Sjaak for your constant support, and being an inspiring role model for me. You are professional, empathetic and enthusiastic, which makes me feel grateful for the opportunity to work together. Thank you for encourage me and give me the opportunity to develop and express my talents.

I want to thank to my O&I colleagues Jan Martijn, Sietse, Fabiano, Slinger, Marjan, Veronica, Sergio, Marco, and Matthieu for sharing UU experiences.

Thank you Basak for our "support team". It is great to be friends and share many adventures.

Agradezco especialmente a mis amigos en la distancia. A Erica por ser mi diario de aventuras. Gracias por escucharme siempre y tener las palabras exactas. Agradezco a Alejandra, Sandra Mateus, Jhon Edison, Jose Fabio, Yosel, Margarita, Lili, Indira y Ana Filomena. Gracias por darme su cariño y motivarme desde la distancia. Agradezco a Esther por su amistad, compañía y oraciones. Agradezco a mis amigos en México Harvey, Doris y Johan por sus consejos, ánimo y compartir conmigo muchos buenos momentos. También en México agradezco a mi amiga Itzel por haber vivido el doctorado conmigo, Itzel, ¡lo logramos!

En Valencia he contado con ángeles terrenales que han cuidado de mí y me han dado su amor. Kathy, gracias por tu cariño y amistad. Gracias por ser tan especial y ser mi cómplice. Eres una mujer a la que admiro mucho y de la cual estaré eternamente agradecida.

Ana, gracias por compartir conmigo tu visión de vida. De ti he aprendido mucho y he forjado mi personalidad. Gracias por ser mi hada madrina, cuidar de mí y apoyarme. Gracias por gestar conmigo mis proyectos de investigación, crearlos y dar a luz. Gracias por nuestra amistad que durará para siempre.

Marielle, gracias por ser mi hermana Parisina. Gracias por compartir conmigo tus aventuras y escuchar las mías. Gracias por ser tan especial y permitirme ser parte de tu familia. Raúl, gracias por abrirme las puertas de tu casa, ser mi colega y amigo.

Paqui, gracias por tu alegría y compañía. Tú has contribuido a la felicidad de mi estancia en Valencia. Tu apoyo e inteligencia me ha permitido sacar mi PhD adelante y vivir esta etapa lo mejor posible. Gracias por tu cariño y ser una mujer a la que admiro profundamente. Gracias por las grandes aventuras que ahora viviremos como doctoras.

Hoy no estaría aquí si no fuera por el amor y el cuidado de mi familia. Gracias a mi tía Vicky por su amor y complicidad, gracias por ser un ejemplo para mí de dedicación y sabiduría. Gracias Tere, Tavo, Adriana, Nena, Marta y Mauricio. Ustedes han permitido que tuviera una infancia muy feliz y especial. Gracias por tanto cariño y recibirme siempre con un gran abrazo.

Agradezco a mis tíos Jaime Alberto, Albeiro, Nidia, Silvia, Cielo, Manuel y Luz Elena, y a mi abuela Ana Luisa. Gracias por su apoyo, cariño y entusiasmo. Me siento muy orgullosa de nuestra familia. Agradezco a mi tía Amparo y Antonio Aparicio, por su cariño y apoyo.

Verónica, gracias por ser mi hermana y estar siempre conmigo. Gracias por cuidar de nuestros padres y hacerlos felices. Me siento muy orgullosa de lo lejos que has llegado y lo mucho que vas a lograr. Gracias por tu sonrisa y ser parte de los momentos más bonitos de mi vida. Gracias por las futuras aventuras que viviremos juntas, porque somos las mejores.

Agradezco a mis padres Jairo y Patricia, ustedes han permitido que me desarrolle en un ambiente muy feliz y seguro. Gracias por cuidar de mí, amarme, confiar en mí y enseñarme grandes lecciones de vida. Gracias por compartir conmigo los logros alcanzados. Gracias por los valores inculcados y darme libertad para desarrollar mi personalidad. De su ejemplo he aprendido a tener un alto sentido de pertenencia y compromiso por mi profesión. Gracias por los consejos para superar los duros momentos. Gracias por darme su compañía a pesar de la distancia. Me siento muy orgullosa de tener unos padres tan maravillosos como ustedes. Sin su compañía y su fuerza yo no hubiera podido terminar mi PhD, gracias por dibujar para mí los mejores escenarios, gracias por desear un hermoso futuro para todos.

Last but not least, I want to acknowledge to the love of my life, Sandro. Thank you Sandro for sharing with me your life. Thank you for let me be and share exciting moments together. Thank you for the encouragement during the writing of my book, you helped me to be focused and strong. Thank you for your patience and cheer me up. Thank you for supporting my crazy ideas and contribute to their development. Thank you for loving me and creating such a beautiful atmosphere that place me in a peaceful and joyful environment. Thank you for all the adventures that we will live together, for the great moments we will keep as treasures in our hearts. I love you endlessly.

# Contents

# Chapter 1    Introduction

*"I believe that when you find something you love,
you should do it your whole life. Why would you
retire from doing what you love? It's just not what
we do" - Steve McCurry*

The universe is in a constant evolution; from the Big Bang to beautiful starred nights,
planets and galaxies are part of an amazing landscape for our enjoyment. The initial
state before the Big Bang is still unknown, which excites the minds of astrophysics
and scientists around the world. To know *how* and *why* the universe has been developed, scientists promote to understand first how stars, galaxies, and planets are
formed. With the focus on *what* conform the universe, its structure, and the ways it
interacts, scientists have created theories about the evolution process.

Each elementary particle of the universe participates actively in the evolution process. Since human beings are part of the universe, human being evolution is indeed
fascinating. Right now, your brain is creating new neuronal connections and memo-
ries based on the information that is given to you through this book; it means that you
will experience a new version of yourself when you finish reading this book.

On the other hand, society is changing. Every day we are creating new ways to
communicate, to analyse and process information and knowledge, to store information, and how to exploit it. The universe exposes new challenges to be confronted.
The context change and we have to evolve at its pace. *"Species come and go through
time, while they exist they change[1]"*. Our genome suffers variations that give extra
survival probability to new contexts. We are in an adaptation process all the time, for
instance, in organisational contexts, companies need to rethink business processes,
infrastructures, technologies, resources, etc. according to new demands from their
environment or changes in their organisational objectives.

Indeed, information systems evolution and software maintenance are activities
that receive significant dedication by industry. Software maintenance costs have been
growing with the passing of the years until almost reach the 100% of software development cost [1]. Fig. 1 summarises the report of Koskinen about software maintenance costs vs. total software development costs from the 80's to 2000.

---

[1] Charles Darwin. 1809 - 1882

© Springer International Publishing AG, part of Springer Nature 2018
M. Ruiz: TraceME, LNBIP 312, pp. 17–32, 2018.
https://doi.org/10.1007/978-3-319-89716-5_1

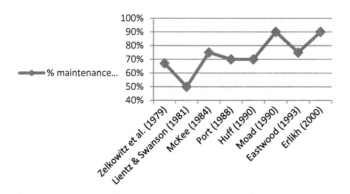

**Fig. 1.** Software maintenance costs in proportion with software development cost [1]

Evidence show how evolution processes demand attention by scientists. New resources and strategies to understand development and evolution are vital for our own evolution. With the perspective of natural selection theory of Darwin, we can see organisational evolution as survival behaviour. Constant organisational change and enterprise innovation must be considered as a fundamental rule of competitive strategy.

Information systems play the main role when evolution is necessary. Software systems, hardware technologies, and organisational actors are adapted to new contexts and environments. Software development seldom starts from scratch. Thus, software development processes are motivated by the need of evolution and adaptation to the environment.

In order to contribute to the requirements engineering field with automated software production methods, this book proposes TraceME to cover the spectrum of activities from requirements to code focusing on organisational evolution. In this sense, the spectrum of activities involves various information systems perspectives of analysis that need to be integrated. For understanding evolution, like astrophysics, we need to understand *what* change is, how it is structured, and how it influences the system.

Providing support to integrate information systems perspectives that are needed for software development processes impose challenging tasks. In this complex setting, traceability and conceptual models are key concepts. Mechanisms to trace software specifications from requirements to code are important to justify *why* each artefact has been specified. Moreover, versions of information systems should be traced in order to get the connection between old and new specifications. The above-mentioned ideas motivate the existence of TraceME.

The Design Science framework proposed by Roel Wieringa shapes the development of TraceME. The analysis of the problem statement, establishing the bases for this research is presented in section 1.1. The research method involving the research goals, research questions, and the tasks to answer the research questions are detailed in section 1.2. The means to achieve the main research goal are presented in section 1.3. A summary of the TraceME method is presented in section 1.4. Finally, an outline of the book is introduced in section 1.5.

## 1.1    Problem statement

### *Model-driven development and model-based engineering*

Since the PROS Research Centre traditionally has been working in the production of software development methods, the model-driven development paradigm (MDD) is the core of the research group. Successful PhD theses have derived in MDD solutions with tool support, bridging the gap between academy and industry [2] [3] [4] [5] [6] [7] [8].

The benefits of MDD are well known [9], [10], [11]:

- The use of models helps us understand information systems through high level of abstractions.
- MDD technologies provide facilities to automate most of the MDD activities like modelling, model-to-model transformations, and model to text transformations.
- Traceability from requirements to code is ensured.
- Evolution of information systems is platform independent because the primary focus is on the models instead of the code.
- Quality of the final software can be tested from early stages like requirements and design.
- Standards promote the use of models to ensure the compliance with rules and laws.

Information systems development projects seldom start from scratch. The MDD approach from requirements to code rarely is applied in complex real-world situations. Apart of all the benefits of MDD, there is a down side that corresponds with the round-trip engineering tasks. In an information systems development project that applies MDD, once the code is generated, models are not updated any more like the typical project documentation. Several solutions have being proposed in the field of reverse engineering. The objective is to convert code back into model, but usually automated reverse transformations cannot make the same modelling abstractions as humans [12]. This problem is magnified when evolution is necessary. For example, if models are used for information systems evolution and they are not synchronised with software implementations, the evolution project is a failure.

Nowadays, the Object Management Group (OMG) is working to promote an industrial consensus on modernisation of existing application by means of the initiative named Architecture-Driven Modernisation (ADM) [13]. This initiative is based on the MDD paradigm to automate reengineering processes. Nevertheless no full-fledge solutions have been obtained in for the reverse engineering process and evolution process.

To take full-advantage of current MDD solutions for information systems evolution and maintenance, round-trip engineering needs to be tackled. Model-based engineering (MBE) solutions for round-trip engineering seems to be a feasible approach to take the most out of MDD when evolving information systems [14]. We assume that information systems development and reengineering are two views of the same activity, every information systems development involves evolution. If an information systems evolution project requires to keep persistent some characteristics of current implementations, model-based solutions that involve human intervention for modelling design seems to be more adequate than automatic specifications. The benefits of MDD can be fully exploited when the potential for automation get more mature [12].

TraceME takes the best of MDD and MBE to facilitate information systems evolution projects. By taking MDD and MBE, we adopt the Conceptual Schema-Centric Development (CSCD), where conceptual schemas are the basis for systems evolution [15]. Despite we know conceptual schemas are different of conceptual models, in TraceME we make use both as synonyms. The reasoning for this is conceptual models are widely used in the requirements engineering community for the specification functional and non-functional requirements of information systems. Since TraceME takes into account different perspectives of information systems, conceptual models are general enough for different modelling purposes of evolution projects.

TraceME consists in chunks that can be assembled and used according to certain needs of evolution projects. For example, when these projects need support from requirements to code, TraceME chunks can be assembled to answer to this need. In addition, when evolution projects require accurate evolution of old to new specifications, TraceME can be assembled to guide such evolution. In Fig. 2, we illustrate how an evolution project can be configured. TraceME provides a set of chunks, for this illustration we call them A, B, C, D, E, F, and G. The evolution project 1 has certain needs that require the assembling of the chunks A, B, and D of TraceME. Then, the chunks can be applied to the evolution project and the relationships among the chunks can be established to accomplish the needs of the evolution project.

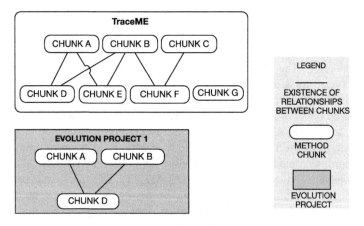

**Fig. 2.** Possible configuration of chunks for an evolution project

## *Why a traceability-based method.*

Traceability support for information systems development and evolution has a significant role. The U.S. Department of Defence currently invests about 4% of its total budget for information technology on traceability issues [16]. Pohl and Ramesh et al. have presented evidence on how failures in software projects traceability have derived in project overruns [17] [18]. Almost 20 years after the publication of the former evidence, software traceability practices are far from mature [19].

In industry, there are two main motivations to apply traceability: because it is mandatory by regulations, and because it is mandatory to apply standards for software quality. Nevertheless, industry seldom implements proper mechanisms to support traceability. The most of the problems to adopt traceability practices in industry rely on the lack of methods and tools [20]. Thus, analysts in charge of information systems projects in the real world are creating their own approaches to manage traceability without any control and discipline. This situation causes high effort to keep traceable information systems development and evolution; also it causes frustration if projects fail because of mistakes in traceability design and implementation.

In the PROS Research Centre, the designs of new methods and techniques are guided by the MDD paradigm. Traceability support is enhanced by its application during model specifications and it is supported in the most of the developed techniques and methods.

The chunks that consist the TraceME method support traceability among models. For example, if the main objective of a certain chunk is to support specification of business process models from goal models, this chunk also provide the traceability facilities from goal to business process models. In addition, if evolution projects require guided evolution of old specifications, the TraceME chunks can be assembled to solve this request by providing traceability among old and new specifications.

The traceability support provided by the TraceME's chunks can be classified by using the study performed by Winkler and Pilgrim summarised in Table 1 [19].

From the perspective of application of traceability in requirements engineering, TraceME supports the traceability usage classified by the ID R2, R7, R8, R10, R11, R12, R14, and R15 (see 0).

Since the model-driven paradigm is applied in TraceME, for the model-driven development classification the following usage ID are supported: M1, M2, M3, M4, M6, and M7.

It is important to clarify that not all the chunks of TraceME support the mentioned traceability usage; it depends on the objective of each chunk that some traceability usage can be profited and exploited depending on the interest of evolution projects.

**Table 1.** Traceability usage in requirements engineering and MDD

| Requirements traceability | | Model-driven development | |
|---|---|---|---|
| **ID** | **Description** | **ID** | **Description** |
| R1 | Prioritising requirements | M1 | Supporting design decisions |
| R2 | Estimating change impact | M2 | Proving adequateness/validation |
| R3 | Providing system adequateness | M3 | Understanding and managing artefacts |
| R4 | Validating artefacts | M4 | Understanding and debugging transformations |
| R5 | Testing the system | M5 | Deriving usable visualisations |
| R6 | Supporting special audits | M6 | Change impact analysis |

| R7 | Improving changeability |
|---|---|
| R8 | Extracting metrics |
| R9 | Monitoring progress |
| R10 | Assessing the development progress |
| R11 | Understanding the system |
| R12 | Tracking rationale |
| R13 | Establishing accountability |
| R14 | Documenting reengineering |
| R15 | Finding reusable elements |
| R16 | Extracting best practices |

| M7 | Synchronising models |
|---|---|
| M8 | Driving product line development |

## 1.2    Research method

For the development of this research project, we conduct a design science project. *Design science is the design and investigation of artefacts in context* [21]. Artefacts are intended to interact with a problem context in order to improve something in that context. For this research project, we design TraceME to support business analysts in their tasks of information systems evolution. The TraceME method is an artefact, and the context consists of business analysts that need to perform evolution projects. For example, a certain business analyst could be performing reengineering activities for adapting the organisation to new regulations, implementing standards, renewing organisational goals, etc.

In design science projects two activities should be considered: design and investigation (see Fig. 3). These activities let us define design problems (DP) related to the design of TraceME, and knowledge questions (KQ) related to finding knowledge about the interaction between TraceME the context where it is applied.

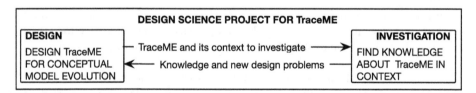

**Fig. 3.** Design science project for the TraceME method

For the design activity, we clarify the social context of the project. It describes the stakeholders that may affect the project or may be affected by it:

- The social context of TraceME involves diverse kinds of stakeholders. Potential users of TraceME, like business analysts, requirements engineers, business consultants, etc., they are part of organisations that need to support their evolution projects. The researchers of this research project: Marcela Ruiz (main researcher), Sergio España (advisor), and Óscar Pastor (advisor), Dolors Costal and Xavier Franch (from Universitat Politècnica de Catalunya), and Camille Salinesi and Raúl

Mazo (from Université de París 1 Panthéon Sorbonne). Industrial partners: everis Spain and SIVSA Spain that have been using the TraceME's chunks; the Univesitat Politècnica de València (UPV) and Generalitat Valenciana (sponsors that provide the budget to support this research).

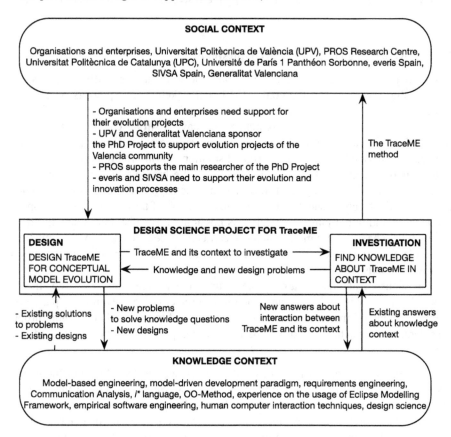

**Fig. 4.** Framework for the design science project of TraceME

For the investigation activity, we describe the knowledge context of this research project:

• The knowledge context of TraceME is founded on model-based engineering and model-driven development. TraceME uses requirements engineering for analysis of information systems from different specification perspectives; some perspectives are supported by the following methods: the Communication Analysis method, the *i** language, and the OO-Method. In addition, the knowledge context contains our experience in the use of Eclipse Modelling Framework for implementing model-driven and model-based tools. In addition empirical software engineering knowledge and human computer interaction techniques are used to validate TraceME in context. We also use our experience in design science projects in order to design the activities of the project.

Fig. 4 presents the framework for the design science project of TraceME. The framework specifies the relationships among the project, social and knowledge context. The framework together with DP and KQ shape the research goals and research questions of this project.

### 1.2.1    Research goals and research questions

In the context of a research project, it is possible to distinguish different goals: the goals of the researcher and the goals of external stakeholders (sponsors or potential end-users).

Apart of our motivation as researchers, we have a strong commitment with the community. We want to improve the way on how software development is performed. We want to provide innovative and original solutions for information systems specifications involving different analysis perspectives. We promote the use of conceptual models as a high level analysis of information systems, models let people communicate and achieve agreements thanks to the instantiation of their ideas in formal specifications. In addition, by using models it is possible to establish traces among different models to have information systems specifications connected. Providing methods and tools for information systems analysis, software development, and evolution, improve our daily life.

The sponsors of this research project support our exploratory research. In this sense, this project is ranked as an exploratory project (a.k.a., technology push projects). This kind of project is motivated by the goals of the researchers without proper consideration of whether or not it satisfies a set of specific stakeholders or end-user needs.

Fig. 5 presents the goal hierarchy of the design science for TraceME. For the hierarchy we focus on the *design science research goals*, which concern to the research goals project. Because of the nature of this Research project has been characterised as exploratory research, *social context goals* (that concern to goals of external stakeholders and real-world problem to improve) are fuzzy. In this state of the project, the social context goals are absent.

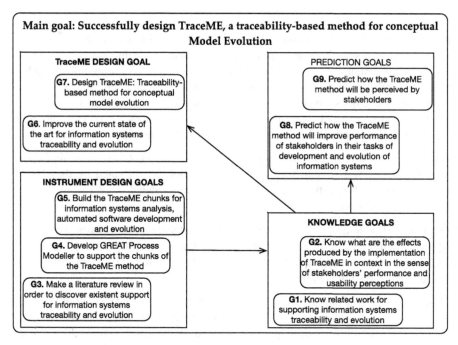

**Fig. 5.** Goal refinement of the design science for TraceME

The TraceME method is the result of an exploratory project. Knowledge goals are dedicated to the exploration of related work for supporting information systems traceability and evolution, and to know the effects produced by the implementation of TraceME in context (G1 and G2). To answer G1, we make a literature review for discovering what the existent solutions (G3) are. Having the description of the related research, we build TraceME with the aim to improve the current state of the art (G6). To answer G2, we build the TraceME chunks and develop a tool for their support (G4 and G5) to perform empirical evaluations. Answering the knowledge question contributes to the TraceME design thanks to the feedback obtained after each experimental task (G7). Here we can distinguish the interaction between the activities of design and investigation described in the framework of design science for TraceME. There are no social context goals; however, TraceME would improve the support for information systems analysis, software development, and evolution.

We design the prediction goals G8 and G9 aiming at generalising the results of empirical exercises to any case of information system evolution where TraceME can be applied. G8 and G9 are high-level goals that would be achieved in the future. Nevertheless, we describe G8 and G9 in this document because these prediction goals are part of the current goal structure for TraceME.

Bellow we introduce the main research goal and the research questions:

> The main research goal is *to successfully design TraceME: a traceability-based method for conceptual model evolution*. To achieve the main goal, we involve model-driven and model-based capabilities to build a set of TraceME chunks to support information system analysis and evolution.

The former goals bring up various challenges that we need to overcome. These challenges derive in a set of research questions. The goals highlight design problems to build TraceME chunks, develop GREAT Process Modeller, and design the TraceME method (TraceME design goal and instruments design goals). In addition, we can deduce knowledge questions (KQ) in order to answer the knowledge goals. Below we present the list of research questions (RQ) derived from design problems (properly called technical research problems- TRP) and knowledge questions.

**RQ1.** (KQ) *What are the existing supports for conceptual model evolution and traceability in information systems?* This research question is motivated by the G1. To answer this research question we establish the current related work for information systems traceability and evolution.

**RQ2.** (TRP) How to design the TraceME method that satisfies model-based and model-driven requirements so that support stakeholders' activities in organisational evolution context? This research question is related to the G6 and G7, which refer to the main research goal of this book.

> **RQ2.1.** (TRP) *How to build the TraceME chunks to support integrated information system analysis, automated software development process and evolution of information systems?* This research question is based on the G5. To tackle this research question we perform a method engineering effort in order to build and assemble the TraceME method chunks.

> **RQ2.2.** (TRP) *How to develop a tool for successfully supporting the TraceME chunks?* This research question is funded on the G4. Due to our experience in the development of CASE tools, we selected the plug-in architecture of Eclipse for supporting each TraceME chunk. The plug-in architecture facilitates further chunks assembling processes when TraceME is applied.

**RQ3.** (KQ) What are the effects produced by the implementation of the TraceME method in real-world contexts in the sense of stakeholders' performance and usability perceptions? This is an empirical research question related with G2. To answer this question we perform an evaluation experience for each TraceME chunk. We perform a comparative experiment, a sensitivity analysis, an action research, and various laboratory demonstrations. As a result, we answer the research questions derived by the knowledge problems placed by each TraceME chunk effects evaluation.

## 1.2.2    Engineering, design and empirical cycles

Since the development of TraceME is in the frame of a design science project, we describe the activities of designing and investigating by means of three tasks (T) that are part of a design cycle: T1 Problem investigation, T2 Treatment design, and T3 Treatment validation.

Since this manuscript describes six years of work on this project, for the sake of brevity, we do not describe all the iterations that we performed over the tasks of the design cycle; instead we present the design cycle that summarises all the iterations (see Fig. 6).

The design cycle for TraceME is part of a larger cycle called engineering cycle, which involves the transference of the treatment design to the real world and its evaluation (this tasks are called implementation and implementation evaluation. It means that the design is implemented to solve real problems in real contexts).

We conceive a system engineering execution sequence for TraceME where implementations are not attempted (because of the nature of this project is exploratory). Fig. 7 presents the tasks of the engineering cycle; it includes the specification of the implementation tasks that could be performed for future research endeavours.

For the tasks related to the treatment validation, we follow the empirical research structure of empirical cycles. Three research cycles have been designed in order to validate some TraceME chunks: Comparative experiment for the *iStar2ca guidelines*, Sensitivity analysis for the *ca2oom integration framework*, and technical action research in everis: validation of the Delta Analysis. The empirical cycle consists of five main tasks: research problem analysis, research and inference analysis, validation, research execution, and data analysis. In general, different validation protocols have been applied according with the population, knowledge questions, and goals of study. For example, for the Delta Analysis technique (one of the TraceME's chunks) we decided to perform a technical action research in the Spanish consulting company everis.

Laboratory demonstrations have been performed to validate the feasibility of TraceME, they are mentioned by are not detailed in the system engineering execution of TraceME for sake of brevity.

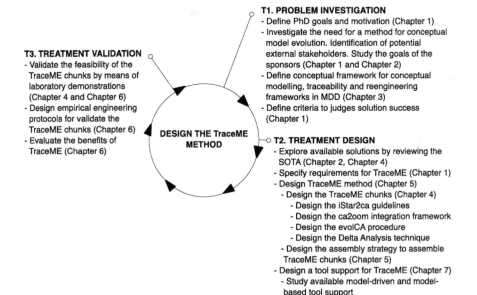

**T1. PROBLEM INVESTIGATION**
- Define PhD goals and motivation (Chapter 1)
- Investigate the need for a method for conceptual model evolution. Identification of potential external stakeholders. Study the goals of the sponsors (Chapter 1 and Chapter 2)
- Define conceptual framework for conceptual modelling, traceability and reengineering frameworks in MDD (Chapter 3)
- Define criteria to judges solution success (Chapter 1)

**T3. TREATMENT VALIDATION**
- Validate the feasibility of the TraceME chunks by means of laboratory demonstrations (Chapter 4 and Chapter 6)
- Design empirical engineering protocols for validate the TraceME chunks (Chapter 6)
- Evaluate the benefits of TraceME (Chapter 6)

**DESIGN THE TraceME METHOD**

**T2. TREATMENT DESIGN**
- Explore available solutions by reviewing the SOTA (Chapter 2, Chapter 4)
- Specify requirements for TraceME (Chapter 1)
- Design TraceME method (Chapter 5)
  - Design the TraceME chunks (Chapter 4)
    - Design the iStar2ca guidelines
    - Design the ca2oom integration framework
    - Design the evolCA procedure
    - Design the Delta Analysis technique
  - Design the assembly strategy to assemble TraceME chunks (Chapter 5)
- Design a tool support for TraceME (Chapter 7)
  - Study available model-driven and model-based tool support
  - Design plug-ins for each TraceME chunk

**Fig. 6.** Design cycle for TraceME and the indication of the chapters that detail the design cycle's tasks

**T1. PROBLEM INVESTIGATION/**
- Define PhD goals and motivation (chapter 1)
- Investigate the need for a method for conceptual model evolution. Identification of potential external stakeholders. Study the goals of the sponsors (chapter 2 and chapter 1)
- Define conceptual framework for conceptual modelling, traceability and reengineering frameworks in MDD (chapter 3)
- Define criteria to judges solution success (chapter 1)

**T2. TREATMENT DESIGN**
- Explore available solutions by reviewing the SOTA (chapter 2, chapter 4)
- Specify requirements for TraceME (chapter 1)
- Design TraceME method (chapter 5)
  - Design the TraceME chunks (chapter 4)
    - Design the iStar2ca guidelines
    - Design the ca2oom integration framework
    - Design the evolCA procedure
    - Design the Delta Analysis technique
  - Design the assembly strategy to assemble TraceME chunks (chapter 5)
- Design a tool support for TraceME (chapter 7)
  - Study available model-driven and model-based tool support
  - Design plug-ins for each TraceME chunk

**T3. TREATMENT VALIDATION**
- Validate the feasibility of the TraceME chunks by means of laboratory demonstrations (chapter 4 and chapter 6)
- Design empirical engineering protocols for validate the TraceME chunks (chapter 6)
- Evaluate the benefits of TraceME (chapter 6)

**REPRISE OF TASK 2**
- Changes on the TraceME design based on empirical results

**T19. TREATMENT IMPLEMENTATION**
- Implement TraceME in a company

**T20. IMPLEMENTATION EVALUATION**
- Establish stakeholders' goals and define a criteria to judge implementation success
- Evaluate effects of the application of TraceME in a company
- Prepare a report with improvements to be included in TraceME (if any)

-Establish the research questions of the comparative experiment, variables and hypothesis.
**T5. RESEARCH AND INFERENCE DESIGN**
- Define the experimental context
- Design the experiment
**T6. VALIDATION**
- Evaluate the experimental design
- Review the instruments for collecting data
- Analyse threats on the experiment validity
**T7. RESEARCH EXECUTION**
**T8. DATA ANALYSIS**
- Analysis of collected data: practitioners' performance and usability perceptions
- Application of statistical tests and corroboration of hypotheses

*Sensitivity analysis for the ca2oom integration framework*

**T9. RESEARCH PROBLEM ANALYSIS**
- Define the goal of the sensitivity analysis
**T10. RESEARCH AND INFERENCE DESIGN**
- Define the research team
- Design the training material for GREAT
- Design the environment where will be carried out the evaluation exercise
- Install the transformation module
- Design the focus group session
**T11. VALIDATION**
- Evaluate the material for the sensitivity analysis
- Check the correct installation of the transformation module
**T12. RESEARCH EXECUTION**
**T13. DATA ANALYSIS**
- Lessons learns
- Reports

*Technical action research in everis: validation of the Delta Analysis*

**T14. RESEARCH PROBLEM ANALYSIS**
- Establish the research questions, variables and hypothesis for the TAR in everis
**T15. RESEARCH AND INFERENCE DESIGN**
- Plan the action research, procedures and protocols
- Design the focus group session
- Define the instruments for measurement
**T16. VALIDATION**
- Analyse threats on the validity
**T17. RESEARCH EXECUTION**
- Study of the everis' context
- Perform the application of delta analysis for the everis' case
- Perform the focus group with the everis' stakeholders
**T18. DATA ANALYSIS**
- Answer research questions
- Analyse and tag the recording with the focus group session

Systems engineering execution sequence                    Empirical cycles

**Fig. 7.** System engineering execution sequence for TraceME

## 1.3    Means to achieve the main research goal

To achieve the main research goals and solve the research questions, four main means
are conceived:

a)  Expert views. We are experts in the model-driven paradigm and model-based
    engineering to provide solutions of the addressed design problems. In addition,
    we have experience in empirical software engineering to design empirical valida-
    tion protocols in order to answer the proposed knowledge questions.
b)  Technical experience. We are expert in model-driven tools as Eclipse. This way,
    we have the necessary knowledge to provide a tool support for TraceME.
c)  Collaboration with other research groups. Our collaborations with other research
    groups increase our assortment of solutions to offer the best designs for
    TraceME.
d)  Action research experiences. We bring the solutions offered by TraceME to in-
    dustry. The main benefit is to make steps to further implement TraceME, also
    learn from the implementation of TraceME in real-world conditions.

## 1.4    The TraceME method in a nutshell

TraceME is a traceability-based method for conceptual model evolution. The
TraceME method is based on a fragmented architecture where various chunks can be
assembled in order to solve needs of evolution projects. We follow the model-driven
development paradigm and model-based engineering techniques to design each
TraceME chunk. With the models as the main artefact for information systems analysis, traceability support is the core of the method as to let the conceptual models to be
traceable. As a result, traceability benefits can be obtained such as estimation of
change impact, understanding the system, tracking rationale, supporting design decisions, proving validation, maintaining artefacts, change impact analysis, and round-
trip engineering tasks.

There are several requirements that one would expect from a method to support information systems evolution. For TraceME we define the following requirements:
i.    It needs to be formally described;
ii.   It needs to be designed in a fragmented manner to allow situational adaptation
      according to the evolution project where it can be applied;
iii.  Provide assembling processes to some predefined evolution projects;
iv.   It need to be supported by tools;
v.    Empirical studies should demonstrate the benefits of TraceME and perceptions of
      potential practitioners; and
vi.   Traceability should be supported.

The mentioned requirements guide our research in the development of TraceME. The
TraceME's chunks offer the following solutions for evolution projects (see Fig. 8): a)
integrative analysis of information systems perspectives, b) delta analysis and meas-

urement for information system evolution, and c) evolution guidance for information systems.

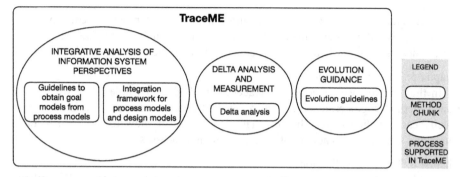

**Fig. 8.** Overview of the TraceME chunks

The TraceME method involves method chunks for goal modelling, communication-oriented business process modelling, and object-oriented modelling. The former method chunks are formally integrated by following ontological integration and method engineering techniques.

Each TraceME chunk is validated by empirical studies in order to analyse its feasibility and stakeholders' perceptions. The feasibility of the method was evaluated by means of analysing subjects' performance. In general, the results present great performance of subjects when applying TraceME. In addition, stakeholders' usability perceptions have been also positively evaluated.

TraceME chunks are implemented in an Eclipse-based tool named GREAT Process Modeller (Global Reengineering Environment for Automated Transformations). The most positive aspect of the tool is the possibility to transfer TraceME to industry by supporting evolution projects.

## 1.5    Outline of the book

This book is organised as follows:

Chapter 2: Related work.

We present a review of the literature to highlight relevant advances in respect of information systems evolution support. The analysis of related work allows us to understand current problems and their impact. The related work is part of the problem investigation tasks for this research project.

Chapter 3: Theoretical framework.

We prepared a theoretical framework in order to establish a commitment about the terminology defined for this research project. In addition, it facilitates a common understanding around the topics discussed in the book. This chapter contributes to the treatment design tasks.

Chapter 4: TraceME chunks: the design.

Since TraceME is a fragmented method, in this chapter we present how each chunk is designed and developed. All the details and formalisations like metamodels and ontologies are described here. This chapter refers to the treatment design tasks.

Chapter 5: The TraceME method.

In this chapter, we describe the TraceME method as a whole. Here we specify how a method engineering effort was applied in order to assembly the method and specify each method chunk. In this chapter, we describe how to use each method chunk and some samples about possible assembling processes.

Chapter 6: TraceME validation.

In this chapter, we describe the validations performed for the TraceME method. We detail each validation experience performed for each method chunk. In addition, we highlight the use of empirical software engineering to formally validate requirements engineering methods. This chapter details the treatment validation tasks.

Chapter 7: Tool support.

In this chapter, we outline the tool support that has been developed for TraceME. It corresponds to various prototypes that support the TraceME chunks. This chapter describe tasks of the treatment design.

Chapter 8: Final discussion.

In this chapter, we discuss the main contributions of the book. We also describe some envisioned short and middle term projects to perform as next steps derived from this research project

# Chapter 2    Related Work

*"Every successful individual knows that his or
her achievement depends on a community of per-
sons working together" - Paul Ryan*

This book has born motivated by our inner desire to contribute to the science with
innovative and fresh information systems evolution methods. Our driver is technology
push [22], which means that our invention (i.e., the TraceME method) does not have
proper consideration of whether or not it satisfies a set of specific user needs (there is
not a concrete market or real industry needs that motivates the development of a solution). Thus, this chapter has two main objectives: 1) to motivate the originality in the
design of TraceME, and 2) to present a literature review that reflects current problems
and impact on information systems evolution projects. We found out that there are no
solutions to the highlighted problems, and then we conclude by providing TraceME.

We investigate research projects that confront information systems traceability
(section 2.1), model evolution measurement (section 2.2), reengineering frameworks
(section 2.3), goal-driven requirements engineering (section 2.4), evolution requirements and information system co-evolution (section 2.5). As a practical case, we present the state of the software productions methods developed in the PROS Research
centre before TraceME. In addition, we describe how TraceME is connected with the
PROS framework increasing its offer of MDD solutions.

## 2.1    Traceability in conceptual model evolution

In a world that lives in continue change; information systems evolution becomes an
inherent activity in the software development process. "Requirements engineering
becomes instead a "relational" process in which the name of the game is continuing
customer engagement" [23]. This relational process happen thanks to the nature of
continues change in requirement models in order to satisfy stakeholder's business and
organisational needs. Thus, analysts (and/or software developers) must to keep a relationship with stakeholders in order to ensure an updated version of software. Resulting software materialises continuing interactions between analysts and stakeholders in
order to support information systems evolution.

In continuing customer engagement, traceability is the core of a new type of "customer relationship management" system [23]. From the point of view of analysts,
traceability makes explicit the connection between information systems evolution and
the impact on stakeholders' organisations.

Practices and benefits of traceability are strongly related with the context of information systems projects and stakeholders goals. Despite many organisations look
at traceability as a mandate to be satisfied (e.g., to follow standards and/or regulations

© Springer International Publishing AG, part of Springer Nature 2018
M. Ruiz: TraceME, LNBIP 312, pp. 33–54, 2018.
https://doi.org/10.1007/978-3-319-89716-5_2

like the Capability Maturity Model Integration (CMMI) and ISO/IEC 15504-5 (2006)), some organisations perceive traceability as an important component for implementing a quality system-engineering program [24].

Mäder & Gotel review the role of traceability in information system evolution projects and traceability maintenance [25]. They highlight why information systems traceability is the core of reengineering and evolving projects. The authors discuss the application of traceability strategies to manage changing requirements in an effective way. The main objective is to assure consistency among evolved models, analyse the impact of software evolution on models, analyse local impact on model evolution, establish traces among models from different information systems perspectives, model versioning, model refactoring, and support software development projects (e.g., agile projects).

Some evidence on the usage of traceability for information systems, problematic and impact are presented in the following subsections.

### *Traceability for managing requirements change.*

Cleland-Huang et al. find information systems traceability strategies as an effective solution to mitigate software failures and manage requirements change [26]. The authors recognise how an inadequate traceability is the major contributing factor that is present in unsuccessful projects. They focus on how traceability is important for supporting impact analysis amongst heterogeneous software engineering components, a vital activity to handle changing requirements effectively.

Cleland et al. confront the aforementioned problems by means of applying an event based traceability (EBT) architecture for information systems analysis and software development [26]. They introduce a monitor to the EBT architecture that identifies changes events on requirements specifications. The authors provide an algorithm aiming at identifying seven change events, which are: create new requirement, inactive requirement, modify attributes, merge two or more requirements, refine requirement, decompose a requirement, and replace one requirement with another. As a result, the algorithm avoids possible introduction of errors and omission of information when the detection of change events and traceability specification is performed manually. The algorithm provides the guidelines to identify changes and establish traceability links that are valuable enough to make evolution analysis without tool support. This approach highlights the current need to provide guidelines to support traceability links specification and changes identification.

### *Traceability for consistency assurance between models and software in evolution scenarios*

Engels et al. have identified the lack of support of software evolution at the model level [27]. Because of models are the central artefacts in model-driven software development projects, and due to the usage of model-based development have became an industrial standard, the evolution of models within software engineering projects requires support for incremental consistency and analysis techniques of a new version of the model after evolution. Several techniques have been proposed to overcome evolution problems at the code-level; if model-driven shall be successful, similar solutions are required at the model level. Models describe a system from different points of view in order to reduce the complexity of analysis. Having the need of specify information systems using different perspectives in mind, consistency assurance between models and software is very important because is the evidence that there exist implementation satisfying all requirements specified in models.

Engels et al. based in the former motivations, have proposed a method for checking semantic consistency requirements for UML models in software evolution projects [28] [29]. They face model evolution as a set of model transformations performed to a model in order to fulfil a set of requirements. The focus in this project is to ensure the preservation of consistency properties by applying traceability strategies after models have evolved. They account elementary evolution steps as creation, deletion, and update of model elements. Each transformation rule is checked in order to analyse if the model is consistent and if it involves some evolutionary steps. As an advantage here, the model is checked just in the case that an evolutionary step is performed. Here the objective is to analyse the evolution locally in order to avoid huge testing task and re-iteration of modelling for model checking consistency.

## Traceability for model refinement and versioning

[30] explore the idea of refinement applied to the software development process. The authors conceive refinement relationships as one of the forms of representing changes within information systems under development with a progressive establishment of traces among models. Models specify information of information systems from different levels of abstractions (from abstract models that specifies requirements of the information system to more concrete models like databases models).

To support model versioning and evolution, [31] have emphasised the necessity for management of change propagation and traceability management. As a practical case, they explore the evolution of UML models mainly working on the target to support consistency checking. Nevertheless, Mens et al. argue that to provide a traceability management, establishment and a control of change propagation is still a challenge for the requirements engineering community.

## Traceability for agile projects

The most important characteristics of agile projects are the importance of people interaction during software development process and the incrementally evolution of software according to a predefined set of iterations. Because of the application of agile methodologies have gained adepts in the last decade, traceability strategies also are applied in the sake of standards fulfilment. For example, in safety-critical projects, traceability among models, code, and test cases is necessary because of government standards and international laws. Cleland-Huang [32] highlights the most important benefits of tracing in agile projects: Change impact analysis, product conformance, process compliance, project accountability, baseline reproducibility and organisational learning. The open challenge here is to provide traceability techniques and strategies to be exploited by software development projects according to their needs and goals. The challenge is to provide "light-traceability" solutions where the benefits of traceability are ensured with affordable resource costs.

## 2.2    Measuring conceptual models evolution

Measurement in software engineering has become a trendy topic for requirements engineers and academics. Qualitative and quantitative information about software and software process are very valuable for decision-making. Industry is especially motivated to get the most out of information systems and its support, measurement in this context play a main role as an activity to provide evidence based on real situations. There exist proposals to measure software change and information systems evolution. In evolving contexts, measurement is vital and necessary.

Regarding to metrics and analysis of software evolution, there are several works dealing with how to measure software systems in changing context. Researchers that work in the field of information system evolution have highlighted the importance of measuring evolution as a strategy to transfer requirements engineering solutions to industry and real world practices. Indeed, information systems evolution projects have different goals and measurement activities must be adapted to context and environmental circumstances. Here the challenge is the provision of metrics and requirements engineering solutions aiming at supporting evolution measurement. The following researchers have endeavoured to discover the need of information system evolution measurement and its impact on industrial practice.

### *Evolution measurement before and after the evolution has occurred*

Mens and Demeyer establish a distinction between the uses of software metrics before and after the evolution has occurred: predictive and retrospective analysis [33]. For example, Gall et al. have proposed a technique to identify changes in code modules after the evolution has occurred (a retrospective strategy) in order to analyse possibilities to restructuring or reengineering opportunities [34]. Below we study how metrics have been applied before and/or after evolution.

**Before evolution:** metrics can be applied for predictive analysis aiming at informing about which parts need to be evolved, which parts are likely to be evolved, and which parts can suffer from evolution [33].

In practice, metrics have been used to assess the quality of software systems. In this case, the results are accounted for discovering which parts need to be evolved (in cases of bad quality). As a result, refactoring techniques are applied for re-designing purposes; metrics are also applied to recognise the most appropriated refactoring technique. Organisations find this metrics very usable because they demonstrate lacks on their quality information technology systems, also this kind of metrics point directly which modules must be evolved.

Another practical usage of metrics is to discover duplicated code; this problematic appears commonly after systems evolve. In addition, metrics are used to detect incomplete code and obsolete code. As a solution of these problems, evolution projects must be performed having the focus on the detected modules to change (i.e., lines of code that are candidate to be changed).

Metrics have been used to detect part of systems that are likely to be evolved; it corresponds to the changeability nature of software requirements. In this case, metrics are based on release histories of software. These kinds of metrics are very sensible and need an active participation of system analysts in order to make decisions on the evolution.

In addition, metrics are needed in order to detect sensitive parts of information systems that can cause problems after an evolution process. In this case, metrics are motivated to find cohesion and coupling of systems modules.

**After evolution**: metrics can be applied to analyse the previous and evolved software to find out whether its quality has improved. In addition, the evolution process is also important to be measured. Evolution process inform about how systems have changed and where the most substantial or intrusive changes were performed.

By analysing previous and evolved software systems, analysts can review if goals of evolution have been achieved. As we mentioned before, in [34] is presented a proposal of coupling metrics based on the analysis of the evolved system.

By analysing the evolution process analysts can understand where and how the changes where performed, also it is possible to analyse why such changes took place [33]. The analysis of why changes have been applied is valuable because it inform about the rationale of the evolution process. The analysis performed on the evolution process is also used to assess cost estimation on the evolution of software systems.

### Evolution measurement as a real world need

Meir Lehman was a very important researcher in the field of software evolution. His contributions have established an important base, which is used by computer scientists around the world. One of the most famous works of Lehman is the laws of software evolution [35]. The Lehman laws have been applied for addressing problems of the real-world [36]. Also, Lehman's laws have been used for specifying metrics to assess software evolution.

In this line of work, in [37] is discussed the need to provide metrics for software evolution and costs estimation. Several points are highlighted:

- It is necessary to provide mechanisms to estimate the amount of human effort and related schedule for accomplishing software evolution tasks.
- Understand and change software is requires a high amount of human effort; it is necessary to provide metrics to measure this effort and provide rationale that justify such effort.

To predict costs of information system evolution is a hard task that demands processing several amounts of data about the project context. Metrics to estimate costs are necessary; these metrics must be general enough in order to make them suitable to any kind of evolution project.

Lehman's laws are general enough to be operationalised in metrics and further customised to be applied in concrete evolution projects. Analysts and managers in charge of evolution projects are needed of methods and techniques that guide the application of metrics and it customisation to fulfil evolution projects requirements.

## *Model measurement*

Models are indeed essential in software evolution processes. They are the point of agreement between analysts and stakeholders. Models are contracts that specify information systems to be developed; they also need to be evolved and evaluated to guarantee their alignment with information systems.

In [38] the importance and impact of model evolution is studied. We review this work, in which we want to highlight the following:

- Understanding information systems evolution requires models that reflect communication and feedback mechanisms that can be used to validate them by observation and measurement of real-world properties and events. Metrics are needed to measure models and conclude about the evolution process. In addition, interpretation guidelines for observing and making decisions are also needed. Interpretation guidelines are context-dependent and they are difficult to be generalised. Empirical evaluations are necessary in order to provide knowledge about evolution that can be generalised.
- As information systems must evolve to keep a pace of the dynamic world, models that specify applications must also be changed and evolved.
- Because of models specify the system in a high level of abstraction, analysis of evolution and improvements performed in the model level have a direct impact on cost and productivity factors. In fact, evolution analysis on models includes the reduction of time to detect, analyse, and correct defects. Also, evolution analysis in the model level increases reliability factors in the sense that it is possible to appreciate quality improvements and performance of information systems.
- A process improvement must be visible and preferably measurable, then the evolution process provide benefits to be perceived by stakeholders and user communities. It is important to provide evolution reports outside the programming process, and then the impact is easily demonstrated to stakeholders. Only the information related about evolution of information systems, which specify stakeholders' processes, resources, etc. has meaning value in the real world. In this context, models play the main role in information system evolution analysis.
- Models that reflect change with sufficient precision and details are no sufficient. A framework must be provided to constitute a realistic environment for model validation, assessment, and analysis of evolution processes. Mechanisms must be provided in order to adjust frameworks to specific evolution cases.
- Analysts and stakeholders must be involved in the process of evolution, and then they must to be accounted when researchers provide frameworks and mechanisms to support the analysis of model evolution.

## *Final remarks and challenges*

As is discussed in [33], several open challenges need to be confronted by scientist. We want to highlight the following:

- It is necessary to provide metrics that are language independent. Mostly, metrics are conceived to measure evolution of software modules (lines of code) of a concrete programming language. Other metrics are specified to measure evolution of requirements models that follow a specific method or modelling language. It is necessary to provide language-independent evolution metrics. Later on, analysts can adapt such metrics to their particular interests and information technology environments. In this way, it is necessary to provide frameworks and methods that guide analysts on the application of evolution metrics.
- It is important to scope the evolution analysis. Analysts should clarify the amount of data to have into account for the analysis of the evolution of a certain software system. Configuration systems to identify the artefacts to account in the evolution analysis become necessary to help analysts in the task of analysing evolution.
- Empirical validations to evaluate methods and techniques for supporting information systems evolution are needed. Toy-examples or laboratory demonstrations are good to demonstrate the feasibility of research results. Nevertheless, controlled experiments and case studies are vital to understand how produced methods and techniques can be applied in real-world cases. It is important to discover how profitable academic solutions are. Industrial involvement or the participation of practitioners is important to guarantee that research results can be applied and transferred to industry.

## 2.3 Model-driven organisational reengineering frameworks

This section reviews related research in order to exemplify alternatives to support the model evolution process in model-driven reengineering frameworks. We study challenges and motivation to research in this field.

In short, reengineering frameworks consists of three processes and four artefacts (see Fig. 9). The first process is the reverse engineering process; whose input is the first artefact, the *as-is* system (current system). The result of the reverse engineering process is the second artefact, the *as-is* models (that represent the As-Is system in an abstract way). The second process is the evolution process; whose input are the *as-is* models. As a result, the output of the evolution process is the third artefact, *to-be* models (evolved models). The third process is the forward engineering process; whose input are the *to-be* models and the output is the fourth artefact, the *to-be* system (system that results from the reengineering process and fulfils the new goals and needs of the organisation).

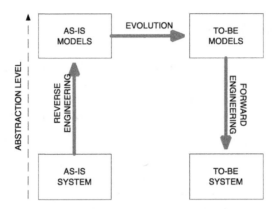

**Fig. 9.** Reengineering framework

## *Supporting the processes of the reengineering framework*

Traceability links are defined as relations between the elements belongs to different specifications. Omote et al. propose an approach to establish traceability links among models belongs to different information systems requirements specifications [39]. As a particular case, they use use-case models. In short, the idea is to maintain the traceability among diagrams at different levels of abstraction and at different stages of evolution (*as-is* system and *to-be* system). This work proposes the evolution of these models as "changes in use-case model", where a use-case model consists of use case-diagrams, activity diagrams and object models (class diagrams and sequence diagrams). Here the open challenge is how to establish traceability links among *as-is* and *to-be* models. In addition, it is necessary to provide guidelines that indicate how to generalise the traceability support for other kind of organisational models. The support of traceability in the evolution process is still demanded and research on this field is needed.

Research in model weaving attempts to handle fine-grained relationships among elements of different models [40]. Due to the complexity of establishing links among models, Didonet et al. propose a weaving metamodel that could be adapted to support different domains (i.e., requirements models and goal models). Then, solutions provided in model weaving need to be materialised by providing guidelines of use and application in concrete cases. For instance, the application of model weaving for tracing *as-is* and *to-be* business process models for analysing model evolution.

From the point of view of business process modelling, business process models change according to the requirements of an application domain. The work in [41] provides an infrastructure that supports the adaptation of both process modelling languages and process models (specifically, a multi-level metamodelling framework). The idea is to provide a metamodel to specify a standard for process modelling language and to specify the changes based on the new requirements in the language. The standard process modelling language is aligned with its specialisations (domain-specific process modelling language). In this way, all language definitions will be based on the same metamodel and will share a common set of modelling constructs.

This holistic solution is very convenient when organisational and methodological evolution is necessary. Nevertheless, guidelines on the usage of infrastructures to evolve information systems from its organisational and methodological perspectives are still needed.

The impact of evolving a system on both organisational and methodological is expensive and from the industry point of view, it is necessary to justify the advantages on performing evolution projects that involves several layers of information systems; in this case, it is involved the organisational specification and the methods that are used for information systems understanding.

Model management confront problems in many databases application domains (e.g. data warehousing, semantic query processing, meta-data management, meta-data integration, schema evolution, etc.); research projects in this area are aiming at providing high-level abstractions artefacts in order to offer a generic solution [42, 43]. As a result, there are works in model management to deal with manipulation of models [44]. Hence, representations of models and model mappings are proposed as formal specifications in high-level algebraic operations. Bernstein [45] propose management operators, for instance, the operator match takes two models as input and returns a mapping between them.

In [45], mapping between models is defined as mapping between objects or combination of objects. The matching process highlights the equality or similarity of concepts between the models that have been matching. In addition, in [46] is presented a proposal for model management, where, formal descriptions of models are manipulated by means of mappings or relations among them. The idea is to define the semantics of the operators in enough detail to face three model management activities: model integration, model evolution, and round-trip engineering. Bernstein et al. works offer solutions for supporting the analysis of the difference between two models; in the case of evolution projects, differences between *as-is* and *to-be* models are operationalized for further analysis. Reengineering projects are needed for supporting this evolution analysis tasks. It is important to find how to involve model analysis techniques in reengineering frameworks.

Although, supporting model evolution by means of model-driven techniques is an open challenge, requirements engineers have done several steps to provide solutions. Nevertheless, methods and guidelines that can be adapted to different evolution projects are still needed and demanded by industry.

## 2.4 Goal-driven requirements engineering

Several related works focus on the integration of goal and business process perspectives in the domain of business process management and maintenance. Those approach goal-oriented business process reengineering from diverse angles.

Some works focus on modelling the *as-is* system (the reverse engineering process in reengineering frameworks). For instance, Andersson et al., [47] propose a goal elicitation method to deepen the understanding of current processes. The authors conclude that a suitable semantic and representation to relate goal and business process models is needed. Guizzardi et al., [48] discuss the alignment of goal and process modelling methods (using Tropos and ARIS, respectively) and propose a three-stage method to model the as-is system.

Other works focus on supporting the evolution of the business process model, i.e., from the *as-is* to the *to—be* systems. Cardoso et al., [49] propose a goal-based pattern definition language for business process evolution, where processes are trajectories in a space of all possible states and goals are final states. Soffer and Wand present a formal approach to analyse the dependency of softgoals on processes [50]. As a practical result, they enable the evolution rationale to be modelled.

Other works focus on modelling the *to-be* system (forward engineering). Kueng and Kawalek present an informal, seminal approach in which goals provide a basis for process definition [51]. Kavakli and Loucopoulos define a method that takes an *as-is* business process model as input and produces a *to-be* goal model and a *to-be* business process model [52]. Leonardi and Giandini propose a set of heuristics in order to specify business process models (based on the Communication Analysis method) from goal-oriented specifications [53]. This work provides a strategy to link processes and organisational objectives in *to-be* scenarios.

Some of the above-mentioned works elaborate a conceptual framework to clarify definitions [51], [52], [48], [49] and [50] even builds upon an existing ontology. However, none of them performs an ontological analysis to guide the integration of the modelling methods.

With regard to modelling language integration, Kavakli and Loucopoulos [52], rely on EKD metamodels (goal and business process perspectives are integrated *a priori*), but, noticeably, none of the above-mentioned works report a proper, rigorous metamodel integration (Guizzardi et al., [48] does mention it as future work).

Some works analyse semantic relations between goals and business processes [54], [55], [56] and [57]. Similarly, the pattern-based approach in [49] could be adapted to the context of goal and business process models.

It is worth mentioning approaches that enrich goal models in order to include information related to business process. Lapouchnian et al., [58] propose adding textual annotations to goal models in order to add control flow details for subgoals (e.g., data dependencies, precedence constraints). Ghose et al., [59] enrich goal models with precedence relationships, which facilitates the derivation of business processes. Similarly, Kazhamiakin et al., [60] define a set of formal annotations in goal models in order to add constraints in goal models for future operationalization of goals. All these approaches extend the expressiveness of goal modelling languages. However, common practices in the area of enterprise modelling architecture promote to separate modelling perspectives to facilitate analysis and decision making [61]. Stakeholders and organisational users can recognise the evolution performed and the rationale behind the evolution process when the analysis is done over information systems perspectives separately. Then, without involving goals and business process models, it is possible to recognise what are the processes or tasks that have changed the impact and change propagation. In fact, goals can be justified and then linked with other specifications of the information system, as interaction models and object models.

## 2.5 Evolution requirements and information system co-evolution

For this section, we want to discuss the works of Salinesi, Rolland, Etien and their co-workers on the field of evolution requirements. They highlight challenges and open gaps based on their experience in industrial projects. Problematic and impact on how evolution projects are performed in industry are analysed.

Because of software systems evolve in order to fulfil the requirements of organisational business, they must evolve together. As is defined in [62], evolution requirements are gaps and similarities resulting from change processes (*as-is* to *to-be* movement). The authors discuss the differences between evolution requirements as they are conceived in academia and how they are treated in real world cases. In academia, evolution requirements are specified only in *to-be* models. In industry, evolution requirements are captured according to the *as-is*, and then a movement to the *to-be*.

In this work, gaps express transformations of *as-is* models into *to-be* models. Similarities specify what the *as-is* and the *to-be* should have in common.

Frameworks and methods that include the analysis of evolution requirements are needed to transfer academic solutions to industry. Here the challenge is how to provide solutions generic enough to be adopted in real cases. Guidelines that indicate the feasibility of application of evolution requirements analysis are needed. This is vital for further usage and implementation.

Requirements change according to the nature of systems evolution. In [63], the authors confront the evolution of information systems from the requirements level as an answer to cope with the problems from the requirements models levels, where the needs of stakeholders and users are specified. In fact, traceability among stakeholders' goals and evolved elements is vital to analyse the rationale of evolution processes. Because information systems development do not start from scratch, legacy system play an important role in order to recognise *what*, *where*, *when* and *why* the information system change. As we already discussed, an analysis on the *as-is* system is performed in the moment to propose a *to-be* solution. As a result, *as-is* models play an important role in evolution projects; nevertheless their importance is unrecognised by companies in the moment to perform evolution tasks.

Authors make explicit the advantages on the analysis of differences among *as-is* and *to-be* models. According to industrial experiences, measurement on evolution requirements clarify what has to change and why, and it acts as an agreed contract on the changes. In addition, measurement results are specifications of software changes to be carried out in the code level. Elicitation process of change requirements is also a demanding intellectual process. It is necessary then to provide solutions that can provide automatic elicitation of change requirements, their measurement, and guidelines for analysis.

On the other hand, Etien & Rolland have proposed to analyse the relationship between business processes and information technology as a fitness relationship, which means a correspondence between components [64]. The authors establish the idea that fitness relationships are measurable. By means of metrics, it is possible to guide and control co-evolution of information systems.

## 2.6    TraceME and related MDD solutions

TraceME has been proposed as part of the model-driven reengineering solutions provided by the PROS Research centre. To support the reengineering framework, various
theses have been developed aiming at supporting the forward engineering process.
For example, specification of information systems requirements from a communicative perspective [7]; modelling of business process perspectives [6]; establishment of
a framework for method integration [65], capturing of interaction requirements for
generation of web and desktop applications [3]; support of automatic interoperability
of languages [5]; production of web 2.0 applications by means of web engineering
[4]; and development of web and desktop application following an object-oriented
perspective [2].

The previous proposals build upon the methodological core of the OO-Method
proposed by [2]. Some of these proposals extend the method with modelling techniques aimed at a specific type of software system. Fig. 10 presents a big picture of
the reengineering framework and the solutions available in the PROS Research Centre
before this book. It is evident were the efforts have been dedicated and future open
projects that can be developed in order to increase the PROS solution offers.

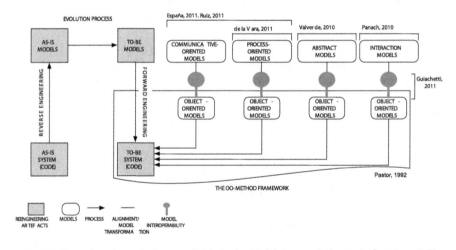

**Fig. 10.** Reengineering solutions available in the PROS Research Centre before TraceME

In the rest of this section, we summarise our efforts in order to support the forward
engineering process by following a business process communicative-oriented perspective. We describe our attempting to bridge the gap from requirements to fully
functional software code in a MDD way. We have integrated two existing methods:
Communication Analysis (a communication-oriented business process modelling and
requirements engineering method) [66] and the OO-Method (an object-oriented model-driven development framework with automatic code generation capabilities[2]) [67].
Mainly, the PhD thesis of España has contributed with an MDD method that covers

---

[2] Integranova Model Execution System http://www.integranova.com/integranova-m-e-s/.

the software development lifecycle from requirements engineering to code generation [7]. In addition, the MSc thesis of Ruiz has contributed with a model-driven framework to integrate Communication Analysis and OO-Method.

As a first step, we have conceived a general framework that defines stages, phases, and tasks that aim at integrating requirements methods in MDD environments. This framework takes into account modelling activities and model transformation activities (for more details of this framework please see [68]). By putting into practice the proposed framework, we integrate Communication Analysis and OO-Method (See Fig. 11).

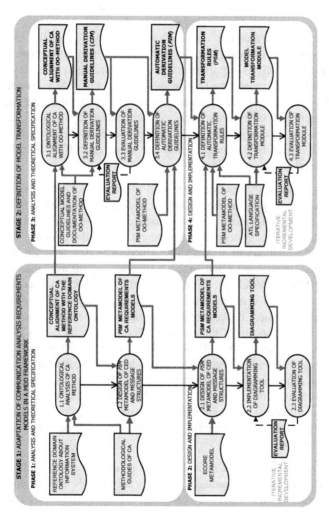

**Fig. 11.** Model-driven framework to integrate Communication Analysis and OO-Method

Each stage of the framework is divided into two phases, and each phase has several tasks. We have decided to differentiate each stage according to the tasks involved in the MDD process. We distinguish between the stage related to modelling tasks (Stage 1) and the stage related to model transformation tasks (Stage 2).

Model-Driven Architecture (MDA) is an approach that uses models in software development. MDA proposes the well-known and long-established idea of separating the specification from the system operation [69]. The application of this concept for developing frameworks to integrate methods allows us to build artefacts with different levels of abstraction. This means that artefacts are available at different abstraction levels according to the MDA layers. The MDA layers are computation-independent models (CIM), platform-independent models (PIM), and platform-specific models (PSM).

Since a metamodel is a model, the MDA approach can be applied to support requirements engineering methods, i.e., we differentiate the abstract representation of the Communication Analysis requirements models according to MDA layers. For this reason, we distinguish between the PIM metamodel and the PSM metamodel. Having the metamodel at different levels of abstraction allows us to implement the PIM metamodel in different target platforms according to the technological platform chosen.

In the same way, we apply the MDA architecture to build the artefacts corresponding to the Stage 2. The derivation guidelines are specified in CIM and PIM layers to allow different technological platforms.

Stage 1 involves some activities that are related to metamodel specifications and construction of diagramming tools. Four products have been obtained at this stage: The first is the conceptual alignment of Communication Analysis with the reference ontology of the information system. This alignment allows the principal concepts and primitives of the Communication Analysis method to be distinguished. Some examples of conceptual frameworks and ontological analyses are available in [70]. The second is the PIM metamodel specification of Communication Analysis requirements models. This metamodel contains a set of elements (metaclasses) and relationships (associations) that represent the concepts of the method. Each metaclass and association corresponds to a concept of the ontology. The metamodel is at a PIM level because it does not have technological information (i.e., the target platform has not yet been considered). The third is the PSM metamodel specification of Communication Analysis requirements models. This metamodel specifies metaclasses and associations with platform-oriented information. The fourth is the diagramming tool. This supports the modelling activities of the Communication Analysis requirements models (communicative event diagrams and message structures). For more details about this stage, please see [71] and [68].

Stage 2 involves some activities related to model transformation from requirements models to conceptual models. These activities are aimed at the generation of software code in an automatic way.

## The OO-Method, the Communication Analysis, and the integration of both methods

The level of abstraction of software engineering methods has been lifted over the years, in order to tackle with the ever increasing complexity of software development projects: from assembler code, to structured programming languages, object-oriented programming languages, aspect-orientation, service-orientation... A new paradigm referred to as model-driven development (MDD) has recently placed all the emphasis on the role of models, to the point of changing the motto "the code is the model" to "the model is the code" [72]. "Software has the rare property that it allows us to directly evolve models into full-fledged implementations without changing the engineering medium, tools, or methods"[3]. Ideally, the computerised information system is specified in an abstract model and then, by means of model transformations, subsequent models are obtained until the source code is automatically generated. The advent of the Model-Driven Architecture (MDA) [73] as a development paradigm and the Unified Modelling Language (UML) as a *de facto* standard notation have paved the way for viable MDD proposals (e.g. Extreme Non-Programming [74], Conceptual Schema-Centric Development [75]).

However, despite the importance of requirements engineering as a key success factor for software development projects, there is a lack of MDD methods that cover the full development lifecycle from requirements engineering to code generation. Most MDD methods range from conceptual modelling to code generation and do not address requirements. There are definitely many open research challenges in model-driven requirements engineering [76]. Furthermore, the code generation capabilities of most MDD methods are currently limited to create-read-update-delete (CRUD) operations and reactions that are more complex need to be programmed manually.

### The OO-Method

The OO-Method was first proposed in the academy [77], on top of a formal object-oriented algebra named OASIS. Soon a spin-off company named CARE Technologies was created, with the aim of creating the tool to support the OO-Method. The result of this endeavour was the Integranova Model Execution system. The suite of tools includes Integranova Modeler, a computer-aided software engineering (CASE) tool that allows specifying the Conceptual Model, and a model compiler. Both the OO-Method and the Integranova technology are used in practice to develop enterprise information systems.

---

[3] Bran Selic and John Hogg have expressed this idea in a number of presentations (e.g. Selic keynote at Workshop on Critical Systems Development with UML, San Francisco, CA, USA, October 2003)

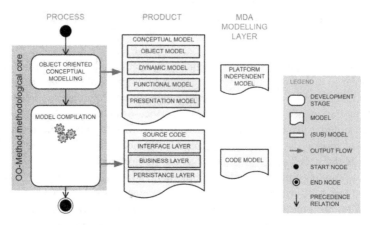

**Fig. 12.** Methodological core of the OO-Method

### *The conceptual modelling core*

The OO-Method methodological core is the *object-oriented conceptual modelling* stage, the result of which is the *Conceptual Model*, an object-oriented model that describes the computerised information sub-system disregarding the implementation platform. This way, the OO-Method Conceptual Model corresponds to the Platform Independent Model (PIM) layer of the Model Driven Architecture. It is comprised of four interrelated models:

- The *Object Model* allows specifying the static aspect of the system in the form of a UML-compliant class diagram. This model allows describing the following elements of the computerised information sub-system (among others): the business objects in terms of classes of objects, structural relations among classes of objects, agents of the system (an abstraction of the users of the software system) and relations among agents and class services.
- The *Dynamic Model* specifies the possible sequences of method invocations that can occur in the life of an object; it is expressed as a State-Transition Diagram.
- The *Functional Model* specifies the effect that the method invocations have in the state of the objects; it is expressed as generic pseudo-code specifications (which is independent of any programming language).
- The *Presentation Model* offers an abstract description of the computerised information sub-system interface. This model is structured in three abstract pattern levels.

After the conceptual modelling stage, a model compiler takes as input the conceptual model and a set of compilation parameters (e.g. the selected database management system and programming language) and it generates the source code of a software application that is functionally equivalent to the conceptual model (i.e. the application fulfils the specifications determined by the model). The automatically generated software application is fully functional and it is organised in a three-layer architecture: interface, business logic, and persistence.

We focus on the communication-oriented approach since it has been fully integrated with the conceptual modelling stage and tool support has been provided, for both creating and transforming models.

## Communication Analysis

Since information systems are a support to organisational communication [78], a communicational approach to information systems analysis is necessary. Communication Analysis is a requirements engineering method that analyses the communicative interactions between the information system and its environment; it was, therefore, a good candidate for completing the catalogue of requirements engineering approaches within the OO-Method framework.

The methodological core of Communication Analysis is the *information system analysis* stage, the result of which is an *analysis specification*, a communication-oriented documentation that describes the information system disregarding its possible computerisation. This way, the analysis specification produced by Communication Analysis corresponds to the CIM layer of the Model Driven Architecture.

Communication Analysis offers a requirements structure and several modelling techniques for business process modelling and requirements specification. The *Communicative Event Diagram* is intended to describe business processes from a communicational perspective. A *communicative event* is a set of actions related to information (acquisition, storage, processing, retrieval, and/or distribution), which are carried out in a complete and uninterrupted way, on the occasion of an external stimulus. Business process model modularity is guided by unity criteria [79]; there are evidence that the application of these criteria improve the quality of models [80]. The *Event Specification Template* allows structuring the requirements associated to a communicative event. Among other requirements, it contains a description of the new meaningful information that is conveyed to the information system in the event. This is specified by means of *Message Structures*, a modelling technique that is based on structured text. Previous work [81] presents the grammar of Message Structures and provides guidelines for their application during analysis and design (they are used differently in each development stage). To create the message structures, the analyst interviews the users and analyses the available business forms. They merely describe messages and are, therefore, an analysis artefact. The structure of message fields lies vertically and field properties can be arranged horizontally; e.g. information acquisition operation, field domain, an example value provided by users, etc.

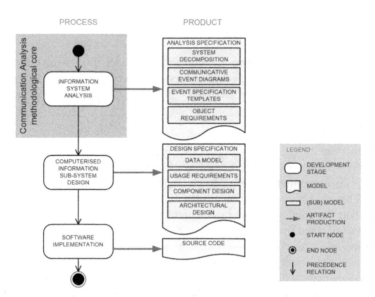

**Fig. 13.** Methodological core of Communication Analysis

At the time we undertook the integration of Communication Analysis into the
OO-Method, a strong theoretical foundation and several specifications of the requirements engineering method were available [82]. There was experience with the method
in action. By means of technology transfer projects, the method had been adopted by
several companies: (a) the Valencia Port Authority, (b) the Infrastructure and
Transport Ministry of the Valencian Regional Government, (c) and Anecoop S. Coop.
However, requirements models were mainly specified using word processors and
general-purpose diagramming tools. In addition, no attempts to integrate Communication Analysis in an MDD framework had been made. Either the final software implementation was carried out within the organisation or it was outsourced.

### *Integration*

The first steps were aimed at improving the method specification, providing more
rigorous definitions for the underlying concepts [66] and designing the artefacts needed for a successful integration into an MDD framework, such as a method metamodel.
Also, an Eclipse-based tool was implemented in order to support the creation of
Communication Analysis requirements models [83]. Then the concepts of both methods were aligned in order to provide a sound theoretical basis and to envision how the
integration should be performed. As a result, a flow of activities has been defined (see
Fig. 14). The activities from Communication Analysis that correspond to the information system analysis stage have been preserved, but those related to design have
been substituted by the OO-Method conceptual modelling stage.

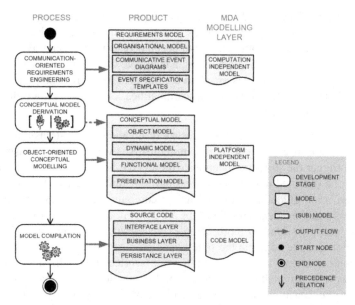

**Fig. 14.** Activities of the integrated method

Furthermore, a derivation technique aimed at obtaining a first version of the conceptual model from a requirements model has been proposed. Two kinds of derivation are provided: namely, a manual derivation intended to be performed by an analyst, and model transformation that automates the process as much as possible. Depending on the development project context (e.g. expertise of the team, organisational culture concerning MDD), one of the alternatives is to be chosen.

The manual derivation technique consists of a set of guidelines that allow to systematically reasoning the elements of the conceptual model, including the Object Model, the Dynamic Model and part of the Functional Model. The Presentation Model is, for the moment, out of the scope since many improvements are being made on human-computer interaction [84], [85], [86] and the derivation should take these into account once they are consolidated.

The derivation of the Object Model consists of three main steps. Firstly, the scope of the derivation is defined; that is, the analyst may want to derive the conceptual model for the whole requirements model or just for some part of it (e.g. only the sales management business process). This is done by marking which communicative events are intended to be supported by the conceptual model. In the former case, all events are marked by default. In the latter case, the marked communicative events are added to a diagram, including the precedences between them; then, the diagram is extended by including any other events that are precedent to the marked ones. Secondly, the communicative events in the transformation-scope diagram are sorted according to their precedences to later process them in order. These two steps prevent inconsistencies in the conceptual model such as referencing an inexistent class. The third step implies processing each communicative event to create its class-diagram view; that is, producing the portion of the class diagram that corresponds to the communicative event. For this purpose, the message structure is processed, and other requirements in the event specification templates are taken into account (e.g. restrictions). By incrementally integrating all the class-diagram views, a complete object model is obtained. Not only the classes and relationships are derived, but also most of their properties; for instance, attribute properties, relationship cardinalities, class services and their arguments. See [87] for more details.

The derivation of the Dynamic Model consists of creating a state-transition diagram for each class that is affected by several communicative events, so as to constrain how the users can trigger the software functions over a given business object. The Dynamic Model can be obtained mainly by processing the Communicative Event Diagram. The main derivation guideline is the following: communicative events are converted into transitions and precedence relationships are converted into states. However, business process gateways lead to more complex state-transition diagrams. Also, additional transitions can be added to the state transition diagram; for instance, transitions that correspond to atomic edition and destruction services (e.g. edit and destroy, respectively), as well as transitions that correspond to atomic services that take part in a transaction (these transitions appear as a result of processing the event specification templates). See [88] for more details.

Last but not least, the derivation of the Functional Model completes the conceptual model by specifying the reaction of the class services. Valuation rules provide the meaning to atomic services, whereas transaction formulas allow defining more complex behaviours.

### *Open challenges*

There are many open challenges in the area of MDD, especially in industry adopted MDD methods. We now enumerate some areas where our proposal can be improved.

First of all, we acknowledge that practitioners are usually reluctant to use nonstandard notations. We therefore plan adopt the Business Process Modelling Notation (BPMN) to support Communication Analysis business process modelling. The BPMN Choreography Diagram is the first candidate to represent communicative event diagrams. Three challenges stem from this decision. First, a careful investigation needs to be carried out to adopt the notation while preserving the concepts and criteria of the method. Second, the derivation technique needs to be adapted to deal with the new notation. Third, a proper tool support needs to be provided, in order to facilitate validation, promote adoption, etc. With regards to the latter challenge, there are plenty of business process management suites in the wild these days; among them, Oryx[4] stands as a clear candidate because of its open, academic nature; also Modelio[5], since it has recently moved to open source.

---

[4] http://oryx-project.org
[5] http://www.modeliosoft.com

Furthermore, we plan to investigate how other analytical perspectives (e.g. goal or value orientation) may extend our approach and become useful under certain project circumstances, like projects that involve an evolution process. In Communication Analysis, business processes are means to fulfil the business goals; however, no methodological support is provided to elicit or model goals. This research line is still active due to its many open challenges [89].

Moreover, ontological analyses, lab demos and controlled experiments have been carried out, but further validations of the derivation technique are planned. This includes an action research application. Several controlled experiments have already been carried out and their data is being analysed; others are being designed. There is a long way ahead, but we are confident that the scientific community will work together to fulfil the vision of the MDD paradigm: providing full model-driven support to all the activities of a software project.

## 2.7    Summary

Traditionally in software system development, the evolution process and information systems maintenance have been faced by means of the reengineering process, traceability management, evolution requirements, evolution metrics, goal-driven requirements engineering and model management. For this reason, we explore current solutions in these fields in order to find related research that confronts conceptual model evolution.

The reengineering process is commonly defined and widely used by the scientific community by means of the metaphor of the "horseshoe" model, which purpose is to present the reengineering process in a figure (the horseshoe is basically a left-hand side, a right-hand side and a bridge between the sides). In general terms, the left-hand side of the horseshoe model consists of an extraction from an existing system to get the system specification, the right-hand side consist of conventional software development activities, and the bridge between the sides consists of a set of transformations from the old system to the new one [90]. Both, the left-hand side and right-hand side represent different levels of abstraction of the system. Nowadays, the Object Management Group (OMG) is working on promote an industrial consensus on modernisation of existing application by means of the initiative named Architecture-Driven Modernisation (ADM) [13]. This initiative is based on the MDD paradigm to automate the horseshoe model. However, full support for the evolution process (the bridge between the sides) is still missing. The authors of [91] aimed to automate the horseshoe model, although it is not severely applied.

Goal-driven requirements engineering approaches faced goal modelling from different perspectives of use. Some of those uses are: understanding the current organisational situations and need for change, decision making, relating business goals to functional and non-functional system components and validation of compliance between system specification and stakeholders' goals [92]. Co-evolution approaches has been proposed in order to understand reciprocal evolution of system components [93].

Nevertheless, goal specification related with change models and specification of evolution grains is still an open research field.

Systems changes and stability analysis in order to derive or facilitate system evolution is confronted by [94]. A method to support the elicitation of evolution requirements and a generic syntax to specify them is explored in [95]. Also, metrics for classifying and measuring software evolution are analysed by [96] and [36]. Nevertheless, specification of evolution in with formal conceptual models and measurement techniques to provide meaningful to kick start analysis is still needed.

Model management confront problems in many databases application domains (e.g. data warehousing, semantic query processing, meta-data management, meta-data integration, schema evolution etc.); research projects in this area are aiming at providing high-level abstractions artefacts in order to offer a generic solution [43] [42]. Bernstein presents a full description of all of the model management operators [45]. Moreover, no complete frameworks to support enterprise information system evolution and traceability management have been proposed yet.

The problems and open challenges detected are the motivations in which this research project is founded. As we discussed in the preview chapter, our main driver is a technology push attempt. Literature review results and the state of the model-driven solutions provided by the PROS Research Centre before this book, demonstrate that TraceME can be accepted by industry. The fragmented nature of TraceME is motivated by our desire to transfer TraceME to industry; where reengineering tasks demand attention and TraceME should be adapted according to stakeholders' needs and goals.

# Chapter 3     Theoretical Framework

*The beginning of wisdom is the definition of terms*
*- Socrates*

We strongly believe that one of the main activities in research is dissemination. A scientist that does not communicate his/her findings is condemned to die. Human beings are in a constant movement and evolution process. The concepts that we learn during our evolution are the consequence of our environment, context, race, nationality, family inheritance, experiences, and several factors that influence our way to think and perceive the world. Communication is possible when people are aligned to the same conceptual commitment; when people agree about the meaning of concepts.

As scientists, how can we ensure communication and well understanding of our findings? In order to minimise possible misunderstanding during the study and communication of our research results, we contribute to the scientific community with a research project based on strong foundations. Hence, a theoretical framework becomes vital.

Theoretical frameworks (a.k.a., conceptual frameworks) have been widely used and proposed aiming at defining the concepts that relies to a certain theory in order to facilitate conceptual commitment. To establish theoretical frameworks, reference ontologies have been applied (e.g., FRISCO [97] and UFO [98] have been used as reference purposes). To build the theoretical framework for this research, we use FRISCO because it offers the facility to define information systems concepts, UFO because it facilitates a domain-independent definition of basic concepts and definitions of concepts proposed in information systems works.

Because the TraceME method follows the model-driven paradigm, we establish a theoretical framework for model driven development. Furthermore, we provide a theoretical framework for organisational reengineering. Here we define the concepts of the reengineering framework and adapt it to organisational contexts. Important concepts for the design and validation of TraceME are defined in the design and validation chapters. Basic concepts for the definition of information systems are presented as the base for the rest of the concepts.

Throughout this book, to define concepts, we use the acronym CD (Concept Definition) followed by a number (in order to identify the definition of a concept, e.g. CD1), a given name to the concept in bold and underlined style (e.g. **Thing**), and a definition. When a defined concept is re-used in future definitions, it is underlined.

© Springer International Publishing AG, part of Springer Nature 2018
M. Ruiz: TraceME, LNBIP 312, pp. 55–63, 2018.
https://doi.org/10.1007/978-3-319-89716-5_3

## 3.1    The basics

We start defining some basic concepts that underlies TraceME. The most important concept is system; because the rest of the concepts defined in this research build upon this concept. For the basic concepts we apply the FRISCO and the UFO ontologies [97] [99].

CD1.  **Thing** is anything perceivable or conceivable [99].

CD2.  **Set** is a thing that has other things as members [99].

CD3.  **Domain** refers to things and/or sets that are under consideration.

CD4.  **System** is a purposely abstracted, clear, precise and unambiguous conception, whereby all the things contained in that conception are transitively coherent, i.e. all of them are directly or indirectly related to each other form a coherent whole [97].

CD5.  **Organisational system** is a special kind of system, being normally dynamic, active and open, and comprising the conception of how an organisation is composed (i.e. of specific actors and actands) and how it operates (i.e. performing specific actions in pursuit of organisational goals, guided by organisational rules and informed by internal and external communication), where its systemic properties are that it responds to (certain kinds of) changes caused by the system environment and, itself, causes (certain kinds of) changes in the system environment [97].

CD6.  **Information** is the knowledge increment brought about by receiving action in a message transfer [97].

CD7.  **Information system** is a sub-system of an organisational system, comprising the conception of how the communication- and information–oriented aspects of an organisation are composed (e.g. of specific communicating, information-providing and/or information-seeking actors, and of specific information-oriented actands) and how these operate, thus describing the (explicit and/or implicit) communication-oriented and information–providing actions and arrangements existing within that organisation [97].

It is important to clarify that the concept system refers to information systems.

## 3.2    A theoretical framework for model-driven development

The Model-Driven Development paradigm (MDD) has the potential to overcome some of the difficulties related to the industrial adoption of requirements engineering practices. Information system requirements specifications have documented the need for organisations that provides the necessary support for work practices and commu-nications [100]. Since specifications are essentially models, the MDD paradigm can get the most out of them: For instance, requirements models can be used to derive organisational models and the management of trace links can be facilitated. This new role of requirements models, which surpasses their current status of documentation to become the main development artefact, increases their industrial value.

In this section we define a set of terms that describes how MDD is used in the TraceME method. As the MDD paradigm promotes to specify information systems by means of models, we start the MDD theoretical framework defining what is conceptual modelling. Mylopoulos defines conceptual modelling as the activity of formally describing some aspects of the physical and social world around us for purposes of understanding and communication [101]. In contrast with mathematical of formal modelling, conceptual modelling supports structuring and inferential facilities that are psychologically grounded. Conceptual modelling is an activity to be performed by humans, not machines. Fig. 15 presents an overview of the concepts involved in the activities of information system analysis, and conceptual model specification and design. Below we define conceptual modelling for information systems analysis.

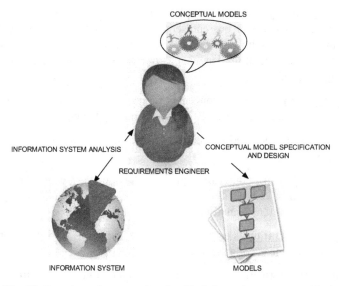

**Fig. 15.** Overview of concepts involved in information systems analysis

CD8. **Conceptual modelling** is the activity of formally describing some aspects of the physical and social world around us for purposes of understanding and communication of relevant parts of <u>information systems</u> or <u>organisational systems</u> [101]. The main result of conceptual modelling activities is the <u>conceptual model</u>.

CD9. **Conceptual model** is an abstract conception of an <u>information system</u>. This abstract conception relies on the perspective from which the <u>information system</u> and/or <u>organisational system</u> is viewed.

CD10. **Information system perspective** is the purpose of analysis (point of view), which can be to analyse processes, communication, security, information, data, users, user interaction, etc., of <u>information systems</u>.

CD11. **Organisational system perspective** is the purpose of analysis (point of view), which can be to analyse processes, goals, behaviour, interaction, communication, security, etc. of organisational systems.

CD12. **A conceptual model specification** is the representation of a conceptual model formed by elements and relationships. The elements and relationships of a model are instance of the same metamodel. The representation of a model is possible by means of a modelling language. This representation can be concretised by means of a piece of paper or modelling tools. In order to reduce the number of words, we will refer conceptual model specification as **model**.

CD13. **Modelling language** consists of concrete syntax and abstract syntax on how modelling elements can be represented and combined into meaningful statements about the modelling domain.

CD14. **Concrete syntax defines** the graphical appearance of a modelling language. The concrete syntax can be represented by means of textual languages, this mean that it defines how to form sentences. Graphical languages define the graphical appearance of the language concepts and how they may be combined into a model [102].

CD15. **Abstract syntax** defines the concepts of a language and their relationships. The abstract syntax can be represented by means of a metamodel [102].

Conceptual models are specified by means of modelling languages based on concrete syntaxes and abstract syntaxes.

CD16. **A metamodel** is the model of a model. Metamodels are widely used in the MDD community in order to perform a set of tasks as model transformations and model to text transformations.

CD17. **Model transformation** is an activity where a source model is transformed to a target model by means of a set of transformation rules.

At the end of the transformation process, source and target models are different. Models can be textual or graphical specifications.

CD18. **Transformation rules** are a set of instructions that indicate how a source model must be transformed into a target one. Traceability relationships are necessary to keep trace among information systems, their changes, and how requirements are aligned with baseline models.

CD19. **Traceability relationship** is a relationship between two modelling elements that are part of different models. Traceability relationships are bidirectional as is described by Gotel and Finkelstein: Traceability relationship is "The ability to follow the life of a requirement in both a forward and backward direction" [103].

CD20. **Vertical traceability** relationship is the traceability relationship between two modelling elements whose metamodels are different. For instance, vertical traceability can be established among modelling elements belonging to requirements <u>models</u> and modelling elements belonging to architectural <u>models</u>. Fig. 16 presents an example of a vertical traceability relationship established between the goal insurance provided that is instance of the metaclass GOAL of the *i\** metamodel, and the communicative event SALE 5 instance of the metaclass COMMUNICATIVE_EVENT from the Communication Analysis (CA) metamodel.

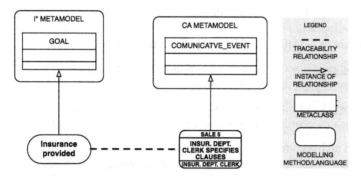

**Fig. 16.** Example of vertical traceability between *i\** models and CA models

CD21. **Horizontal traceability relationship** is the <u>traceability relationship</u> between modelling elements that are instance of the same immediate <u>metamodel</u>. For instance, in a <u>model</u> evolution scenario, a <u>horizontal traceability</u> relationship can be established between an element belong to an *as-is* <u>model</u> and an element belonging to a *to-be* <u>model</u> (<u>models</u> that specify the current and desired <u>information systems</u>). In this case, *as-is* and *to-be* <u>models</u> are instance of the same immediate <u>metamodel</u>. Fig. 17 exemplifies a horizontal relationship between two communicative events belonging to as-is and to-be models instance of the CA metamodel.

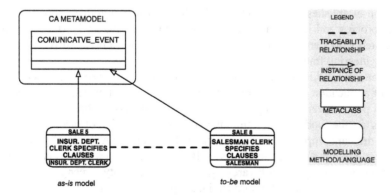

**Fig. 17.** Example of a horizontal traceability relationship between *as-is* and *to-be* models instance of the CA metamodel

To use MDD in practice, scientists and requirements engineers have designed guide-lines, tools, techniques, frameworks, approaches, and methods in order to bring requirements engineering advances to real and practical cases in information systems analysis. We customised each term for the development of information systems; they are defined below.

CD22. **Guideline** establishes where, when, how and who performs a task in an <u>information system</u> development process.

CD23. **Tool** is an element to be used in order to perform a task in an <u>information system</u> development process.

For instance, a <u>modelling tool</u> is a <u>tool</u> to specify <u>models</u>.

CD24. **Technique** is a set of <u>guidelines</u> and <u>tools</u> in order to perform a task in an <u>information system</u> development process.

CD25. **Framework** is a black box that includes an overview of a set of elements and its relationships in order to confront a problem in <u>information system</u> analysis.

Model driven architecture (MDA) is an approach that separates the fundamental logic behind a system specification from its particular technological implementation [104]. MDA provides a framework to specify the system accounting models for the logic layer and models for implementation layer.

CD26. **Approach** is a <u>method</u> without validation to prove its efficiency in real scenarios.

CD27. **Method** is a set of instructions (recipes) that involve people, processes, techniques, and artefacts in order to achieve goals. Following the definition of [105], a method offer <u>guidelines</u> for work and explains what to do in different situations to arrive at certain goals.

## 3.3   A theoretical framework for organisational reengineering

This section establishes a consistent set of concepts and terminology about the reengineering process and its artefacts. The aim is to facilitate the analysis and comparison of related works and set the theoretical foundations for a model-driven organisational reengineering framework.

There are many different definitions of the reengineering process, depending on the field of application or the nature of the evolving system. For instance, in the field of business process reengineering, Hammer and Champy have defined the reengineering process as "the fundamental rethinking and radical redesign of business processes to achieve dramatic improvements in critical, contemporary measures of performance such as cost, quality, service, and speed" [106]. The definition proposed by Arnold [107] is widely used by the software engineering community, "reengineering is the whole process of reverse-and-forward engineering".

Several works define the reengineering process as having three basic processes (reverse engineering, improvement, and forward engineering) and four basic artefacts (*as-is* system, *as-is* models, *to-be* models, and *to-be* system). Based on these definitions, we can establish the following general definition for the reengineering process.

CD28. **Reengineering process** is the whole process, which consists of a set of thre activities (reverse engineering, evolution process, and forward engineering) aimed at evolving systems from a current situation (*as-is* system) to a future, improved/desired situation (*to-be* system):

(1) the *as-is* system is abstracted as a model (*as-is* model)

(2) an analysis on the current needs is performed in order to improve the system's current limitations, and the changes of the *as-is* models are reflected in a new improved set of models (*to-be* models).

(3) the *to-be* system is developed based on the *to-be* models.

Fig. 18 presents an outline of the reengineering process. The three basic processes (reverse engineering, evolution process, and forward engineering) are represented by means of arrows that link the four basic artefacts (*as-is* system, *as-is* models, *to-be* models, and *to-be* system) that are represented by means of rectangles. Note that the *as-is* system and the *to-be* system can exist at two different moments in time, so they can be considered to represent either two distinct systems or a single system that has evolved. Following Fig. 18, we establish the definition of the three processes and the four artefacts that conform the reengineering process. The first basic process is the reverse engineering process.

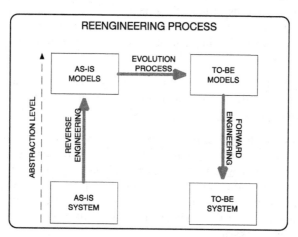

**Fig. 18.** Overview of the reengineering process

CD29. **Reverse engineering** is the process of analysing the current system to identify the system's components and their interrelationships and create representations of the system in another form or at a higher level of abstraction (we adapted this concept from [108]). When the current limitations or risks of a system make a reengineering process advisable, then the current system is analysed in order to identify disconnects (e.g. inconsistencies between the functions of a process that cause the existing process to fail to achieve its goals) [109]. The first artefact is the *as-is* system.

CD30. *as-is* **system** is the current system that needs to be aligned with the new requirements of the environment and is the input of the reverse engineering process. The system's abstraction is part of the reverse engineering process and is represented by means of models. The creation of the models is guided by the use of the various modelling methods available (business process models, activity diagrams, conceptual models, etc.). The system's models allow time, costs, resources etc. to be analysed. This analysis highlights the concepts and relationships that need to be reengineered [110]. The result of the reverse engineering process is the second artefact, the *as-is* models.

CD31. *as-is* **models** are a set of models that represent the *as-is* system at a high level of abstraction. The *as-is* models are the artefacts to evolve. The second basic process is the evolution process.

CD32. **Evolution process** aims at identifying alternatives to the current situation (represented by means of *as-is* models) that satisfy the strategic goals or needs of the desired system. Thus, the input of the improvement process is the *as-is* models. The improvement process has several names; restructuring [108] and producing of alternatives [110] are two of them. The improvement process is an iterative process that leads to the creation of the models that represent the desired system by means of modelling methods [111]. In short, the *as-is* models are analysed and aligned with the goals and needs of the desired system. As a result, the output of the improvement process is the third artefact, the *to-be* models.

CD33. *to-be* **models** are a set of models that result from the improvement process and, thus, represent the desired system at a high level of abstraction. The third basic process is the forward engineering process.

CD34. **The forward engineering** process is the process of moving from high-level abstractions and logical implementation-independent designs to the physical implementation of a system (we adapted this concept from [110]). The input of the forward engineering process is the *to-be* models, and the output is the implemented system, which corresponds to the desired system that is delimited by the goals and needs of the environment. The result of the forward engineering process is the *to-be* system.

CD35. **The *to-be* system** is the system that results from the reengineering process. The *to-be* system fulfils the goals and needs of the desired system.

In practice, there are some recurring general themes: most reengineered processes tend to align with several jobs that are combined into one; decision-making falls to the workers and not the managers; process steps are performed logically and naturally; checks and controls are reduced or eliminated; hands-off are minimized; [106]. In addition, as-is model specifications and the reverse engineering processes are not valuable from the practical point of view. Reengineering can involve just evolution and forward processes. These real cases are discussed in the section of related work (see the Chapter 2)

## 3.4    Summary

In this chapter, we presented two theoretical frameworks where the TraceME method is based: a theoretical framework for model-driven development (Section 3.2) and a theoretical framework for organisational reengineering (Section 3.3). In addition, some basic concepts are presented as a base where the concepts of the research are built (Section 3.1)

The model-driven theoretical framework is indeed a vital base where the TraceME method is built.

The theoretical framework for organisational reengineering is also important for the TraceME method because of its evolution nature. It defines the artefacts and processes that are part of TraceME and place it in practical and real world usage conditions.

The terms defined in this section are used in the Chapter 4 and Chapter 5, where the TraceME method design is presented. In addition, the Chapter 6 uses the terms for describing the validations performed.

# Chapter 4    TraceME chunks: the design

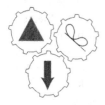

*A designer knows he has achieved perfection not when there is nothing left to add, but when there is nothing left to take away. - Antoine de Saint-Exupery*

## 4.1    Introduction

TraceME is a traceability-based method for conceptual model evolution. Mainly, traceability-based and model-based strategies are the core of TraceME. TraceME is intended to support the evolution of information systems specified by means of conceptual models. For this research project, we focus on three information systems perspectives applied in information systems evolution: the intentional perspective, the business process and communicational perspective, and the object perspective. Further perspectives can be involved like interaction perspectives. The architecture of TraceME is based on chunks that can be applied and assembled according with certain needs of evolution projects.

For the specification of information systems evolution, we select three well-known methods for information systems: the *i\** language, the Communication Analysis method, and the OO-Method. The *i\** language is selected as a language to specify the intentional perspective of information systems. Communication Analysis method serves as a purpose to specify the business process and communication-oriented perspectives of information systems. The OO-Method stands for the object-oriented design of information systems. Since the *i\**, the Communication Analysis method, and the OO-Method were defined before the development of TraceME, we make them part of the TraceME chunks as given methods for information systems specification. In addition, those methods serve as a base for building the new method chunks that are presented in this book.

In this chapter, we present the design of each TraceME chunk and a summary of the given chunks: the *i\** language, the Communication Analysis, and the OO-Method. First, we present an ontology-driven framework for integrating goal and business process perspectives called the GoBIS framework (see section 4.3). For the GoBIS framework we make a method engineering effort in order to integrate the *i\** language and the Communication Analysis method. Two scenarios that can be confronted by applying the GoBIS framework are the top-down and evolution scenarios. In this way, we design the *iStar2ca* guidelines for obtaining Communication Analysis models from *i\** models (see section 4.4), and the *evolCA* procedure for evolving Communication Analysis models (see Section 4.5).

© Springer International Publishing AG, part of Springer Nature 2018
M. Ruiz: TraceME, LNBIP 312, pp. 65–141, 2018.
https://doi.org/10.1007/978-3-319-89716-5_4

On the other hand, to support the specification of design models, we design the *ca2oom* integration framework, a top-down scenario for the creation of OO-Method models from Communication Analysis models (see Section 4.6). Last but not least, we present the Delta Analysis, which is a TraceME chunk to specify, measure, and analyse differences and similarities of pair of models. Mainly, Delta Analysis is applied for analysing the evolution of information systems (see Section 4.7).

Fig. 19 presents an overview of the TraceME chunks. It presents the given chunks for information systems specification (*i*\* language, Communication Analysis, and OO-Method), the chunks that we design to conform the TraceME method (*iStar2ca* guidelines, *evolCA* procedure, *ca2oom* integration framework, and Delta Analysis technique), and the relationships among given and designed chunks.

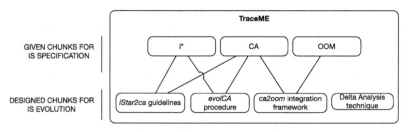

**Fig. 19.** Overview of the TraceME chunks

## 4.2 Background and running example

This section presents an overview of the *i*\* language and Communication Analysis (CA). Throughout this chapter, we use a running example based on the case of Super-Stationery Co., which is an intermediary company that buys and sells office material. The focus of the example is on the intentional and operational aspects of sales management.

### 4.2.1 The i\* framework in a nutshell

The *i*\* framework is a goal- and agent-oriented requirements engineering method [55]. It proposes two models: a Strategic Dependency (SD) model, which represents the intentional level; and the Strategic Rationale (SR) model, which represents the rational level. An SD model consists of a set of nodes that represent actors and a set of dependencies that represent the relationships among them, expressing that an actor (depender) depends on other actor (dependee) in order to obtain an objective (dependum). The dependum is an intentional element that can be a resource, task, goal, or softgoal. An SR model allows the intentional elements to be visualised inside the boundary of an actor in order to refine the SD model with reasoning capabilities. The dependencies of the SD model are linked to intentional elements inside the boundary of the actor. The elements inside the SR model are decomposed according to three types of links: task-decomposition links, means-end links, and contribution to softgoal links.

Actors can be specialised into agents, roles, and positions. Agents are actors with a concrete physical manifestation. Roles are abstract characterizations of the behaviour of a social actor within a context. A position covers roles.

Fig. 20 shows an excerpt of an *i\** model for the SuperStationery Co. case. For the sake of brevity, the SR diagram is shown only for some of its actor roles: `Client`, `Supplier`, `Truck driver`, and `Insurance dept clerk`.

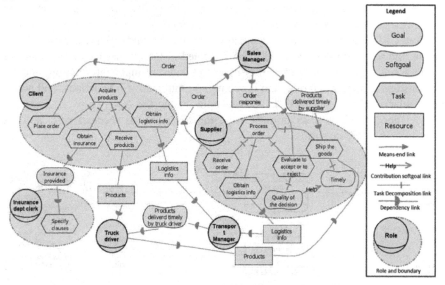

**Fig. 20.** Excerpt of an *i\** model for the SuperStationery Co. case

### 4.2.2    The Communication Analysis method in a nutshell

CA is a requirements engineering method that analyses the communicative interactions between information systems (IS) and its environment [66]. CA provides business process modelling and gets the most out of communicational techniques in order to analyse business processes. In this way, it improves conventional proposals for business process modelling. Therefore, the method focuses on external IS functions: information acquisition, and distribution. CA offers requirements structure and several modelling techniques: 1) the Communicative Event Diagram (CED) describes business processes from a communicational perspective; 2) the Event Specification Template allows the structuring of the requirements; and 3) Message Structure specifies the description of new meaningful information that is conveyed to the information system in the event [112].

Fig. 21 shows an excerpt of a CA model for the SuperStationery Co. case. It includes the CED for the management of a sale. The CED (see 0) consists of communicative events (CE). A CE is an organisational action that is triggered because of a given change in the world (e.g., `A client places an order`) and accounts for that change by gathering information about it. A CE is structured as a sequence of actions that are related to information (acquisition, storage, processing, retrieval, and/or distribution), which are carried out in a complete and uninterrupted way. CE are identified by the guidelines (referred as unity criteria) which act as modularity guidelines [113]. CE can be specialised by means of event variants, which are alternative transitions that define the composition of a CE (e.g., in Fig. 21, `Supplier evaluates the order` is specialised into `Order is rejected` or `Order is accepted`). In addition, CED specifies primary roles that trigger the CE and provide the input information, the receiver roles that need to be informed of the occurrence of an event, the interface roles that are in charge of editing and entering input information, and the relationships to specify ingoing and outgoing communicative interactions, and precedence relationships among CE. In the example, in the CE `A client places an order`, the `Client` acts as primary role, the `Manager` as receiver role, and the `Salesman` as interface role.

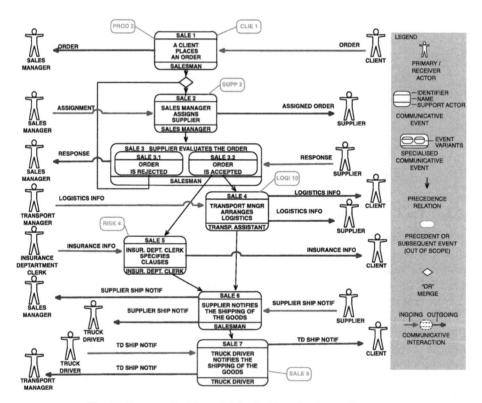

**Fig. 21.** Excerpt of a CA model for the SuperStationery Co. case

## 4.3    The GoBIS framework

Organisations are aware of the importance of evolving to keep pace with changes in the market, technology, environment, law, etc. [114]. As a result, continuous improvement and reengineering have become common practices in information system (IS) engineering. Understanding organisations and their needs for change often requires several interrelated perspectives [55, 115]. The IS engineering community has contributed with a number of modelling languages that are typically oriented towards a specific perspective, requiring approaches to their integration [116].

As a first stage, we focus on extending a business process perspective with intentional aspects of organisations. Business process modelling languages provide primitives to specify work practice (i.e., activities, temporal constraints, and resources). Despite the fact that processes are widely accepted as a means to achieve organisational goals [54], process models give little attention to the strategic dimension [48], [117]. The analysis, prioritization, and selection of organisational strategies are the scope of intentional modelling languages, which focus on the business roles, their goals, and their relationships.

Business processes and goals are intrinsically interdependent [118], [117] and several works provide detailed arguments in favour of combining both perspectives: (i) An integrated approach allows understanding of the motivation for processes [48], [117]; (ii) in a non-integrated approach, goals may be used to guide process design [51]; (iii) traceability is enhanced, which is necessary for enterprise management [56] and facilitates the sustainability of organisations [57]; (iv) integration also helps in identifying cross-functional interdependencies during business change management by supporting the identification of the goals that motivate evolution and the analysis of their impact on processes [51], [52], [57].

The GoBIS framework (Goal and Business Process Perspectives for Information System Analysis) pursues this aim by integrating a goal-oriented and a business process-oriented modelling language. One would expect several criteria from modelling language integration. For the framework definition, we highlight the following: (i) The languages to combine need to be formally described; (ii) the integration itself should be well founded in theory; (iii) it should clarify the scenarios where the integrated approach can be applied and provide some scenario-dependent guidelines; (iv) it should provide tool support; (v) empirical studies should demonstrate some benefits to potential adopters. These criteria guided our research. A comparative review (see Section 2.4) reveals that proposals with similar aims do not fulfil one or several of the above-mentioned criteria, revealing that the challenge remains open.

In this section we present our design science endeavour [119] from the problem investigation to the solution design. The implementation of a modelling tool and the solution evaluation are presented in the Chapter 6 and Chapter 7. We have chosen to integrate the languages proposed by $i*$ [55] (a goal-oriented modelling method), and Communication Analysis (CA) [66] (a communication-oriented business process modelling method).

For the scenario-dependent guidelines, we envision three possible application scenarios: top-down scenario, evolution scenario and bottom-up scenario. Note that the scenarios are closely related with the three main processes of reengineering frameworks. Since there are various solutions for bottom-up scenarios, for this research project, we embrace the top-down scenario (see section 4.4) and the evolution scenario (see section 4.5). Nevertheless, we conceived for our futures research tasks to explore the bottom-up scenario by offering specific solutions under the light of the GoBIS framework.

### 4.3.1 Research Method

We structure our research in terms of design science since it involves creating new artefacts and acquiring new knowledge (see Fig. 22). Our research method follows the cycles described by Wieringa [119]. We performed one engineering cycle (EC1) that mainly create an integrated metamodel for the *i** language and the CA method. Further, this metamodel is implemented in an Eclipse based tool to support integrated modelling tasks. It is important to mention that this engineering cycle for GoBIS is the forefather of two engineering cycles for the design of the *iStar2ca* guidelines and the *evolCA* procedure. The two engineering cycles are detailed in sections 4.4 and 4.5.

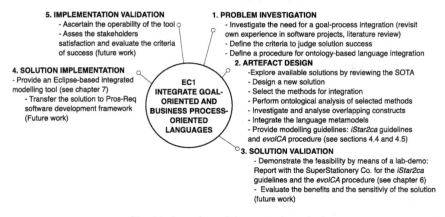

**Fig. 22.** Overview of the research method

### 4.3.2 Modelling language integration

In order to combine the process and intentional perspectives, we undertake a method engineering effort [120], where *i** and CA are considered method chunks. Note that the analysis of project situations is out of the scope of this research project. Instead, the focus placed on integrating the product and the process models of the methods. Taking the integration map proposed in [120] as reference method, Fig. 23 presents how we have operationalized each of its intentions and points to the corresponding section.

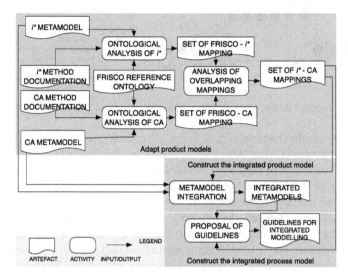

**Fig. 23.** Flow of modelling language integration

### 4.3.3    Ontological mapping between i* and CA

Integrating the product models of two methods requires identifying pairs of constructs that have the same semantics to merge them later. When the two product models have different terminology, as in the case of *i*\* and CA, Ralyté and Rolland suggest adapting the product models by means of name unification and transformation [120]. We have opted for ontological analysis, which is an equivalent strategy that offers strong theoretical foundations to method analysis and comparison. In an ontological analysis, the constructs of a method are mapped to the constructs of reference ontology. This is commonly used to assess to what extent the method covers the constructs of the ontology, and vice versa. For example, the UFO ontology is used as analysis tool for designing a modelling language for the ARKnowD method (Agent-oriented Recipe for Knowledge Management Systems Development) [121], [122]. ARKnowD has been created by mapping two distinct modelling languages: Tropos (for requirements analysis) [123] and AORML (for system design) [124].

Among other different possible ontologies (e.g., BWW, Chisholm's, DOLCE, UFO, etc.), we have chosen FRISCO as the reference ontology [97]. FRISCO is intended to provide a conceptual framework and suitable terminology for the most fundamental concepts in the information system field, including the notions of information, communication, organisation, and information system. Therefore, it naturally fits the analysis of methods such as *i*\* and CA, which offer different perspectives for information system engineering. In fact, we have experienced the appropriateness of this ontological analysis in a previous analysis related to one of the two methods, CA [125].

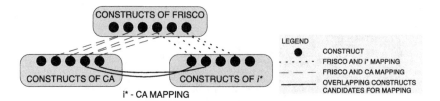

**Fig. 24.** Ontological analysis as a means to map constructs and guide method integration

The procedure is illustrated in Fig. 24. We have performed a separate ontological analysis of each method, establishing a complete mapping first between the constructs of *i** and the constructs of the FRISCO ontology and then between the constructs of CA and those of the FRISCO ontology. These complete mappings are reported in [126]. Since we are not interested in the criteria commonly applied in ontological analyses (e.g., construct excess, laconicism), we instead identify which pairs of constructs from each method are mapped onto the same ontological FRISCO construct (this is an alternative way of verifying construct similarity [120]). These constructs are considered overlapping, and, therefore, they are candidates for the *i**-CA mapping. Finally, we analyse the overlap and decide whether to map the concepts unconditionally (i.e., in all cases) or under certain conditions (see [127] for details).

Fig. 25 summarises the overlapping constructs found in this analysis. Each row describes a pair of constructs that overlap. FRISCO mappings consist of FRISCO constructs (underlined) that are qualified when necessary. It is common to find ontological analysis where the constructs of a method do not map directly (one-to-one) with the constructs of reference ontologies. For example, the OPEN Modelling Language (OML) has been mapped with the BWW and FRISCO ontologies, giving as a result the definitions for each OML construct based on one or several constructs from BWW or FRISCO [128].

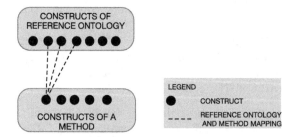

**Fig. 25.** Ontological analysis where one construct of a method map to more than one construct of a reference ontology

The ontological mapping between the constructs of *i** and the FRISCO ontology, and between the constructs of CA and FRISCO is not one-to-one in all cases. e.g., one construct of *i** do not map directly to just one construct of the FRISCO ontology in all cases, and the same for the mapping CA and FRISCO. For this case, FRISCO-based definitions have been established using more than one FRISCO construct for the *i** and CA constructs that required more than one FRISCO construct. For example, *istar.agent* maps with *FRISCO.actor, FRISCO.human actor* and *FRISCO.goals.* The FRISCO-based definition is: "<u>actor</u> with a concrete physical manifestation, for instance, a <u>human actor</u> that carries out actions to achieve <u>goals</u> by exercising its know-how" (see the first row of Table 2).

At the moment to perform the mapping between the constructs of *i\** and CA, the FRISCO-based definitions established for each *i\** and CA constructs are analysed. Then, the mappings are performed between the FRISCO-based definitions established by the *i\** and CA constructs. For example, *istar.agent* maps with a *FRISCO.actor with a concrete physical manifestation, for instance, a FRISCO.human actor that carries out actions to achieve FRISCO.goals by exercising its know-how*. The FRISCO definition for the <u>human actor</u> construct is: *FRISCO.human actor is a responsible FRISCO.actor with the capabilities and liabilities of a normal human being, in particular capable of performing FRISCO.perceiving actions, FRISCO.conceiving actions and FRISCO.representing actions*. On the other hand, for CA we find that *CA.organisational actor maps with a FRISCO.goal-pursuing actor*. The FRISCO definition for <u>goal-pursuing actor</u> is: *FRISCO.goal-pursuing actor is a FRISCO.actor performing an FRISCO.action, who deliberately aims at a specific FRISCO.goal when involved in that action*. The reasoning is, since *FRISCO.human actor* and *FRISCO.goal-pursuing actor* are specialisations of *FRISCO.actor;* we can conclude that *iStar.agent* and *CA.organisational actor* are equivalent.

Table 2 also indicates the ontological mappings between *i\** and CA that were decided in view of the FRISCO mappings (additional information of the methods was necessary). They are unconditional except in two cases. The CA method provides a set of unity criteria to identify and encapsulate communicative events that help to define them at an appropriate level of modularity (see [113] for details). Therefore, an *istar.task* is aligned to a *ca.communicative event* only if it satisfies the unity criteria. An *istar.resource* is aligned to a *ca.message structure* only if it is informational (e.g., a delivery note). Hence, *istar.physical resource* is not aligned to *ca.message structure* (e.g., a pallet of boxes is not a message structure).

**Table 2.** Mappings of candidate overlapping concepts

| *i\**– FRISCO mapping | | CA – FRISCO mapping | | *i\**– CA mapping |
|---|---|---|---|---|
| *i\** | FRISCO-based definition | CA | FRISCO-based definition | |
| agent | <u>actor</u> with a concrete physical manifestation, for instance, a <u>human actor</u> that carries out actions to achieve goals by exercising its know-how | organisational actor | <u>goal-pursuing actor</u> | equivalent |

| role | type of actors such that it characterizes the behaviour of agents | organisational role | type of goal-pursuing actors | equivalent |
|------|------|------|------|------|
| goal | goal that is an intentional desire of an actor | organisational goal | goal of an actor of an organisational system | equivalent |
| task | action that involves one actor in its pre-state and in its post-state | communicative event (CE) | composite transition | CE -> task / task -> CE (1) |
| resource | input actand of an action (if it is physical) or data that is the input actand of an action (if it is informational) such that an actor desires its provision and there are no open issues about how it will be achieved | message structure (MS) | type of messages; it is an input actand of a composite transition (i.e., the "communicative event") | MS -> resource / resource -> MS (2) |

Mapping conditions: (1) task satisfies unity criteria (2) resource is informational

Using ontological analysis to guide the *i** and CA concepts integration has provided us with a systematic way to map concepts and has prevented possible biases due to our subjective preconceptions (e.g., *istar.task* and *ca.communicative event* may look equivalent intuitively, but the systematic analysis has shown that they only map under specific conditions). More specifically, the lessons learned from the application of ontological analysis are the following: (1) the systematic ontological analysis has helped us to focus only on concepts with objective reasons for being candidate overlapping concepts (i.e., only concepts that map into the same or related FRISCO concepts are candidates for mapping); (2) the FRISCO mappings have provided the rationale to decide whether two concepts are totally equivalent or they map under specific conditions; and (3) in the latter case of concepts mapping under specific conditions, the FRISCO mappings have contributed to identifying those conditions.

### 4.3.4    Metamodel integration: the GoBIS metamodel

To integrate the *i** and CA metamodels, we analysed the *i**-CA mapping of concepts presented in Section 4.3.3. For each pair of mapping constructs, we need to decide whether we keep both corresponding metaclasses (one for each modelling method) or just one metaclass. We provide some heuristics to make this decision and the implications of each choice (see Fig. 26.a for the starting point).

In some cases, the two constructs are totally equivalent in the sense that their mapping is clear-cut (the constructs in the first three rows in Fig. 26 fall into this category). In these cases, the simplest solution is to keep only one metaclass and it needs to be decided which of the two involved metaclasses is removed. Then, the relationships in which the removed metaclass participated must be connected to the metaclass that is kept (see Fig. 26.b). In other cases, the mapping of two constructs is qualified with a condition specifying under what circumstances both constructs can be mapped (the constructs in the last two rows of Fig. 26). Thus, we propose to keep both metaclasses and create a relationship between them to provide traceability in cases where the specific constructs are mapped (see Fig. 26.c). The application of these heuristics to our case is summarised in Table 3.

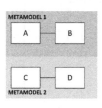   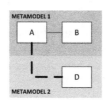   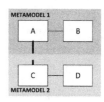

| (a) Example of two metamodels to integrate | (b) Case in which the constructs are totally equivalent (A≡C) and we decided to keep A | (c) Case in which the mapping is conditional (A≅C) |

**Fig. 26.** Deciding which metaclasses to keep

**Table 3.** Metamodel integration

| *i** meta-class | CA metaclass | Metaclasses kept | Rationale |
|---|---|---|---|
| AGENT | ORGANISATIONAL_ACT | AGENT | - Equivalent con- |
| ROLE | ORGANISATIONAL_ROLE | ROLE | structs |
| GOAL | GOAL | GOAL (from *i**) | - *i** provides more detailed definitions |
| TASK | COMMUNICATIVE_EVEN | Both | - Equivalent un- |
| RESOURC | MESSAGE_STRUCTURE | Both | der specific condi- |

To create the integrated GoBIS metamodel (see Fig. 27), we have started from: (1) the i* metamodel presented in [129] (adapted to be compliant to the *i** wiki version taken as reference in this work), and (2) the CA metamodel [125]. Both source metamodels are described in detail in [126] along with a discussion on why we selected them among other options. Following Table 3, all metaclasses from the source *i\** metamodel have been kept in the GoBIS metamodel. Conversely, metaclasses ORGANISATIONAL_ROLE, ORGANISATIONAL_ACTOR and GOAL that are part of the CA metamodel have been removed. A detailed description of the integrated metamodel is presented in [126].

It is important to clarify that all the concepts from the CA and *i\** metamodels have been considered for the ontological analysis. In this research just the ones with detected mappings between *i\** and CA are described. The full ontological analysis can be found at [126].

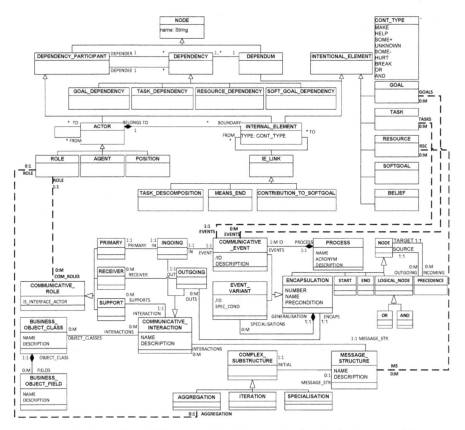

**Fig. 27.** Integration of *i\** metamodel and Communication Analysis metamodel

## 4.4  iStar2ca guidelines: top-down scenario guidelines

The objective of this section is to present the reasoning of the *iStar2ca* guidelines together with a running example to facilitate their understanding. In the section 5.5, the *iStar2ca* guidelines are presented as a method chunk of TraceME. The concepts, procedure, notation, and roles are also detailed to facilitate this chunk application. In addition, we present the *iStar2ca* guidelines at a glance to have them "close at hand" when they need to be applied.

We present the *iStar2ca* guidelines version 2.0 for a top-down scenario, an evolution of the *iStar2ca* guidelines V1.0 motivated by the empirical results described in the Chapter 6. The guidelines facilitate obtaining a CA model having as input a given *i\** model and establishing the mappings identified at a metamodel level. They indicate how to derive *ca.communicative events* and *ca.message structures* since these CA elements only map into *i\** elements under specific conditions. As seen in the previous section, *ca.organisational actors*, *ca.organisational roles*, and *ca.goals* are always mapped from *istar.agents*, *istar.roles*, and *istar.goals*.

Due to the strategic focus of *i\** models, some informational *istar.resources* or some *istar.tasks* that should map into *ca.message structures* or *ca.communicative events* may not be explicitly represented if they do not add strategically relevant knowledge. The *iStar2ca* guidelines not only provide advice on how to obtain CA elements from explicit *i\** elements but also on how to derive CA elements from *i\** elements that are not explicit but whose existence can nevertheless be deduced from the model. For example, the existence of an implicit informational *istar.resource* Insurance info can be deduced from the istar.goal Insurance provided (see 0).

CA focuses on communicational interactions among roles. Therefore, most guidelines involve *i\** dependencies among roles because satisfying the dependency will generally require some type of interaction. Each type of dependum has an associated guideline except resource dependums since informational and physical resources require different treatment.

The rationale of the guideline 1 deals with the case of dependums that are informational resources that (according to our metamodel alignment) map into *ca.message structures*. As a result, dependums that are informational resources induce communicative events. Thus, corresponding primary role is dependee role; corresponding receiver role is depender role; ingoing and outgoing interactions are the specification of message structures; if any of the SR elements of dependums' dependee and depender roles are tasks, they map into communicative events.

In our SuperStationery Co. case (see Section 4.2), the resource Order of the dependency from Sales Manager to Client maps into the CA message structure Order (see ingoing interaction in Table 4). The dependency for the Order from the Sales Manager to the Client indicates that the communicative event A client places an order (which allows the Client to communicate the order to the Sales Manager) is needed.

**Table 4.** Guideline 1 applied to dependency for Order from Sales Manager to Client

| *i\** | CA |
|---|---|
|  |  |

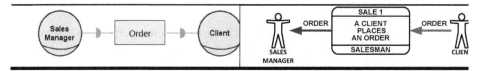

The rationale is that the *dependency* indicates that the *depender* expects to receive information from the *dependee*, and, therefore, a *communicative event* is needed to allow the *dependee* to communicate that information to the *depender*.

The *ca.interface actor*, however, cannot be determined from the *i\** model. It may or may not coincide with the *primary actor*. It may even be an actor that does not appear in the *i\** model at all because it is not strategically relevant. In the previous example, the *ca.interface actor* Salesman does not appear in the *i\** model.

Two *istar.tasks* (i.e., one for the *dependee* and another for the *depender*) may map into a single *communicative event*. The reason is that *i\** provides a separate SR diagram for each actor and then the behaviour of a single *communicative event* with two involved actors appears distributed in two *istar.tasks* that are visualized inside the boundary of the two actors. In our example, the task Place order in the Client SR maps into this new communicative event and a task of the Sales Manager SR (not shown in Fig. 21 for reasons of space) also maps into it.

A dependency may be connected to SR elements that are not tasks, thus indicating that the task of communicating the resource information is implicit in the *i\** model.

Guideline 1 is also applied to the dependencies for Order (from the Supplier to the Sales Manager), Order response (from the Sales Manager to the Supplier), and Logistics Info (from Supplier and Client to the Transport Manager) in order to map to the communicative events SALE 2, SALE 3, and SALE 4, respectively.

The rationale for the following group of guidelines deals with the rest of the dependency types (i.e., where dependums are goals, tasks, softgoals, or physical resources). Although these dependum types do not map directly into *ca.message structures*, they may indicate the existence of informational resources that are not explicit in the *i\** model.

We define an abstract guideline that yields to four actual guidelines that correspond to the rationale of the rest of the dependency types (from Guideline 2 to 5). The abstract guideline indicates that the dependee of a certain dependum that is required to give information to the depender about the <u>intentional satisfaction</u> of the dependum, this dependum induces a message structure. For these cases, dependums induces communicative events; corresponding primary role is dependee role; corresponding receiver role is depender role; ingoing and outgoing interactions are the specification of message structures; if any of the SR elements of dependums' dependee and depender roles are tasks, they map into communicative events.

We call this dependency an *informationable dependency* (because of the dependers' need to be informed about the intentional satisfaction of a certain dependum). The actual guidelines refine the notion of *intentional satisfaction* according to the type of the dependum.

The rationale for the guideline 2 is related to the case when the dependum is a goal. Thus, the notion of <u>intentional satisfaction</u> of the abstract guideline refines into attainment of this goal.

The informational resource mapping into the new *message structure* is implicit in the *i\** model. In our example, the goal dependency for `Insurance provided` from the `Client` to the `Insurance dept clerk` is an informationable dependency because the client needs to receive the clauses of the insurance. The message structure `Insurance info` represents this information. The communicative event `Insur. Dept. clerk specifies clauses` is obtained with communicative roles `Insurance Dept Clerk` and `Client`. The tasks `Specify clauses` (of the `Insurance Dept Clerk`) and `Obtain Insurance` (of the `Client`) map into this event.

The rationale for the guideline 3 is related to the case when the dependum is a task, the notion of <u>intentional satisfaction</u> of the abstract guideline refines into accomplishment of this task. The guideline 4 reviews the cases when the dependum is a softgoal, the notion of <u>intentional satisfaction</u> of the abstract guideline refines into level of satisfaction of this softgoal.

In our example, the softgoal dependency for `Products delivered timely by supplier` from the `Sales Manager` to the `Supplier` is an informationable dependency because the sales manager needs to be informed about the time when the products are shipped in order to supervise its timeliness. The message structure `Supplier ship notif` represents this information. The communicative event `Supplier notifies the shipping of the goods` is obtained with the communicative roles `Supplier` and `Sales Manager`. There is another informationable softgoal dependency for `Products delivered timely by truck driver` from the `Transport Manager` to the `Truck Driver`. The event `Truck Driver notifies the shipping of the goods` is obtained with communicative roles `Truck Driver` and `Transport Manager`.

Finally, for physical resources, the notion of <u>intentional satisfaction</u> of the abstract guideline refines into the provision of this physical resource (this rationale derives in the guideline 5).

The dependency for the physical resource `Products` from `Truck Driver` to `Supplier` leads to the creation of the communicative event `Supplier notifies the shipping of the goods`, which is merged with the notification that the `Supplier` gives to the `Sales Manager` (`SALE 6`). Thus, we add the receiver role `Truck Driver` to `SALE 6`. Similarly, the dependency for `Products` from `Client` to `Truck Driver` leads to the addition of the receiver actor `Client` to `SALE 7`. In the general case, the decision of merging events is not derivable from the *i\** model only and must be decided in an ad-hoc way by analysing whether the events can be performed simultaneously. Specific cases in which event merging can be deduced from the *i\** model are captured by Guideline 8.

If the information of an actor is necessary, which relevant information and must be registered in the IS; a communicative event and its corresponding message structure must be specified in order to register the actor information. This rationale conforms the guideline 6.

In our example, a message structure is required for Client in order to keep a registry of clients. Some of the information to be kept is: VAT number, Client name, Telephone, Registration date, Client Addresses. The communicative event Clie 1 is also specified; it is not visible in Fig. 21 because it is part of another process (i.e., Client management; acronym CLIE).

In general, an i* model does not provide information to deduce the ordering of the communicative events obtained from it or whether several communicative events can be merged into a single one and be performed simultaneously. However, there two are specific cases in which we can obtain the ordering of events as described in Guideline 7 and the merging of events as described in Guideline 8.

In some cases where there are two dependencies with the same dependum in an i* model, a precedence between the two mapped communicative events is implicitly induced. The rationales to establish precedences relationships are: if two dependencies have the same dependum, it means that the induced communicative events of each dependum have a precedence relationship; if the depender of a certain dependum is the dependee of other dependum, it means that there is a precendence relationship among the induced communicative events of each dependum. This rationale conforms the guideline 7.

In our example, there are two dependencies with the same dependum Order such that the Sales Manager is the depender in one and the dependee in the other. This indicates that the communicative event A client places an order where the Sales Manager receives the order must precede the event Sales Manager assigns supplier where the Sales Manager provides the order to the Supplier. Similarly, from the two dependencies with the dependum Products, it follows that the event Supplier notifies the shipping of the goods must precede the event Truck driver notifies the shipping of the goods.

If an i* model has two dependencies with the same dependum and dependee role, this indicates that the two mapped communicative events should be merged. This rationale is the base for the guideline 8.

In our example, the two dependencies for the Logistic Info from Supplier and Client to the Transport Manager map to the communicative event SALE 4 according to Guideline 1. Note that that the resulting communicative event is a merge of the communicative events induced by each dependency. The communicative event has the common dependee role (Transport Manager) as primary actor and its ingoing and outgoing interactions specify the message structure corresponding to the common dependum. In this case, the resulting communicative event has two receiver roles, which correspond to the depender roles (Supplier and Client).

For traceability purposes, the rationale of the guideline 9 provides some tips for naming the elements of the CED obtained by the guidelines. This guideline applies in the case where the dependee's SR related element is a task. Because the names of the CED elements are derived from the i* elements, we suggest following the good practices for naming i* elements reported in [55]:

- Communicative events are based on the name of Dependums' dependee + the name of the SR related element of the dependee+ the name of Dependums' dependum (optional)
- Primary roles' name are based on the name of Dependums' dependee role
- Receiver roles' name are based on the name of Dependums' depender role
- Message structures are based on the name of dependums if they are informational resources; otherwise, message structures are based on the name of the intentional satisfaction that corresponds to its corresponding dependum.

In our example, the communicative event SALE 1 is derived from the dependency for Order from Sales Manager to Client. Then, the names of the dependee (Client), the Client's SR related element (Place order), and Order are used to give a name to SALE 1 (A client places an order). The name of the dependee is used as the name of the primary role (Client), and the name of the depender is used as the name of the receiver role (Sales Manager). The message structure for the ingoing and outgoing relationships takes the name of the dependum Order since this dependum is an informational resource.

The CA elements obtained by applying the proposed guidelines are part of those that conform Communicative Event Diagrams (CEDs). On the other hand, the internal structure of *ca.message* structures is not obtained by applying the guidelines because *i** models do not provide the details about the resources. It is necessary to explore organisational documents to obtain it.

The *iStar2ca* guidelines at a glance are presented in the section 5.5.

## 4.5    evolCA procedure: evolution scenario procedure

We present the *evolCA* procedure 1.0 for an evolution scenario. We detail the design of the procedure and we explain it by applying it in a running example. The *evolCA* procedure at a glance can be consulted in the section 5.7 together with the details on how it is applied as part of the TraceME method.

The *evolCA* procedure facilitates obtaining an evolved CA model and establishing the traces identified at a metamodel level. As depicted in Fig. 28 the procedure has as input a given CA model that requires to be evolved (we call it CA_as-is); and a given *i** model that specifies the strategic conditions to be supported in the desired CA model (called CA_to-be). Thus, we propose with the *evolCA* procedure a goal-driven solution to evolve CA models.

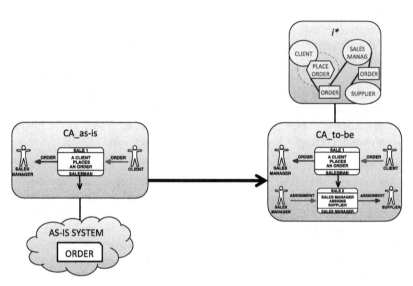

**Fig. 28.** Overview of the input and output of the *evolCA* procedure

In order to exemplify the procedure, let us assume that the CA_as-is model presented in Fig. 29 needs to evolve to a CA_to-be model in order to meet new business goals. These requirements of the *to-be* system are specified in the *i\** model (see Fig. 20 in section 4.2.1). To refer the elements of both CA_as-is and CA_to-be models we use the sub indexes $_{AS\text{-}IS}$ and $_{TO\text{-}BE}$ (e.g., a communicative event C of the CA$_{AS\text{-}IS}$ model is called C$_{AS\text{-}IS}$).

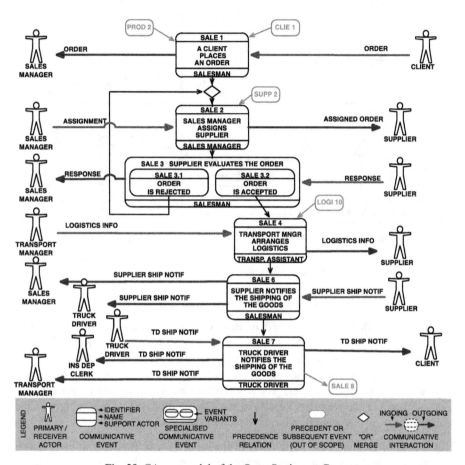

**Fig. 29.** CA_AS-IS model of the SuperStationery Co. case

The procedure of evolution is divided in four main steps that are illustrated in Fig. 30. For each step, we design a set of guidelines. We recommend applying the steps in the prescribed order.

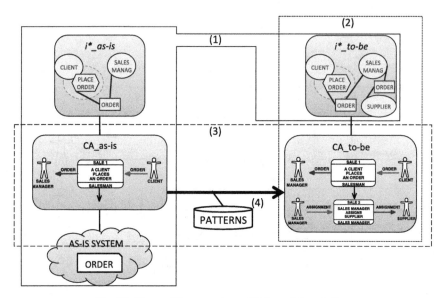

**Fig. 30.** Steps of the procedure of CA model evolution

The steps are the following (we later specify the guidelines of each step in detail):

**(1) Analysis of elements supported in the *as-is* system.** Revision of the *i\*_to-be* model in order to identify all the elements that need to be supported in the $CA_{TO-BE}$ and are already supported in the *as-is* system. Identified elements should be specified in the $CA_{TO-BE}$ model. As a result of this step, the $CA_{TO-BE}$ model will be formed by a set of elements from the $CA_{AS-IS}$. We say that the elements created in the $CA_{TO-BE}$ model will reflect the elements kept from the $CA_{AS-IS}$ model (i.e., it is a copy of the elements of the *as-is* system that should be kept in the $CA_{TO-BE}$).

**(2) Analysis of elements not supported in the *as-is* system.** Revision of the *i\** model in order to identify the elements that are not supported in the *as-is* system. Identified elements should be specified in the $CA_{TO-BE}$ model. Because of this step, the $CA_{TO-BE}$ model will reflect new elements that are no supported in the $CA_{AS-IS}$ model.

**(3) Analysis of elements that should be kept.** Revision of the $CA_{AS-IS}$ model to analyse the elements that were not selected in the step 1 to be kept in the $CA_{TO-BE}$ model. One possible reason why they were not selected is that the *i\** model is incomplete; that is, it does not specify all the strategic rationale of the *as-is* system. There may be two reasons for such incompleteness:

- It can occur when the *i\** model is focused on specifying dynamic goals (just the evolution part of the goal models) instead of specifying static goals. In this case, the analyst should decide which elements of the $CA_{AS-IS}$ should be kept in the $CA_{TO-BE}$ despite the fact that they are not explicitly equivalent with elements in the *i\** model.
- It can also occur due to the fact that goal models and business process models have a different nature; this way, business process models typically in-

clude information outside the scope of a goal model, such as the flow of business activities (e.g., *i\** models do not define the order of istar.tasks.

As a result of this step, the CA$_{TO\text{-}BE}$ model will include elements from the CA$_{AS\text{-}IS}$ that should be kept.

**(4) Application and/or creation of evolution patterns.** If the organisation has established rules about how their business process models should evolve, some evolution patterns are provided in order to facilitate evolution cases. In addition, we provide the facilities for creating new patterns. This is a practical option to specify good evolution practices and business rules for innovation. Because of this step, the CA$_{TO\text{-}BE}$ model will include elements that have evolved from the CA$_{AS\text{-}IS}$ and are justified by organisational evolution patterns. Also, since new patterns could emerge or being modified, a result of this step could also include modification in the pattern repository.

### *Guidelines for the step (1)*

Below we describe the guidelines belong to the step (1) (see Fig. 31). Here the focus is on the analysis of elements in the *i\** model that are supported in the *as-is* system. The dashed lines in Fig. 31 represent the traceability relationships that are established. Implicitly, there is a traceability relationship between the *i\** model and the *as-is* system, as well as there is a traceability relationship between the CA$_{AS\text{-}IS}$ and the *as-is* system. After the application of the guidelines for the step (1), the traceability between the CA$_{AS\text{-}IS}$ and CA$_{TO\text{-}BE}$ is established. In the same way, the traceability relationships between the *i\** and the CA$_{TO\text{-}BE}$.

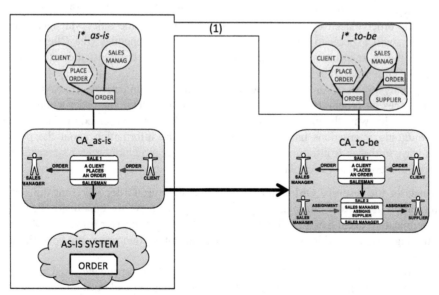

**Fig. 31.** Step (1) of the *evolCA* procedure

According to our integrated metamodel (see Fig. 27), an istar.resource is traced to a ca.message structure only if it is informational. In this case, we say that a certain informational resource is equivalent to a message structure if both of them specify the same information in an information system. Fig. 32 illustrates the reasoning for a first guideline, the guideline 1. This guideline deals with the analysis of $i^*$ models to identify dependums that are informational resources and specify certain phenomena of *as-is* information systems (see the dashed link between i* models and the *as-is* system). In addition, this guideline stands for identifying the message structures in $CA_{AS\text{-}IS}$ models that specify the same phenomena as the informational resources of the $i^*$ model (see the dashed link between the $CA_{AS\text{-}IS}$ and the *as-is* system). Decision making for defining if informational resources and message structures specify the same information is according to the analyst's criteria who is applying the guideline.

The reasoning of the guideline 1 indicates the following: if both a certain dependum of a dependency that is an informational resource and a Message structure of a $CA_{AS\text{-}IS}$ model ($M_{AS\text{-}IS}$)represent the same information in an *as-is* information system, we say that the dependum and the $M_{AS\text{-}IS}$ are equivalent. In this case, the $CA_{TO\text{-}BE}$ model should contain the $M_{AS\text{-}IS}$ such that: (1) the $M_{AS\text{-}IS}$'s communicative event ($C_{AS\text{-}IS}$) is specified in the $CA_{TO\text{-}BE}$ as $C_{TO\text{-}BE}$; (2) the $C_{AS\text{-}IS}$'s primary role is specified in the $CA_{TO\text{-}BE}$ as $C_{TO\text{-}BE}$'s primary role; (3) the $C_{AS\text{-}IS}$'s receiver role is specified in the $CA_{TO\text{-}BE}$ as $C_{TO\text{-}BE}$'s receiver role; (4) $C_{AS\text{-}IS}$'ingoing and outgoing interactions are specified in the $CA_{TO\text{-}BE}$ as $M_{TO\text{-}BE}$; (5) if any SR element of dependum's dependee and depender roles are tasks, those tasks are traced with $C_{TO\text{-}BE}$.

In the $i^*$ model of our SuperStationery Co. case (see section 4.2.1), the resource Order of the dependency from Sales Manager to Client specifies the informational resource about the order placed by the Client. In this dependency, the Sales Manager is the depender who expects to receive information from the dependee (the Client). This way, in the *as-is* information system the resource Order represents the information about the Order placed by a Client.

By analysing the $CA_{AS\text{-}IS}$ model, we discover the communicative event SALE 1 (A client places an order) that allows the Client to communicate the order to the Sales Manager. This way, the message structure Order (which is represented by the ingoing and outgoing interactions named Order) specifies the information about the order. This way, in the *as-is* information system the message structure Order represents the information about the Order placed by a Client.

Because of the resource Order and the message structure Order represent the same information in the *as-is* information system, we say that they are equivalent. Then, the communicative event SALE 1, the primary role Cient, the receiver role Sales Manager, the ingoing interaction order, and the outgoing interaction order, are specified in the $CA_{TO\text{-}BE}$.

Guideline 1 is also applied to the following pairs of dependency and message structure: Order (from the Supplier to the Sales Manager) and Assignment (of the communicative event SALE2); Order response (from the Sales Manager to the Supplier) and Response (of the communicative event SALE3); and Logistics Info (from the Supplier to the Transport Manager) and Logistics info (of the communicative event SALE4). As a result, the communicative events SALE2, SALE3 and SALE 4 with their corresponding primary actor, receiver actors, message structure, ingoning and outgoing communicative interactions are specified in the CA$_{TO-BE}$. Currently, The CA$_{TO-BE}$ has the appearance presented in Fig. 32.

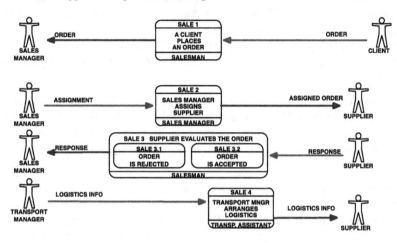

**Fig. 32.** CA$_{TO-BE}$ model after the application of the Guideline 1

After the application of the guideline 1, the traceability relationships among elements belong to the CA$_{AS-IS}$ and CA$_{TO-BE}$ are established according to the reasoning of the guideline. We call these traceability relationships as horizontal traceability relationships because they are established between models that are instance of the same metamodel (the concept of horizontal traceability relationship is defined in the Chapter 3). In this case, the horizontal traceabilities are established among the elements of two communicative event diagrams that are instance of the Communication Analysis metamodel.

Vertical traceability relationships should be established between the CA$_{TO-BE}$ elements and the $i^*$ model. Following our integrated metamodel (see Fig. 27), for each pair dependency D and message structure M identified as equivalent, create traceability relationships between the elements in the CA$_{TO-BE}$ and the $i^*$ elements such that: C$_{TO-BE}$'s primary role is traced with D's dependee role; C$_{TO-BE}$'s receiver is traced with D's depender role; C$_{TO-BE}$ is traced with the dependum and the SR tasks of D's dependee and depender roles if any.

The following group of guidelines deals with the rest of the dependency types (i.e., when dependums are goals, tasks, softgoals, or physical resources). As we can deduct from our metamodel (see 0), these dependum types are not directly related with *ca.message structures*, they may indicate the existence of informational resources that are not explicit in the $i^*$ model. We define an abstract guideline that yields to four guidelines (from guideline 2 to 5) depending on the type of dependum.

The reasoning for the abstract guideline yield with the identification if both a certain dependum of a dependency and a certain message structure of a CA$_{AS-IS}$ model

($M_{AS-IS}$) represent the same information in an *as-is* information system, then we say that de dependum and the $M_{AS-IS}$ are equivalent. Also, if dependum's dependee is required to give information to the dependums's depender about the *intentional satisfaction* of this dependum, the $CA_{TO-BE}$ model should contain the $M_{AS-IS}$ such that: (1) the $M_{AS-IS}$'s communicative event ($C_{AS-IS}$) is specified in the $CA_{TO-BE}$ as $C_{TO-BE}$; (2) the $C_{AS-IS}$'s primary role is specified in the $CA_{TO-BE}$ as $C_{TO-BE}$'s primary role; (3) the $C_{AS-IS}$'s receiver role is specified in the $CA_{TO-BE}$ as $C_{TO-BE}$'s receiver role; (4) $C_{AS-IS}$'ingoing and outgoing interactions are specified in the $CA_{TO-BE}$ as $M_{TO-BE}$; (5) if any SR element of dependums's dependee and depender roles are tasks, those tasks are traced with $C_{TO-BE}$.

We call this dependency an *informationable dependency*. The following guidelines (from 2 to 5) refine the notion of intentional satisfaction according to the type of dependum. For example, the reasoning for the guideline 2 is: When the dependum is a goal, the notion of intentional satisfaction of the abstract guideline refines into the attainment of this goal.

In our SuperStationery Co. example, the goal dependency for Insurance Provided from the Client to the Insurance dept clerk is an informationable dependency because the client needs to receive the clauses of the insurance. By reviewing the *as-is* information system, we distinguish that there is no support for Insurance provision. In the $CA_{AS-IS}$ model, we identify that there are no an equivalent message structure that represents provision of insurances in the *as-is* information system. In this situation, the guideline 2 cannot be applied because we do not find an equivalent specification of this goal neither in the *as-is* information system or $CA_{AS-IS}$. As a conclusion, no changes are introduced in the $CA_{TO-BE}$ model for the SuperStationery Co.

Otherwise, if the $CA_{AS-IS}$ model would contain a message structure for insurance provision to the Client, the guideline 2 could be applied by specifying all the information related to this message structure to the $CA_{TO-BE}$ model.

We treat the cases when the elements of *i\** models and $CA_{AS-IS}$ models are no equivalents in the guidelines 6.

The reasoning for the guideline 3 says that when the dependum is a task, the notion of intentional satisfaction of the abstract guideline refines into accomplishment of this task. For the guideline 4, we treat the case when the dependum is a softgoal. Thus, the notion of intentional satisfaction of the abstract guideline refines into level of satisfaction of this softgoal.

In our SuperStationery Co. case, the softgoal dependency for Products delivered timely by supplier from the Sales Manager to the Supplier is an informationable dependency because the sales manager needs to be informed about the time when the products are shipped in order to supervise its timeliness. By reviewing the *as-is* system, we recognise the support for shipping notification. In addition, in the $CA_{AS-IS}$ model there is a message structure (See the ingoing interaction Supplier ship notif from the primary actor Supplier to the communicative event SALE 6) that stands for this purpose. Thus, the softgoal Products delivered timely by supplier is an informationable dependency and the message structure Supplier ship notif are equivalent; which lead the application of the guideline 4 by specifying in the $CA_{TO-BE}$ the following elements:

the communicative event SALE 6, the primary actor Supplier, the receiver actor Sales Manager, and the ingoing and outgoing interactions Supplier ship notif.

The guideline 4 is also applied to the softgoal Products delivered timely by truck driver. As a result, the communicative event SALE 7 (with the Truck driver as a primary actor, the Transport Manager as a receiver actor, and ingoing and outgoing communicative interactions) is specified in the $CA_{TO\text{-}BE}$ model.

For the reasoning of the guideline 5, we establish that when dependum is a physical resource, the notion of <u>intentional satisfaction</u> of the abstract guideline refines into the provision of this physical resource.

In the SuperStationery Co. case, two physical resources are identified: Products from Truck driver to Supplier and Products from Client to Truck Driver. Both physical resources are specified in the *as-is* system and corresponds to the message structures Supplier Ship notif of the communicative event SALE 6, and the message structure TD ship notif of the communicative event SALE 7. We merge then this information and we specify the receiver actors Client (for SALE 6) and Supplier (SALE 7) in the $CA_{TO\text{-}BE}$. Here the merging decision is justified because the softgoals and physical resources are specifying the same information of the *as-is* system.

After the application of the guidelines 4 and 5, the $CA_{TO\text{-}BE}$ has evolved to the appearance presented in Fig. 33.

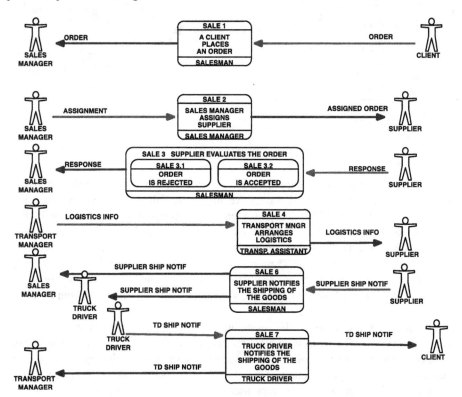

**Fig. 33.** $CA_{TO\text{-}BE}$ model after the application of the guidelines 4 and 5

## *Guidelines for the step (2)*

Below we describe the guidelines belong to the step (2) (see Fig. 34). Here the focus is on the analysis of elements of the *i\** model that were no supported in the *as-is* system. As we see in Fig. 34, no dashed lines are connecting the *i\** model with the *as-is* system and the CA$_{AS\text{-}IS}$. In this case the traceability relationships are established among the elements of the *i\** model and the CA$_{TO\text{-}BE}$.

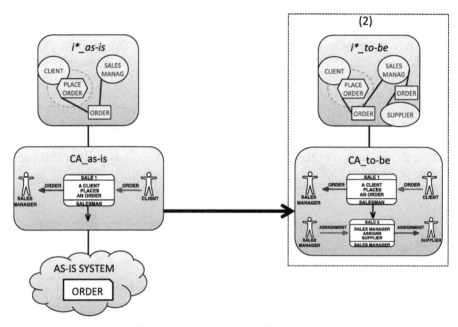

**Fig. 34.** Step (2) of the *evolCA* procedure

For the elements that are no supported in the *as-is* system (consequently these elements are not supported in the CA$_{AS\text{-}IS}$), we suggest to follow the top-down scenario guidelines *iStar2ca guidelines 2.0* presented in the section 4.4. The rationale is that there are no elements specified in the *as-is* system that can be kept for the CA$_{TO\text{-}BE}$ model. As a result, new elements should be created in the CA$_{TO\text{-}BE}$ model in order to support the requirements of the *i\** model. The *iStar2ca guidelines* 2.0 stand for this situation, when new elements are specified as requirements in evolution scenarios. Thus, the *iStar2ca guidelines* indicates how to specify this requirements from *i\** models to CA models.

The guideline 6 establishes the reasoning to apply the *iStar2ca guidelines* 2.0 in evolution scenarios. The reasoning is when a certain dependum of a dependency does not specify the information of an *as-is* system; consequently this dependum is not equivalent to a message structure of a CA$_{AS\text{-}IS}$ model (M$_{AS\text{-}IS}$). Thus, this dependum represents new requirements to be supported in the CA$_{TO\text{-}BE}$ model. In this case, apply the *iStar2ca guidelines* 2.0 to create the new elements in the CA$_{TO-BE}$ corresponding to the dependum (see the reasoning of the iStar2ca guidelines in the section 4.4 or the iStar2ca guidelines at a glance in the section 5.5).

By analysing our *i\** model for the SuperStationery Co. case, we discover that the informational resource Logistics Info from Client to Transport Manager is not actually specified neither in the *as-is* system or in the CA$_{AS-IS}$ model. Then, we apply the guideline 1 of the *iStar2ca guidelines* in order to create the new elements in the CA$_{TO-BE}$ corresponding to the informational resource Logistics Info. As a result, this dependency induces the creation of a communicative event for supporting the management of the logistics and the communication to the Client, which is merged with the notification that the Transport Manager gives to the Supplier. Thus, we add the receiver role Client to SALE 4.

The dependency for the goal Insurance Provided is an informationable dependency because the Client needs to receive the clauses of the insurance. This goal is not supported neither in the *as-is* system or CA$_{TO-BE}$, which trigger the application of the guideline 6. The communicative event Insur. Dept. Clerk Specifies Clauses (SALE 5) is obtained with the communicative roles Insurance Department Clerk and Client (see Fig. 35)

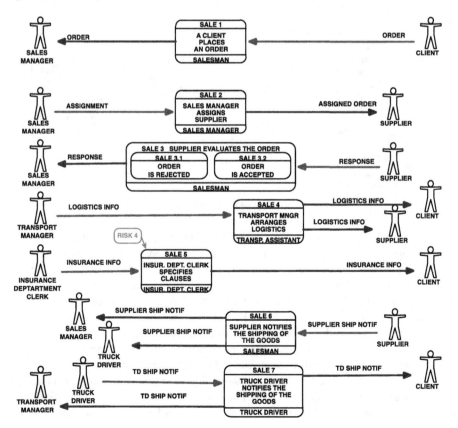

**Fig. 35.** CA$_{TO-BE}$ model after the application of the guideline 6

With the finalisation of the step (2) the analysis of the $i*$ model to specify the $CA_{TO-BE}$ is done. The step (3) stand for the analysis of the elements that are specified in the $CA_{AS-IS}$ and but they do not have an equivalent element in the $i*$ model. For example, precedence relationships and task ordering cannot be deduced. Next section will present how to confront this issue.

### *Guidelines for the step (3)*

Below we describe the guidelines belong to the step (3) (see Fig. 36). Here the focus is on the analysis of elements of the $CA_{AS-IS}$ that should be kept but the requirements for these elements are not specified in the $i*$ model. As is presented in Fig. 36, the traceability relationships are horizontal connecting the $CA_{AS-IS}$ and the $CA_{TO-BE}$.

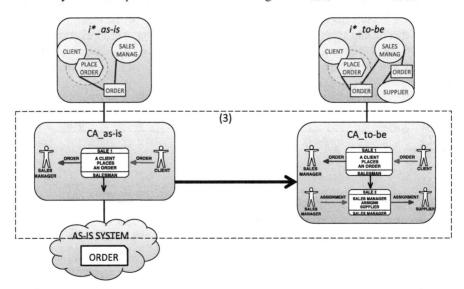

**Fig. 36.** Step (3) of the *evolCA* procedure

We review the elements of the $CA_{AS-IS}$ that does not have any horizontal traceability relationship with the $CA_{TO-BE}$ (i.e., the elements that were no processed in the step (1)). As we introduced before in the step (3), there are two possibilities that explain why requirements of the $CA_{AS-IS}$ could not be explicitly specified in the $i*$ model. One possibility is justified because of the nature of the $CA_{AS-IS}$. There are some elements that cannot be deduced from $i*$ models. For this purpose, first we review the elements that cannot be traced with $i*$ models like precedence relationships and relationships to other processes. On the other hand, other possibility is that the $i*$ model just specify dynamic goals (i.e., new goals or strategies to be implemented in the *to-be*). Nevertheless, some elements of the $CA_{AS-IS}$ are strategically important to be kept for the *to-be*; but they are not specified in the $i*$ model because they are not new. For this situation, we review communicative events and their actors in order to discover elements that were no kept based on the step (1). Thus, the analyst is responsible of decision making in order to specify elements in the $CA_{TO-BE}$. Decisions are taken according to the domain and the requirements that need to be fulfilled by the *to-be* system.

For the former possibilities, the reasoning of the guideline 7 establishes how to proceed:

When the elements of the $CA_{AS-IS}$ are not equivalent with elements in the i* model, they can be specified in the $CA_{TO-BE}$ if (1) they corresponds to elements that cannot be traced with i* models because of their business process nature; or (2) they do not corresponds with dynamic goals but are strategically important to be kept in the $CA_{TO-BE}$. For each possibility do the following:

For (1):

a) Review the precedences relationships of the $CA_{AS-IS}$ and specify all of them in the $CA_{TO-BE}$ if necessary for the *to-be* system.
b) Review the precedences and relationships with other processes of the $CA_{AS-IS}$; then specify all of them in the $CA_{TO-BE}$ if necessary for the *to-be* system.

For (2):
a) Review the communicative events, the primary and receiver actors of the $CA_{AS-IS}$; then specify all of them in the $CA_{TO-BE}$ if necessary for the *to-be* system.

In our $CA_{AS-IS}$ of the SuperStationery Co. case, we distinguish that the precedence relationships among communicative events, the relationships with other processes (e.g., CLIE 1, PROD 2, etc.,), and the receiver actor Insurance Dept Clerk of the SALE 7 are not equivalent with elements of the i* model and for that reason they were no processed in the step (1). By applying the guideline 7, we decide the following:

- To keep all of the precedence relationships that are specified in the $CA_{AS-IS}$. In addition, we decide to create precedences for the SALE 5 because it was no specified in the $CA_{AS-IS}$. We review the new requirements and we discover that the insurance notification should be given to the Client before the Supplier notifies the ship of the goods (see the precedence relationships in Fig. 37).
- To keep all the relationships with other processes of the $CA_{AS-IS}$ because they are necessary for the *to-be* system. The sales management process should be connected with the rest of the processes of SuperStationery Co. as the creation of new Clients, Suppliers, etc. (see the gray rectangles in Fig. 37).
- The receiver actor Insurance Dept Clerk of the SALE 7 is not kept. In the *as-is* system, first the Insurance Dept Clerk received the communication about the shipping of the goods to proceed with the issuance of the clauses. For the *to-be*, this behaviour is changed with the introduction of SALE 5, the Insurance Dept Clerk sent the communication about the insurance information to the Client before to ship the goods. Thus, his/her participation in the process finishes with the communication of the clauses to the Client. Notice that the actor Insurance Dept Clerk of the SALE 7 is not specified in the $CA_{TO-BE}$ in Fig. 37.

Fig. 37 presents the CA$_{TO-BE}$ after the application of the first three steps of the evolution procedure.

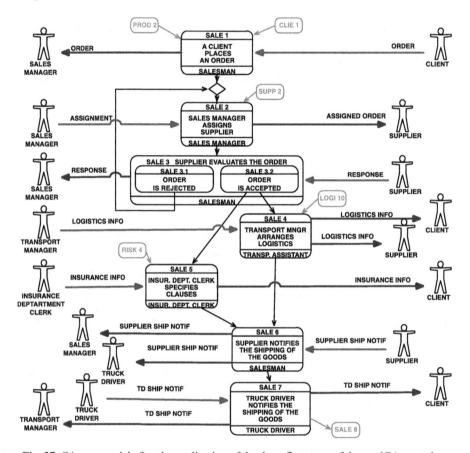

**Fig. 37.** CA$_{TO-BE}$ model after the application of the three first steps of the *evolCA procedure*

## Guidelines for the step (4)

The fourth step is optional because the decision to apply or create patterns depends of the organisation and the context of the information system to evolve. Below we describe the reasoning for the design of the guidelines belongs to the step (4) (see Fig. 38). Here the focus is on the analysis of possible evolution patterns that can be applied or created instead of the guidelines for evolution presented in the steps (1) to (3).

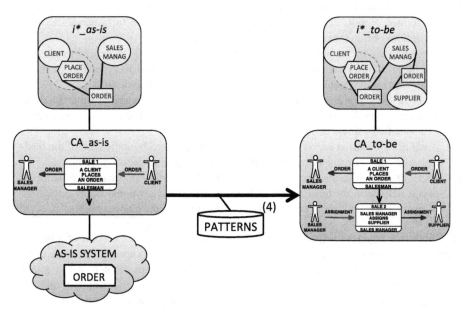

**Fig. 38.** Step (4) of the *evolCA* procedure

España has carried out a revision about communicative behaviour [7]. This revision focus over communicative events and it highlights communicative events that can be revised by both analyst and the users. These communicative events can lead changes in business processes specification.

Due we are aiming at supporting model evolution; we build upon this revision as a starting point for evolution patterns. Hence, we identify a set of business activities behaviour that analyst can revise in order to improve the current business process. As an initial attempt, we identify the following business activities behaviour:

**Table 5.** Business activities behaviour and their corresponding evolution patterns

- *Exception in internal treatments:* A business activity that involves an authorization can demand an exceptional behaviour related to approvals or decision-making.
- *Deviations from optimist assumptions:* A business activity related to carry out orders of resources can lead saturation of resources and it can affect mediator objects that are responsible of a specific management (i.e. saturation of resources, saturation places, over booking, supplies, etc.). As a result, deviation from optimist assumptions can affect basic business activities and it can demand exceptional behaviour related to approvals in order to maintain resource balance.
- *Exceptions in external treatments:* Exceptions in business activities outside the range of action of organisational system or environment. This case is related to a business activity that depends of feedback from a business activity outside range of action of organisational system. These exceptions in external treatments can imply a decision taking in order to offer different alternative.

- *Issuance audit:* Business activities related to issue specific documents can demand an audited output. Consequently, business activities related to issuance can lead exceptional behaviour in order to ensure issuance.
- *Reception audit:* As before business activity, reception audit is related to confirm reception of information. Thus, business activities related to reception of information can lead exceptional behaviour in order to ensure reception.
- *Audit of occurrence:* A business activity needs the occurrence of other business activity. It can demand an exceptional behaviour related to ensure the occurrence of a specific business activity.
- *Audit of information content:* A business activity affected by indicators of the business rules can demand an exceptional behaviour related to decision taking.
- *Audit of normative events:* Business activities related to normative sequence of events defined in the business rules. It can demand an exceptional behaviour where business activities should be reordered in order to fulfil the business rules.

We think that business activities behaviour mentioned above can be part of a body of knowledge to guide business processes evolution. In order to specify business activities behaviour, we propose to take advantage of the concept of pattern. "A pattern describes a problem which occurs over and over again in our environment, and then describes the core of the solution to that problem, in such a way that you can use this solution million times over, without ever doing it the same way twice" [130]. Even though pattern definition was thought in the context of buildings and constructions, software engineering community has used this concept [131]. In order to bring a pattern-driven specification for business processes model evolution, we were inspired in the patterns metamodel for system engineering presented by [132]. As a result, we propose the metamodel presented in Fig. 39.

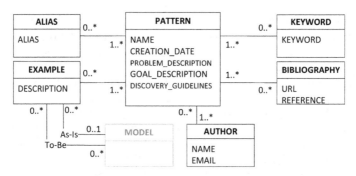

**Fig. 39.** Pattern definition metamodel

The PATTERN metaclass can have multiples keywords (KEYWORD metaclass) to allow its localisation. In addition, PATTERN can have related bibliography or documentation (BIBLIOGRAPHY metaclass). In addition, it is recommendable to specify the author information in order to create contacts or networking to build the pattern repository (AUTHOR metaclass). We advise to specify one example (at least) in order to clarify it use (EXAMPLE metaclass). EXAMPLE metaclass is pointing to MODEL metaclass via two references in order to represent both relation As-Is model and To-Be model. This way, we suggest exemplifying each pattern by means of a description, As-Is and To-Be models. MODEL metaclass is painted grey because is an external metaclass. For instance, BPMN and Activity Diagrams of UML are models that could be used as example for the specification of a pattern. Also, PATTERN metaclass can have a set of alias (also-known-as) (ALIAS metaclass).

## *How to specify new patterns?*

In order to illustrate how to specify new patterns, we use the pattern metamodel presented in Fig. 39 to specify two business activity behaviours: a) exception in internal treatments and b) issuance audit.

**Table 6.** Specification of the pattern of exception in internal treatments

| PATTERN |
|---|
| **Name:** Exception in internal treatments |
| **Creation date:** 01/12/2011 |
| **Problem description:** A business activity that involves an authorization can demand an exceptional behaviour related to approvals or decision taking |
| **Goal description:** Offer possibility of rejections or alternative decisions. |
| **Discovery guidelines:** The analyst should ask the stakeholders the following questions. *Is this business activity just a formal acknowledgement step, or is it a seal of approval? Can it occur that the decision is negative, that the approval is denied?* In case the stakeholders keep dismissing such possibility, the analyst should insist. *Then, it never has occurred that the decision maker communicated a rejection, right? In addition, you consider impossible that this can ever happen in the future, right? Moreover, if it ever happens and the software system does not account for such rejection, the consequences are not important, right?* The intention is to make the stakeholders aware and reconsider whether the alternative path is impossible or it has a small frequency of occurrence but it is still possible. |

| AUTHOR |
|---|
| **Name:** Arturo González |
| **Email:** agdelrio@dsic.upv.es |
| **Name:** Sergio España |
| **Email:** sergio.espana@pros.upv.es |

| KEYWORD |
|---|
| **Keyword:** authorisation, rejection, decision, fork |

| BIBLIOGRAPHY |
|---|
| **Url:** http://riunet.upv.es/handle/10251/14572 |
| **Reference:** S. España, "Methodological integration of Communication Analysis into a Model-Driven software development framework," PhD. Computer Science, Departamento de Sistemas Informáticos y Computación (DSIC), Universitat Politècnica de València, Valencia, 2011. |

| EXAMPLE |
|---|
| **Description:** In the illustrative example, the analyst should also investigate whether the employee could insist in case of rejection; for instance, by providing new proofs of the expenses and a letter justifying the total amount, or by lowering the total amount. In such case, a loopback in the process would appear. |

| As-Is |
|---|

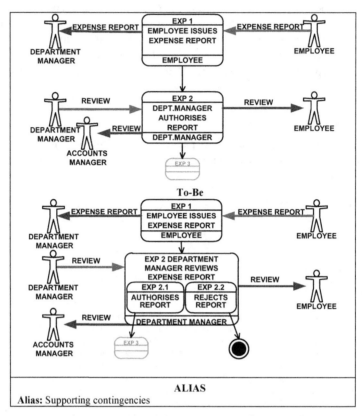

**ALIAS**

**Alias:** Supporting contingencies

Due to the pattern metamodel is not defined for a specific modelling language; we use the communicative event diagrams, a modelling technique of the Communication Analysis method to exemplify the pattern for business activity behaviour of exception in internal treatments [66]. On the other hand, to exemplify the pattern for business activity behaviour of issuance audit, we chose UML activity diagrams (see Table 7).

Afterward, we propose to store pattern specification in a pattern model repository. This way, when an analyst analyses a business process, he/she may require the application of a pattern. Then, analyst chooses patterns from the pattern model repository to apply it to the business process according to its behaviour. Analyst can create new patterns to support business process behaviour that have not been previously considered.

**Table 7.** Specification of the pattern of issuance audit

| PATTERN |
| --- |
| **Name:** Issuance audit |
| **Creation date:** 29/09/2011 |
| **Problem description:** To introduce controls (audit) in a business activity that involves issues of documents or reports can demand exceptional behaviour related to check this issue. |
| **Goal description:** Offer business activities for ensuring an audited output of |

specific issues.

**Discovery guidelines:** The analyst should ask the stakeholders the following questions. *Is this business activity just an issue, or is it necessary to check or approve this issue?* In case the stakeholders keep dismissing such possibility, the analyst should insist. *Then, it never has occurred that information about issue could be checked/ used? In addition, you consider impossible that this can ever happen in the future, right? And if it ever happens and the software system does not account for such checked/used, the consequences are not important, right?* The intention is to make the stakeholders aware and reconsider whether the business activity related to audition is impossible or it has a small frequency of occurrence but it is still possible.

## AUTHOR
**Name:** Arturo González
**Email:** agdelrio@dsic.upv.es
**Name:** Sergio España
**Email:** sergio.espana@pros.upv.es

## KEYWORD
**Keyword:** audit, control, monitor, check

## BIBLIOGRAPHY
**Url:** http://riunet.upv.es/handle/10251/14572
**Reference:** S. España, "Methodological integration of Communication Analysis into a Model-Driven software development framework," PhD. Computer Science, Departamento de Sistemas Informáticos y Computación (DSIC), Universitat Politècnica de València, Valencia, 2011.

## EXAMPLE
**Description:** In the illustrative example, the analyst should also investigate whether the salesman should audit the issue of photographers receipts; for instance, to check who is the person in charge to issue the receipt, each time a photographers receipts is issued, a time stamp and the identifier of the salesman are recorded. This way, an audit in the process would appear.

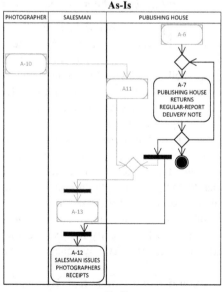

**As-Is**

**To-Be**

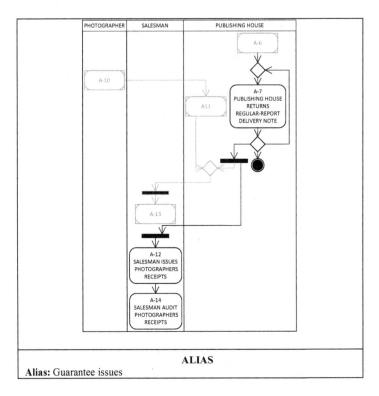

## Establishing the traces among as-is, to-be and goal models

For establishing the traces, we apply concepts of the Delta Analysis technique defined in the section 4.7. Traceability between *as-is* and *to-be* models are called horizontal traceability relationships. To establish horizontal traceability relationships we use delta models because of the facilities provided by delta models to specify delta operators (Bernstain called delta operators as mapping operators). The role of delta operators in an evolution process is to indicate changes in *as-is* models and *to-be* models. In particular, we analyse the operator match; accordingly, we propose a delta metamodel that takes advantage of traceability metamodel proposed by Jouault [133] in order to provide artefacts to store traceability information (details about the design of the delta metamodel is presented in the section for Delta Analysis 4.7). We extend the delta metamodel in order to introduce the pattern support. Fig. 40 shows the delta metamodel with the pattern extension. It contains an EVOLUTION_TRACE metaclass owing an operator attribute to store information about evolution. We conceive an enumerator (EVOLUTION_OPERATOR) to specify four basic evolution operators:

- The first basic evolution operator is equal. By equal, we mean that two model elements are alike.
- The second basic evolution operator is modified. By modified, we mean that two model elements are alike but some properties could be changed. For instance, the property name of a business process could be changed.

- The third basic evolution operator is added. By added, we mean that a model element has been added.
- The fourth basic evolution operator is deleted. By deleted, we mean that a model element has been deleted.

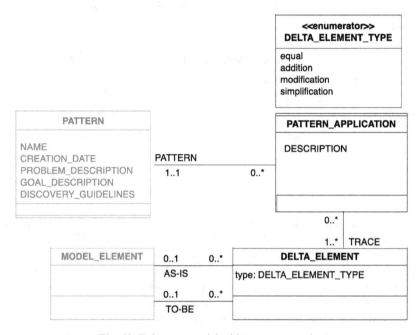

**Fig. 40.** Delta metamodel with pattern extension

TRACE metaclass is pointing to MODEL_ELEMENT metaclass via two references in order to represent both *as-is* and *to-be* relationships from/to TRACE metaclass. MODEL ELEMENT metaclass is an external metaclass (this metaclass is grey in order to indicate that it is part of the metamodel that has been linked with delta metamodel). In order to apply the proposed pattern definition metamodel (see Fig. 41) we define a PATTERN_APPLICATION metaclass. Basically, this metaclass consist of an abstraction to relate patterns definition with a set of evolution traces. PATTERN_APPLICATION metaclass is pointing to PATTERN metaclass and it is pointing to TRACE metaclass. PATTERN metaclass is an external metaclasses from pattern definition metamodel. The objective of PATTERN_APPLICATION metaclass is recording evolution traces when a pattern is applied. This way, we can provide a support to store the set of evolution traces when a pattern is applied; for instance, the information about traces can be recorded in a text log. Finally, the delta operator are established by means of an enumerator (DELTA_OPERATOR <<enumerator>>)

To illustrate, Fig. 42 presents an instance of the delta metamodel with pattern extension. We use communicative event diagram metamodel as business process model [66] (in order to facilitate well understanding, we provide a view of this metamodel in 0).

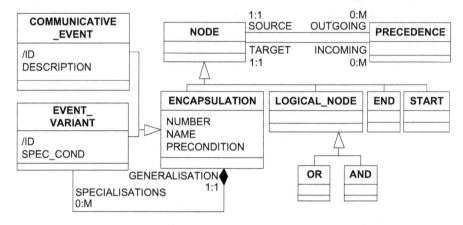

**Fig. 41.** View of communicative event diagram metamodel

Fig. 42 describes the model evolution process of expense report business process model; which corresponds with the example presented in Table 5. Although our evolution process supports the evolution of a set of models, in order to simplify, in this example we describe the evolution traces to evolve from one *as-is* model to one *to-be* model. Note that traces whose attribute is equal do not have association with pattern application. We advise do not store information related to equal delta operations because they do not provide useful information about changes in the *to-be* models. However, we provide support for equal delta operator in the case of the analyst considers its use. We advise to provide enough information in order to provide complete logs or reports about model changes. It is important to focus the attention on the attribute description of the PATTERN_APPLICATION metaclass.

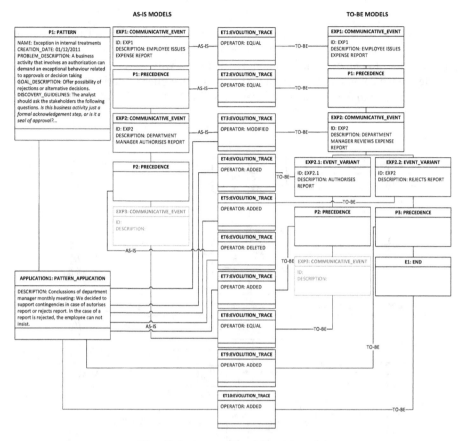

**Fig. 42.** Instance of the delta metamodel

The following guidelines stand for the use of the evolution patterns. The analyst in charge of a certain evolution project should makes decisions about to apply existent patterns already specified in the patterns repository or create new ones based on organisational needs.

The guideline 8 relies on the assumption that an organisation wants to reuse existent patterns defined in the pattern repository for evolving business process models, for example, like the ones presented in Table 5. They want to benefit from common best practices when evolving business process models and traceability support. For the former purposes, we advise to do the following:

(1) Find the most appropriated pattern according to the pattern description in the pattern repository. Thus, apply the pattern

(2) Create an instance of the delta metamodel for establishing the traceability relationships.

For instance, in our SuperStationery Co. case, the *as-is* is presented in Fig. 43. To place an order, most clients phone the sales department and are attended by a sales-

man (this process is related to the communicative event SALE 1). Then the client
requests products. The salesman takes note of the order. Then the sales manager assigns the order to one of the many suppliers that work with the company (this process
is related to the communicative event SALE 2). The supplier authorises the order (this
process is related to the communicative event SALE 3).

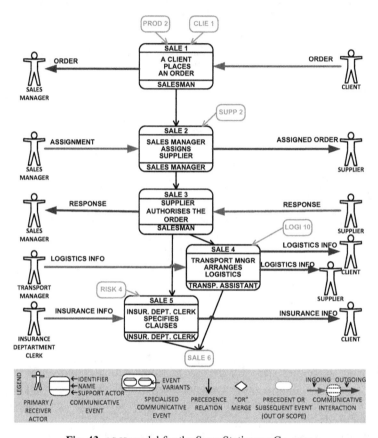

**Fig. 43.** AS-IS model for the SuperStationery Co. case

To carry out the evolution process to a *to-be* situation, we apply the guideline 8. First,
we analyse the pattern repository to discover the behaviour of the business process
with the problem description of the patterns. Then we apply the most convenient the
pattern by means of the delta metamodel. Hence, analysing the *as-is* model, we can
suggest an evolution process focus on the behaviour of the communicative event
SALE 3 because it involves an internal treatment that can be traced with business
activities behaviour analysed in 0. This way, by applying the pattern described, we
analyse both problem description and goal description to relate communicative event
SALE 3 with this pattern. We analyse the discovery guidelines suggested by the pattern to formulate questions below: Is the order always authorised? Is it impossible that
an order is rejected? As a result, we analyse the example provided by the pattern spec-

ification and we decide to apply the pattern. In this case, we apply the evolution met-amodel to use evolution traces. Thus, we start to record each use of evolution traces. For instance, when an order is rejected, the sales manager assigns the supplier to the order to evaluate it again (loopback). In this case, we add an or element in the *to-be* model to indicate that SALE 2 can occur after the occurrence of SALE 1 or it can occur after the occurrence of the event variant SALE 3.1 (see the diamond that precedes communicative event SALE 2).

In order to simplify, for this example we used the notation for delta models to specify the traces (see the section 4.7 for further details). Traces with background grey are related to pattern application and they are stored to create an evolution log. In order to simplify the example, we do not draw each association among evolution traces and pattern application. In contrast, we provide a rectangle that groups the set of evolution patterns associated with pattern application. However the equal evolution operator does not provide meaningful information about the evolution process, for illustrative purposes, we specified it to register the business activities that persist after evolution process.

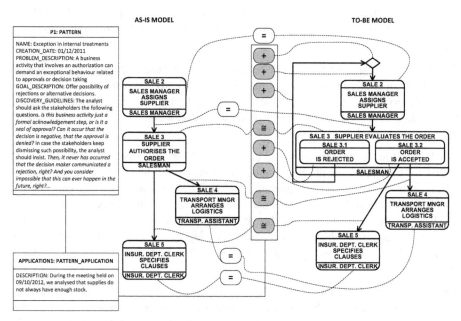

**Fig. 44.** Evolution traces for sales manager business process of SuperStationery Co. case

To conclude, due to the application of the pattern repository and the delta metamodel is not dependent with the modelling language; we can use this approach to support conceptual model evolution in general.

Since the pattern repository is created to let the specification of new patterns and the edition of the existing ones, we specify the guideline 9 in order to guide how to enrich the pattern repository metamodel. Organisations with established organisational rules and best practices to evolve their business process models are the ones that can get the benefits of the pattern repository: formalisation of the best practices and traceability support. To apply the pattern repository, we advise to do the following: (1) Create an instance of the pattern evolution metamodel and specify the new pattern to be stored in the pattern repository; (2) apply the pattern to the certain cases that derived its creation; (3) create an instance of the delta metamodel for establishing the traceability relationships.

We envision that the pattern repository will grow with its application for supporting evolution of real cases.

### 4.6    ca2oom integration framework

The main objective of this method chunk is to support a combined use of the Communication Analysis and OO-Method as part of the forward solutions of the TraceME method.

The *ca2oom* integration framework (*ca2oom*) defines stages, phases, and activities that aim at integrating requirements methods in MDD environments. This framework takes into account modelling activities and model transformation activities. As a result of the execution of all the framework's activities, a diagramming tool and model transformation module are obtained [65]).

We follow the Model-Driven Architecture (MDA) as an approach to develop the *ca2oom*. MDA proposes the well-known and long-established idea of separating the specification from the system operation [134]. The application of this concept for developing frameworks to integrate methods allows us to build artefacts with different levels of abstraction. This means that artefacts are available at different abstraction levels according to the MDA layers. The MDA layers are: computation-independent models (CIM), platform-independent models (PIM), and platform-specific models (PSM).

Since a metamodel is a model, the MDA approach can be applied to support requirements engineering methods, i.e., we differentiate the abstract representation of the Communication Analysis requirements models according to MDA layers. For this reason, we distinguish between the PIM metamodel and the PSM metamodel. Having the metamodel at different levels of abstraction allows us to implement the PIM metamodel in different target platforms according to the technological platform chosen.

In the same way, we apply the MDA architecture to build the artefacts corresponding to the Stages 1 and 2. As a result, the *ca2oom* are specified in CIM and PIM layers to allow different technological implementations. We summarises the *ca2oom* in Fig. 45.

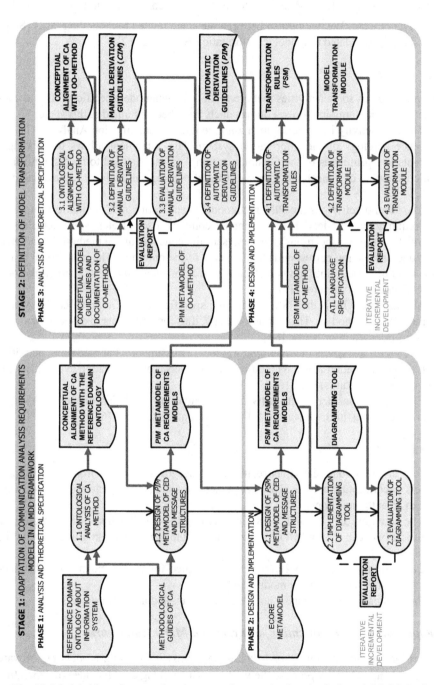

**Fig. 45.** Model-driven framework to integrate Communication Analysis and OO-Method

Each stage of the framework is divided into two phases, and each phase has several tasks. We have decided to differentiate each stage according to the tasks involved in the MDD process. We distinguish between the stage related to modelling tasks (Stage 1) and the stage related to model transformation tasks (Stage 2).

## The stage 1

Stage 1 involves some activities that are related to metamodel specifications and construction of diagramming tools. Four products have been obtained at this stage:

The first activity is the conceptual alignment of Communication Analysis with the reference ontology of the information system. This alignment allows the principal concepts and primitives of the Communication Analysis method to be distinguished. Some examples of conceptual frameworks and ontological analyses are available in [70].

The second activity is the PIM metamodel specification of Communication Analysis requirements models. This metamodel contains a set of elements (metaclasses) and relationships (associations) that represent the concepts of the method. Each metaclass and association corresponds to a concept of the ontology. The metamodel is at a PIM level because it does not have technological information (i.e., the target platform has not yet been considered) [7].

The third activity is the PSM metamodel specification of Communication Analysis requirements models. This metamodel specifies metaclasses and associations with platform-oriented information [65].

The fourth activity is the diagramming tool. This supports the modelling activities of the Communication Analysis requirements models (communicative event diagrams and message structures) [71], [68].

Finally, we consider a fifth activity to promote the validation of the results [65]. The results of the third, fourth and fifth activities are detailed in [65].

## The stage 2

Stage 2 involves some activities related to model transformation from requirements models to conceptual models. These activities are aimed at the generation of software code in an automatic way.

The activities 3.1, 3.2 and 3.3 are concerning the specification of the ontological alignment between CA and OO-M, the design of the transformation guidelines and its evaluation [7].

The activities 3.4, 4.1, 4.2 and 4.3 are designed for the development and implementation of a transformation module [65].

The application of the stage 1 and stage 2 are detailed in the following.

## Adaptation of communication analysis in a MDD framework

Model Driven Architecture™ or MDA is an approach for using models in software development; and MDA propose the well-known and long establish idea of separating the business process specification of the application or implementation of a system [69].

Although MDA is commonly applied to product software development, we think is interesting to apply this concept for developing methods.

To achieve this proposal, we have designed a MDD framework to support the Communication Analysis method; this framework contains different stages and activities [135].

The requirements for the system are modelled in a computation independent model (**CIM**). The CIM describes the situation in which the system will be used. The CIM is a model of a system that shows the system in the environment in which it will operate, and thus it helps in presenting exactly what the system is expected to do. The CIM specification can be represented by means of a textual explanations, technical reports, etc.

The system is described by means of a platform independent model (**PIM**), thus it helps to describe the system but does not show details of its use in a specific technological platform. A PIM consists of enterprise descriptions and it can follow a particular architectural style (object oriented, aspect oriented, etc.).

The PIM can be transformed in a model that specifies how the system uses the chosen platform. Thus, this is a platform specific model (**PSM**). The PSM provide more details about the implementation. A PIM can be transformed to different PSM depending on the target platform.

By applying the MDA approach for method development; our approach applies the MDA concepts in an orthogonal way over the models in a software development process. These metamodels are aligning to a method textual description or an ontology reference for the method.

We focus on the CIM models (requirements models in a software development process) for the Communication Analysis method.

### *Development of a modelling tool*

The tasks for the Stage 1 (Phase 1 and Phase 2) allow us to obtain a modelling environment to specify Communication Analysis requirements models (communicative event diagrams and message structures). By following a set of derivation guidelines [112], it is possible to obtain object-oriented models from Communication Analysis models.

The phase 1 is composed of two tasks: The first task is the ontological analysis of Communication Analysis method. This task is vital for the analysis and the establishment of a theoretical framework for the methods to integrate. In previous works, Pastor et al. have presented the specification of the concepts for Communication Analysis [70]. Later España [125] proposes the ontological alignment for the Communication Analysis Method and OO-Method. The results of this PhD thesis have been used aiming at establishing well-based theoretical specification. In the case that there are no previous ontological analysis for the methods to integrate, we advise to do it in order to provide formal and strong-based solutions.

The second activity is about design of PIM metamodel (PIMm). The PIMm contains a set of elements (metaclasses) and relationships that represents concepts of the method. Each metaclass and relationship corresponds to a concept of the ontology (for the case of Communication Analysis [136]). The Communication Analysis metamodel specifies the abstract syntax to build communicative event diagrams and message structures.

The elements, relationships, cardinalities and roles intend to represent the semantic of the Communication Analysis requirements models. Each modelling decision was taken according to the ontological analysis of the method. For this reason, each element of the metamodel corresponds with one element of the ontology [136].

The phase 2 is composed of three tasks: The first task is the design of the PSM metamodel (PSMm). The PIMm serves as input and as a result, the PSMm specifies all the details required by a certain target platform. For Communication Analysis, we choose Eclipse (http://www.eclipse.org).

By using Eclipse Modelling Framework (http://www.eclipse.org/emf), we build a graphical editor in order to support the modelling of communicative event diagrams (CED) and message structures. In addition, the message structures has a support based on Xtext technologies (https://eclipse.org/Xtext/). Fig. 46 presents a snapshot of the diagraming tool.

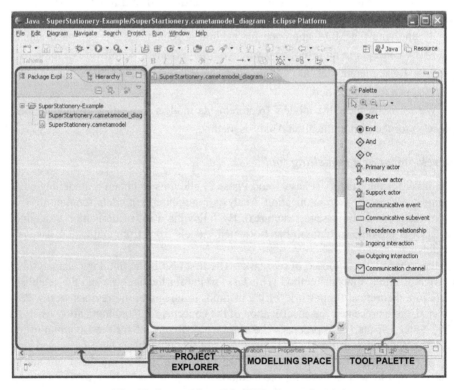

**Fig. 46.** Composition of the CED diagraming tool

To illustrate the usage of the diagraming tool, Fig. 47 presents the CED for the SuperStationery Co. case.

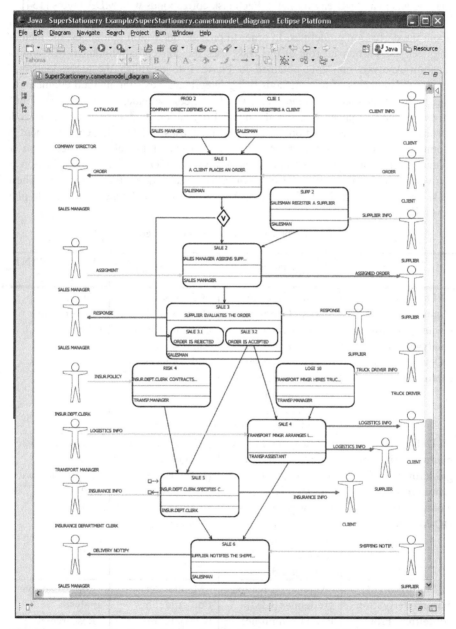

**Fig. 47.** Communicative Event diagram for Sale business process modelled in the diagraming tool

## Development of a transformation module

Stage 2 aims at defining model transformations from requirements models to conceptual models in a MDD environment. Each task corresponds with MDA layers [134].

Stage 2 has two phases (Phase 3 and Phase 4): The goal of Phase 3 is to reason
about the derivation guidelines. In order to provide derivation guidelines, the method
engineer (the participant role of this task) uses the conceptual alignment of Communication Analysis concepts obtained in Phase 1 to establish the correspondences
among the concepts of two methods being integrated. Next, the method engineer designs a set of manual derivations according to the correspondences established. Finally, the method engineer specifies the manual derivation guidelines in a pseudo-code
for their future implementation. Phase 3 has four tasks: 3.1 Ontological alignment of
Communication Analysis with OO-Method conceptual models; 3.2 Definition of
manual derivation from Communication Analysis to OO-Method; 3.3 Evaluation of
derivation guidelines; and 3.4 Definition of automatic derivation guidelines. These
tasks are explained in Table 8. Participant roles are presented. One person can to play
several roles.

**Table 8.** Tasks corresponding to Phase 3 of the integration framework

| TASKS | ENTRIES | OUTPUTS | PARTICIPANT ROLES |
|---|---|---|---|
| **3.1 Ontological alignment of Communication Analysis with OO-Method conceptual models.** | - Conceptual alignment of Communication Analysis concepts with reference domain ontology.<br>- Conceptual model guidelines and documentation of OO-Method. | - Conceptual alignment of Communication Analysis concepts with OO-Method. | - Ontology expert<br>- Method engineer. |
| **3.2 Definition of manual derivation guidelines. From Communication Analysis to OO-Method.** | - Conceptual model guidelines and documentation of OO-Method.<br>- Conceptual alignment of Communication Analysis concepts with OO-Method. | - Manual derivation guidelines (CIM). From Communication Analysis to OO-Method. | - Method engineer.<br>- Representative analyst |
| **3.3 Definition of manual derivation guidelines. From Communication Analysis to OO-Method.** | - Manual derivation guidelines (CIM). From Communication Analysis to OO-Method. | - Manual derivation guidelines (CIM). From Communication Analysis to OO-Method. | - Representative analyst.<br>- Researcher. |
| **3.4 Definition of** | -PIM metamodel of | - Automatic deri- | - Method engi- |

| automatic deriva-tion guidelines. | Communication Analysis.<br>- PIM metamodel of OO-Method.<br>- Manual derivation guidelines (PIM).<br>From Communica-tion Analysis to OO-Method. | vation guidelines (PIM). | neer.<br>- Representative analyst |
|---|---|---|---|

The goal of Task 3.1 is to align the concepts of the two methods. Thus, it is necessary to analyse the concepts of the conceptual models and the concepts of the requirements models. The method engineer has to be an expert in Communication Analysis and OO-Method. If the method engineer is only expert in one method, then the participation of more than one expert must be obtained. The ontological alignment is the step before designing the derivation guidelines. For more details about this task, please see [137].

The goal of Task 3.2 is to establish a set of derivation guidelines in natural language. This guide should offer steps to obtain the conceptual models manually. The conceptual alignment between Communication Analysis and OO-Method is very important because it allows the correspondences among elements of each method to be established. Examples of the application of the manual derivation guidelines are available in [138]. Fig. 48 presents an example of the derivation of a new class. Rule steps, notes, and pattern matching are provided in order to facilitate their reading and understanding.

The goal of Task 3.3 is to evaluate the manual derivation guidelines to improve them and to assess the quality of the derived conceptual models. This task was carried out in the context of a controlled experiment. One set of subjects applied a text-based conceptual model derivation. Another set of subjects applied the derivation guidelines. The results were compared and interesting results were obtained: a significant impact on conceptual model completeness was shown when the derivation guidelines were applied. The results and feedback of the subjects were part of the evaluation report for improving the derivation guidelines. In addition, several lab-demos were carried out to analyse the use of the derivation guidelines.

The goal of Task 3.4 is to represent the manual derivation guidelines as an algorithm. A pseudo-code of the derivation guidelines is obtained after carrying out this task. The PIM metamodel of the two methods were used to define the derivation guidelines.

Three products were obtained of Phase 3: The first product is the conceptual alignment of Communication Analysis and OO-Method. This product is the first step in reasoning about the concepts of each method. The second product is the manual derivation guidelines to derive conceptual models from Communication Analysis requirements models. This product presents the derivation guidelines in natural language for human readers. It was used by students, which gave as a result satisfactory insights about its acceptance. It is important to highlight the MDA layer of this product. This product is in a CIM layer of MDA because technological support is not the objective. The third product is the automatic derivation guidelines. This product was developed to specify the derivation guidelines in a computational language, but disregarding the technological platform. For this reason, this product is at a PIM level in the MDA layers (See Fig. 48).

| **Rule OM4**. Derivation of a new class from an aggregation substructure |
| --- |
| **Pattern matching** |
| Each aggregation substructure within the message structure of the event being processed that *is not* an extension aggregation substructure. |
| **Preconditions** |
| Rule **OM2** has already been applied to the requirements model. |
| **Rule steps** |
| Create a new class. Assign to the name of the class the name of its corresponding aggregation substructure, replacing spaces with underscores and using uppercase letters. In any case, the analyst can choose to give a different name to a class. |
| **Traceability information** |
| Create a trace link of type Class_Derivation between the communicative event and the newly-created class (this can be done after step 2). Create a trace link of type Class_Derivation between the aggregation substructure and the newly-created class (this can be done after step 2). If the aggregation substructure describes an organisational role, then create a trace link of type Agent between the organisational role and the newly-created class (this can be done after step 2). |
| **Notes** |
| In case the analyst is creating the conceptual model using Integranova Modeler, then we advice not using *extended creation* facility optionally offered by the tool (which automatically creates an autonumeric identifier attribute, a creation service, a destruction service, and an editing service). In case this facility is used, the analyst should be aware of the model elements automatically added by the tool and remove those that are not needed. |

**Fig. 48.** Example of manual derivation guide

The goal of the Phase 4 is develop a model transformation tool to carry out model transformation activities among Communication Analysis requirements models and OO-Method conceptual models. In order to provide a transformation module, the analyst uses the PSM metamodel of the requirements models and conceptual models to define the transformation rules. Finally, the analyst should design software evaluation activities for the transformation module. These activities should involve the experts and the final users. Phase 4 has three tasks: 4.1 Definition of automatic transformation rules; 4.2 Definition of transformation module; and 4.3 Evaluation of transformation module. These tasks are explained in Table 9.

**Table 9.** Tasks corresponding to Phase 4 of the integration framework

| TASKS | ENTRIES | OUTPUTS | PARTICIPANT ROLES |
|---|---|---|---|
| **4.1 Definition of automatic transformation rules.** | - PSM metamodel of Communication Analysis requirements models.<br>- PSM metamodel of OO-Method.<br>- ATL language specification.<br>- Automatic derivation guidelines (PIM). | - Transformation rules (PSM) from Communication Analysis models to conceptual models. | - Method engineer. |
| **4.2 Definition of transformation module.** | - ATL language specification.<br>- Transformation rules (PSM) from Communication Analysis models to conceptual models. | - Model transformation module. | - Analyst.<br>- Developer. |
| **4.3 Evaluation of transformation module.** | - Model transformation module. | - Model transformation module. | - Representative analyst.<br>- Researcher |

The goal of Task 4.1 is to define the automatic transformation rules in the specific technological platform ATL[6]. Thus, a study about a transformation engine was carried out. QVT[7] is a standard proposed by the OMG for model transformation that is implemented in the Eclipse[8] environment. ATL is another transformation engine developed in the GMT[9] project of Eclipse. The result of this study allows us to choose ATL as the better option to implement the derivation guidelines. The derivation guidelines are expressed in declarative and imperative sentences, so the hybrid nature of ATL provides patterns and a language to specify kind of heuristics of this kind.

Fig. 49 presents an example of a transformation rule specified in ATL language. The PSM metamodel of the two methods being integrated are used as input to specify the derivation guidelines in ATL language. The PSM metamodels are specified in ECORE language [139].

---

6  ATL, the Atlas Transformation Language. Available: http://www.eclipse.org/atl
7  M2M/QVT, Declarative (QVTd) Available:
   http://wiki.eclipse.org/M2M/Relational_QVT_Language_%28QVTR%29
8  Eclipse.org. Available: http://www.eclipse.org
9  GMT Project. Available: http://www.eclipse.org/gmt

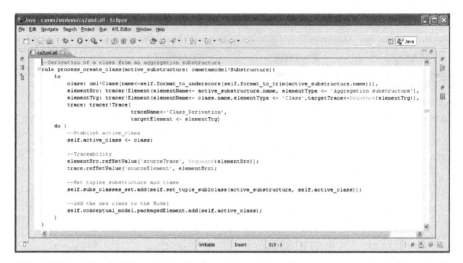

**Fig. 49.** Example of ATL code: Derivation of a new class from an aggregation substructure

The goal of Task 4.2 is to define a model transformation module (an environment to carry out the model transformation activities). The environment has to support the metamodel of both methods. In addition, it is important to provide the correct format for the metamodel (i.e., Ecore format). The environment has to support the model to be transformed and to show the transformation results to the user. In addition, the transformation module has to show messages to the user if something is wrong with the models for future modification.

The goal of Task 4.3 is to evaluate the transformation module to determine whether it is usable. This task is part of the future work discuses

Two products are obtained from Phase 4: The first product is the transformation rules. This product is specified at a PSM level in the MDA layers. ATL language has been used to specify the transformation rules. The second product is the model transformation module. This module has the transformation environment to support the transformation rules.

### Final comment

We consider the implementation of the transformation rules to be an important step in reducing the gap between the requirements models and the final software application. Thus, the *ca2oom* chunk provide an environment supported by tools to model CA models and obtain OOM models by means of the model transformation module. This chunk it is the core to join requirements design an efficient development of information systems prototypes. The integration of the *ca2oom* is presented as a TraceME chunk in the section 5.6.

## 4.7    Delta analysis

In this section, we present the design of the Delta Analysis technique for the analysis of differences and information gathering of two information systems. To compare two information systems, we used the representation of information systems by means of conceptual models. We design a Delta Analysis technique general enough to be applied to any pair of conceptual models (e.g., specification of the information system goals, the perspective of process, the interaction requirements, etc.).

Comparisons of conceptual models are widely applied in order to conclude about information systems evolution. In this case, comparisons are performed between *as-is* and *to-be* models that specifies *as-is* (current) and *to-be* (desired) information systems

In addition, comparisons of conceptual models are used for distinguishing how a certain model is different according to a reference (a.k.a., baseline model). The objective is to detect misalignment with requirements or baseline models. This situation is common when an information system need to report on how it follows well practices and standards.

Several works have been performed in order to support syntactical differences. In model management, Bernstein has provided wide applied techniques in order to match and compare models [45]. For analysing business process alignment, van der Aalst [140] has presented the application of process mining as a tool for delta analysis in scenarios for conformance testing. In software product lines, delta modelling is an approach for defining and deriving products from a core product (different products based on a core product). Clarke et al. [141] have been working on this line by means of providing solutions for the generation of abstract solutions that can be applied to different core context of core products.

We design a Delta Analysis technique that helps to highlight differences between two models in order to analyse the differences and make conclusions. We say that Delta Analysis guides on the specification, measurement, and analysis of syntactical differences. It means that the differences are established according to the syntax of the models under comparison.

CD36. Syntactical difference is the difference between two models specified in a graphical fashion.

Regarding to the analysis of semantical differences of models, different approaches have been proposed in order to enrich delta analysis of information systems. van der Aalst and Basten have proposed an approach to identify semantical differences by means of the analysis of behavioural-inheritance relations [142]. The inheritance relations can be used to guide the reasoning about common super- or submodels of two models. Super- or submodels inform the differences between two models, specially the behaviour of such two models. Another approach to tackle semantical differences is change regions. van der Aalst  has presented a proposal to identify change regions to analyse the behaviour of the change from one system to another, or what is the alignment of two systems [143].

Our Delta Analysis technique helps to identify – in a light way- semantical differences between two models. Semantical differences means differences in behaviour.

CD37. Semantical difference is the difference in behaviour between two models.

The differences between two models can be specified by means of a model that we call delta model.

CD38. Delta model is a conceptualisation of the differences between two conceptual models that are instance of the same metamodel. The two models are called pivot model and satellite model. Fig. 50 presents the conceptualisation of delta model.

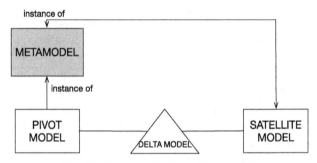

**Fig. 50.** Conceptualisation of delta model

The most important objective of delta models is to communicate differences and make possible its measurement. We measure delta models in order to gather meaningful information about the differences between two models for further analysis. For delta models assessment, in this research we use mathematic formulas that we call metrics.

CD39. Metric is a mathematical formula to measure models.

Metrics' results are interpreted and analysed in order to conclude about the comparison.

For the Delta Analysis technique, we distinguish the following criteria that one would expect from a technique for model comparison: (i) Specification of differences and similarities between models should be guided; (ii) metrics to facilitate measurement should be provided; (iii) dashboard and keys for interpretation should be established to help on the interpretation process of the metrics results; (iv) an interpretations repository should be built in order to use it for further recommendations and well practices.

Delta Analysis technique is shaped by three units that are interrelated (see Fig. 51). Each unit involves artefacts to perform tasks related with Delta Analysis.

*Unit 1: Delta model specification.* This unit corresponds to the guidelines to specify delta models.

*Unit 2: Delta models measurement.* This unit corresponds to the <u>metrics</u> for delta model measurement

Unit 3: Delta models and metrics interpretation report. This unit describes the framework for reporting the interpretation and understanding of delta models and metrics results.

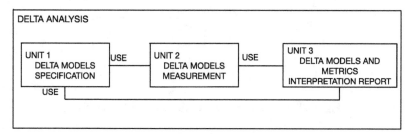

**Fig. 51.** Units of the Delta Analysis technique

For each unit we specify metamodels that serve for purposes of instantiation of the proposal and further implementation.

The core of the Delta Analysis technique is delta models. Delta models specify the difference between pivot and satellite models. To analyse delta models, we conceive a set of metrics that uses delta models to provide quantitative insights about the result of the comparison. Those results are interpreted in order to conclude. To interpret, both delta models and metrics are analysed. As a result, the Delta Analysis provide a whole view about the differences between two models providing delta models, quantitative information of the differences as a results of the metrics application, and conclusions about the differences thanks to the interpretations.

In the following, we describe the design of each unit of the Delta Analysis in the sections 4.7.1 4.7.2 4.7.3. Finally, in the section 4.7.4 we present the Delta Analysis metamodel.

### 4.7.1    Delta models specification

For specification of delta models, we design a set of guidelines that receive as input a pair of models (i.e., pivot and satellite models). As output of the guidelines application, we obtain a delta model that describes the differences and similarities of the two input models. In Fig. 52 we present an overview of the framework for the specification of delta models.

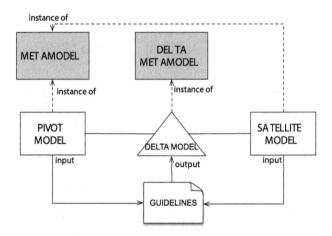

**Fig. 52.** Framework for the specification of delta models

Delta model is a conceptualisation of the differences between conceptual models. For the definition of delta models we were inspired by Bernstein [45], besides, even though we do not pretend to match two models, we consider as an interesting idea mapping representation as an intermediate model. Similarly, we adopt mapping model definition and we establish mapping between objects as a relationship between objects from different models by means of mapping operators (similar, equal, etc.). To illustrate, Fig. 53 presents a mapping example between model A and model B. MAPPING 1 says that CONCEPT A1 and CONCEPT B1 are been mapping by means of mapping operator equal (=), while MAPPING 2 says CONCEPT A2 and CONCEPT B2 are been mapping by means of mapping operator similar (≅).

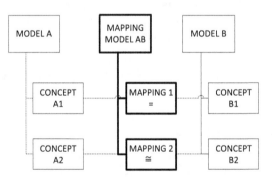

**Fig. 53.** Mapping between model A and model B (This figure has been adapted from [45])

On the other hand, traceability is a concept widely used in MDD. There are proposals in order to support traceability among models. Besides, traceability could be also considered as a model. Jouault presents a simple trace metamodel able to specify relationships among elements without have into account a specific context (i.e. model to model transformation, model to text transformation, etc.) [133].

In order to provide a delta metamodel, we borrow from Bernstein research some mappings operators and its semantics. We call mapping operators as delta operator because its role is to tell us about differences and similarities between two models. In particular, we analyse the operator match; accordingly, we propose a delta metamodel that takes advantage of traceability metamodel proposed by Jouault in order to provide artefacts to store traceability information. We extend this traceability metamodel following the specification for carrying out model mapping presented by Bernstein. Fig. 54 shows our delta metamodel. It contains a DELTA_ELEMENT metaclass owing a type attribute to register information about the comparison. We conceive an enumerator (DELTA_ELEMENT_TYPE) to specify the four basic delta elements:

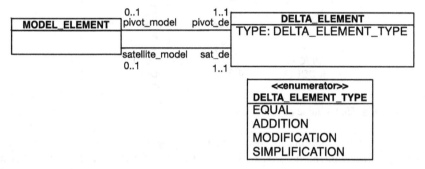

**Fig. 54.** Metamodel view of the Unit 1 of the Delta Analysis. Also called delta metamodel

- The first basic delta element is equal. By equal, we mean that two model elements are alike. The symbol of equal is (=).
- The second basic delta element is modification. By modification, we mean that two model elements are alike but some properties could be changed. For instance, the property name of a business process could be changed. The symbol of modification is (≈).
- The third basic delta operator is addition. By addition, we mean that a model element has been added. The symbol of addition is (+).
- The fourth basic delta element is simplification. By simplification, we mean that a model element has been deleted. The symbol of simplification is (-).

Delta models are instance of a delta metamodel (see Fig. 54). A delta model specifies the differences of one pivot model (reference model, baseline model, *as-is* model, etc.,) and one satellite model (model under analysis, *to-be* model, etc.).

For example, the delta d(A,B) presented in Fig. 55 specifies the differences and similarities of the models A and B; or how model A is turned into model B. Both models A and B are instance of the same metamodel. The delta elements are represented by means of rounded rectangles.

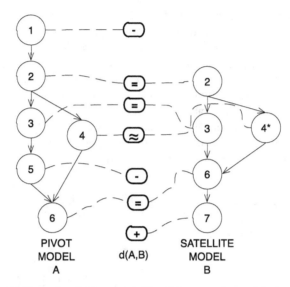

**Fig. 55.** Example of delta model d(A, B) between the models A and B

We distinguish two options to specify delta models. One option is an incremental specification of delta models. For example, the specification of d(A,B) can occur during the change process when model A is turned into B. The creation of the delta model in an incremental way has as input a pivot model and the requirements for change (The requirements for change are the decisions that justify the changes to make in the pivot model to obtain a satellite model). In order to guide this process, we offer the following set of guidelines. A certain situation where the satellite model is not given happen in evolution scenarios and a delta model is needed for a post-analysis of the evolution procedure.

### Guidelines for incremental creation of delta models

Follow these guidelines when creating a delta model having as input the pivot model (A). As a result, a satellite model (B) is obtained.

The following guideline stands when an element specified in the model A needs to be kept in the model B. This situation occurs when the requirements of the model B rule the specification of elements belonging to the model A.

---

**Guideline 1.** Assume that an element *e* that is part of A (*e*A) needs to be kept in the model B. In that case, specify the element *e* in the model B (*e*B) and create an equal element (=) in the delta model that link both *e*A and *e*B.

---

The following guideline stands when an element specified in the model A needs to be kept in the model B. This situation occurs when the requirements of the model B rule the specification of elements belonging to the model A by making some variations.

**Guideline 2.** Assume that an element $e$ that is part of A ($eA$) needs to be kept in the model B with some variations in its attributes. In that case, specify the element $e$ with variations ($e'$) in the model B ($e'B$) and create a modification element ($\approx$) in the delta model that link both $eA$ and $e'B$.

When the requirements for the model B demand the creation of elements that are not specified in A. The guideline 3 indicates how to proceed in this situation.

**Guideline 3.** Assume that the requirements for the model B demand the creation of an element $e$ that is not specified in the model A. In this case, specify the element $e$ in the model B ($eB$) and create an addition element (+) in the delta model linking to the element $eB$.

If the model A has elements that are not required to be specified in the model B, such models should not be kept for the model A. Thus, the delta model will represent this situation with a simplification element (-). The following guideline presents the steps to treat this situation.

**Guideline 4.** Assume that an element $e$ that is part of A ($eA$) should not be kept in the model B. In that case, do not specify the element $e$ in the model B and create a simplification element (-) in the delta model linking to the element $eA$.

Other scenario, in which delta models can be created, is in the case that both pivot and satellite models are given. Situations where pivot and satellite models pre-exist are common when it is necessary to compare a model with a baseline, or for a post-analysis of the evolution of a model.

## Guidelines for creation of delta models

Follow these guidelines when creating a delta model between two models: a pivot model (A) and a satellite model (B). As input models A and B are given, as a result the delta model d(A,B) is obtained

**Guideline 1.** Given two elements $eA$ and $eB$ that are specified in the models A and B respectively. If $eA$ and $eB$ are the same elements, then create an equal element (=) in the delta model that links both $eA$ and $eB$.

E.g., In Fig. 55 the element 2 of the model A is also specified as an element 2 in model B; which induces the creation of an equal element (=) in the delta model d(A, B) that links 2 of model A and 2 of model B.

**Guideline 2.** Given one element $eB$ that is specified in the models B. If $eB$ is not specified in the model A, then create an addition element (+) in de delta model for the $eB$ element.

E.g., In Fig. 55 the element 7 of model B is not specified in model A; which induces the creation of an addition element (+) in the delta model d(A, B) for the 7 element.

> **Guideline 3.** Given one element *eA* that is specified in the models A. If *eA* is not specified in the model B, then create a simplification element (-) in de delta model for the *eA* element.

E.g., In Fig. 55 the element 5 of model A is not specified in model B; which induces the creation of a simplification element (-) in the delta model d(A, B) for the 5 element.

> **Guideline 4.** Given one element *eA* that is specified in the models A. If *eA* is also specified in the model B (*e*'B) but with some variations in its attributes, then create a modification element (≈) in de delta model that links both *eA* and *e*'B.

E.g., In Fig. 55 the element 4 of model A is also specified in model B with some variations on its attributes (the variation is indicated by means of the "*"); which induces the creation of a modification element (≈) in the delta model d(A, B) that links both 4 and 4*.


## 4.7.2    Delta models measurement

To measure something, a clear purpose should be established before to perform the measurement task. For example, to measure a computer monitor in order to know its size, it is necessary to use a tape measure from one corner of the screen to its opposite one. In this case, the objective was clear: To know the size of the monitor screen. To measure delta models, the objective should be clear in order to use the most convenient measurement tool.

We design a framework for delta model measurement (see Fig. 56). In this framework the core are delta models that serve as input for a set of metrics. As a result, metrics results are obtained.

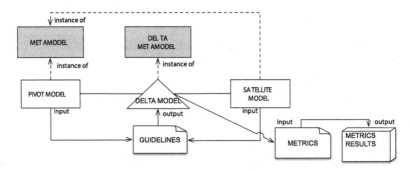

**Fig. 56.** Framework for delta model measurement

To measure delta models, we design a set of mathematical formulas that we call metrics. Fig. 57 presents the conceptualisation of metric and its relationship with delta models. The metaclass METRIC stands for the specification of metrics in the Delta Analysis. The attributes of METRIC are designed in order to provide a consistent specification of metrics. In this way, each metric has an ID with the form of *m#*, the letter *m* comes from metric and the symbol # identify each metric by adding a natural number. The attribute name describes the meaning of the metric in a short manner. The attribute description serves to provide details about the metric. The attribute formula is a mathematical description of the metric to perform measurements. The METRIC metaclass is related with the DELTA_ELEMENT metaclass by means of the attribute measure. A metric can measure 1 or several delta elements that are part of a delta model.

The mathematical formula of each metric is based on this metamodel.

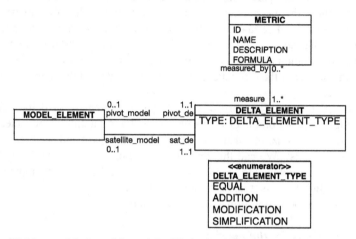

**Fig. 57.** Metamodel view of the unit 2 of Delta Analysis: Delta model measurement

We distinguish three abstract categories of metrics that are oriented to certain objectives (see Fig. 58): 1) delta impact; 2) conceptual impact; and 3) situational impact. For each category, we provide its corresponding set of metrics. In addition, we describe possible practical applications of each category.

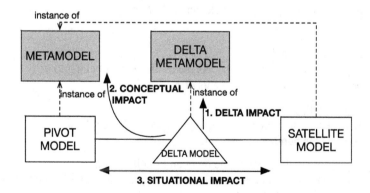

**Fig. 58.** Categories of metrics for delta models

The categories are the following; the metrics and practical applications are presented in detail in the next sections.

1. **Delta impact.** Category of metrics for measurement of delta models to give to know about deltas (see the arrow *1. Delta impact* that is pointing out to the delta metamodel to refer the types of deltas). Results of the metrics inform about the amount of additions, simplifications, equals, and modifications. We say that the quantitative values obtained as a result of the metrics inform about the delta impact.

2. **Conceptual impact.** Category of metrics for measurement of delta models in order to inform about deltas in terms of the concepts that are defined in the metamodels of the compared models (see the arrow *2. Conceptual impact* that is pointing out to the metamodel to refer its concepts). Results of the metrics report about the amount of certain concepts belonging to the metamodel that are detected in the delta model as addition, simplification, equal or modification. We say that the information about delta in terms of the concepts of the metamodel report about the impact of the differences of its concepts. We call this impact as conceptual impact.

3. **Situational impact.** Category of metrics for measurement of delta models by reporting its impact on the elements of the pivot and satellite models (see the arrow *3. Conceptual impact* that is pointing out to the pivot and satellite models to refer its elements). We call this impact as situational impact because it depends on the elements belongs to the pivot and satellite models. It is situational regards to the situation that pivot and satellite models are specifying. As a result, quantitative information will inform about the situational impact.

## *General statements for the metrics*

The following statements are used through the specification of the metrics.

Statements for delta models

Let $\Delta$ represents a delta model; $\Delta_i$ represents an element belong to $\Delta$; $|\Delta|$ represents the number of elements of $\Delta$;

$\Delta_i. type$ represents types of delta elements: $\Delta_i. type \begin{cases} = \\ + \\ - \\ \approx \end{cases}$

Statements for pivot models

Let $\sigma$ represents a pivot model; $\sigma_i$ represents an element belong to $\sigma$; $|\sigma|$ represents the number of elements of $\sigma$

Statements for satellite models

Let $\lambda$ represents a satellite model; $\lambda_i$ represents an element belong to $\lambda$; $|\lambda|$ represents the number of elements of $\lambda$

Statements for metamodels that define pivot and satellite models

Let $M$ represents a metamodel that defines both pivot and satellite models; $M_i$ represents a metaclass belong to $M$; $|M|$ represents the number of metaclasses of $M$;

### *Metrics for delta impact category*

Below we describe the metrics for measurement of delta impact. In Fig. 59 we illustrate the reasoning for this category of metrics by means of the arrow *1. Delta impact*, which is pointing out to the delta metamodel.

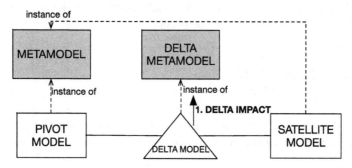

**Fig. 59.** Overview of the delta impact category

To design the metrics to measure the delta impact, we decided to analyse the delta model by blocking the analysis of the delta elements by the four types: equal, modification, addition, and simplification. For example, one metric is to sum the number of delta elements such that the attribute type is addition.

Results of the metrics will provide values between 0 and 1 that can be interpreted as percentages as well.

The first metric of this category is persistency. Here we focus on the amount of equals that are specified in the delta model.

---

*m1*      **Persistency metric**

The persistency metric (P) measures how much a satellite model specifies elements that are part of a pivot model.

$$P = \frac{sumequal}{|\sigma|}$$

$$sumequal = \sum_{i=1}^{|\Delta|} is\_equal(\Delta_i);$$

$$is\_equal(\Delta_i) = \begin{cases} 1 \; iff \; \Delta_i.type \; is" = " \\ 0 \; otherwise \end{cases}$$

---

The next metric is focuses on the amount of simplifications specified in the delta model.

---

*m2*      **Simplification metric**

The simplification metric (S) measures how much a satellite model is simplified according to elements specified in a pivot model.

$$S = \frac{sumsimp}{|\sigma|}$$

$$sumsimp = \sum_{i=1}^{|\Delta|} is\_simp(\Delta_i);$$

---

$$is\_simp(\Delta_i) = \begin{cases} 1 \; iff \; \Delta_i.type \; is" - " \\ \quad\quad 0 \; otherwise \end{cases}$$

In the following metric, we focus on discovering the amount of additions that are specified in the delta model.

### m3 Enrichment metric

The enrichment metric (E) measures how much a satellite model is enriched with elements that are not specified in a pivot model.

$$E = \frac{sumaddi}{|\lambda|}$$

$$sumaddi = \sum_{i=1}^{|\Delta|} is\_addi(\Delta_i);$$

$$is\_addi(\Delta_i) = \begin{cases} 1 \; iff \; \Delta_i.type \; is" + " \\ \quad\quad 0 \; otherwise \end{cases}$$

The metric that stands for the modification delta operator is called adaptation. This metric reports on the amount of modification operator specified in a delta model.

### m4 Adaptation metric

The adaptation metric (A) measures how much elements of a satellite are modified according to a pivot model.

$$A = \frac{summodi}{|\sigma|}$$

$$summodi = \sum_{i=1}^{|\Delta|} is\_modi(\Delta_i);$$

$$is\_modi(\Delta_i) = \begin{cases} 1 \; iff \; \Delta_i.type \; is" \approx " \\ \quad\quad 0 \; otherwise \end{cases}$$

To enrich the analysis of results, we advise to aggregate the results of the first four metrics in a Cartesian plane (see Fig. 60). We propose the Cartesian plane in order to have the results in a graphical fashion to let the analysis of tendencies on how much a satellite model has change or is different to a pivot model.

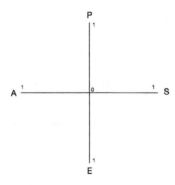

**Fig. 60.** Cartesian plane to specify the results of the metrics P, S, E and A

We design a Cartesian plane where each metric has an axis that meet in the origin or point zero. The values of the metrics are specified in the axis for each metrics (e.g., for the metric persistency (P), the axis to specify its values is P). Values from 0 to 1 can be specified in the Cartesian plane for each metric. As a result of specifying the metrics results in the Cartesian plane, a shape is obtained by joining the four values with a line. Below we provide a set of keys to analyse the tendency of the satellite model. We do not pretend to interpret the meaning of the delta with these keys; the objective is to help on the analysis tasks.

### *Global conservation*

The global conservation tendency (GC) indicates how much a satellite model has changed or is different to the pivot model. Global conservation is the tendency of P against S, E, and A. Three situations can happen:

- P has a higher value than S plus E plus A. It means that the satellite model conserves the most of the pivot model. This can be distinguished in the Cartesian plane because the shape tends to be in the high values of P. Check if it is necessary to keep everything. Are there some elements in the satellite model that need to be kept according to the system requirements?
- P has a lower value than S plus E plus A. This situation happen, when several modifications or differences have been found in the satellite model. This situation is observed in the Cartesian plane because the area of the shape tends to be mostly in the quadrants S - E and E - A. Review what has changed. Evaluate the main purpose of the process, is the process aligned with it purpose? Review dependencies and the requirements of the system in order to ensure that the satellite model fulfil with this requirements.
- P has a same value as S plus E plus A. In this situation, just a half of the satellite model can be consider as persistent according to the pivot model. In the Cartesian plane, this is evident because a half of the shape tends to be in the P axis and the rest in the quadrants S - E and E - A.

### *Consistency*

The consistency tendency (C) indicates how much a satellite model still "good enough" according to its purpose or mandatory requirements. Consistency is the tendency of S against P. When the tendency is to S. It is necessary to check the conformity of the satellite model with it purpose.

### *Enrichment*

The enrichment tendency (E) invites to review if it is possible to find reusable assets in the *as-is* models.

### *Recreation*

The recreation tendency (R) indicates how much a satellite model incorporates new components or simply recreates everything. The key is to analyse the value of S and E against P and A.

*Superficial*

The superficial tendency (SU) indicates how to analyse a satellite model when changes are related on modifications on elements' names. We say that the tendency shows a superficial delta when A has a greater value than P plus S plus E.

## *Metrics for conceptual impact category*

We design a set of metrics to measure the conceptual impact. The conceptual impact informs about the delta in terms of the concepts specified in the metamodels of the pivot and satellite models. We use the term concept to refer a certain metaclass or element belonging to a metamodel. For example, if the metamodel is a business process models, a metric could be to sum the number of delta elements such that attribute type is addition and pivot model element is instance of the concept TASK. Fig. 61 represents the conceptual impact by means of the diagonal arrow *2. Conceptual impact*. The diagonal arrow indicates the relationship between the deltas and the concepts of the metamodel through the pivot and/or satellite model.

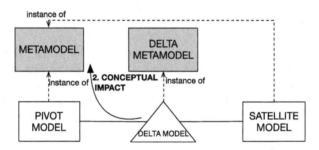

**Fig. 61.** Overview of the conceptual impact category

For the metrics design, we analyse the delta model by blocking the analysis of the delta elements by each of the four types: equal, modification, addition, and simplification and the concept of the metamodel to analyse. By blocking, we mean as to focus the attention on one type delta element together with the concept.

In Fig. 62 we illustrates the reasoning to measure conceptual impact. For this example[10], we want to analyse the concepts ELEMENT (see the metamodel) that are persistent in both pivot and satellite model. To do this, block the delta elements (see the delta model) whose attribute type is equal (=). Then, check if the attribute pivot_model or the attribute satellite model of the blocked delta elements is instance of the ELEMENT metaclass. As a result, from the delta model we select the elements 3 and 6 as persistent elements instance of the concept ELEMENT. It is important to clarify that the attributes pivot model and satellite model (of delta elements) are reviewed regarding the type of delta element. For instance, for delta elements of type addition the attribute pivot model is not instantiated because there is not relationship between addition elements and pivot models.

---

[10] For the sake of clarity of the example we do not specify all the instance of relationships.

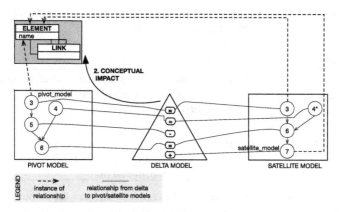

**Fig. 62.** Example of the conceptual impact category

Results of the metrics will provide values between 0 and 1 that can be interpreted as percentages as well. As we defined before in the general statements for the metrics, $M$ represents a metamodel that defines both pivot and satellite models; $M_i$ represents a metaclass belong to $M$. Since for each metric we need to specify a concrete concept (that is specified by means of a metaclass) to be analysed, the letter $m$ stands for input metaclasses.

The first metric of this category is persistency by concept. Here we focus on the amount of equals that are specified in the delta model and are related to a certain metaclass $m$ specified as input.

*m5      Persistency by concept metric*

The persistency by concept metric (PC) measures how much a satellite and pivot models keep elements of a certain concept (m) of the metamodel.

$$PC = \frac{sumequal\ (m)}{|\sigma|}$$

$sumequal(m) = \sum_{i=1}^{|\Delta|} is\_equal(\Delta_i, m);$

$is\_equal(\Delta_i, m) = \begin{cases} 1\ iff\ \Delta_i.type\ is\ "="\ and\ \Delta_i.pivot\_model\ is\ instance\_of\ m \\ 0\ otherwise \end{cases}$

Since for the delta elements of type equal is indifferent the attribute pivot or satellite model, we decided to build the metric taking the attribute pivot model.

The following metric stands for the analysis of the amount of elements of a certain concept that has been simplified in the satellite model

*m6      Simplification by concept metric*

The simplification by concept metric (SC) measures how much a satellite model has been simplified according to a certain concept (m) of the metamodel.

$$SC = \frac{sumsimp(m)}{|\sigma|}$$

$sumsimp(m) = \sum_{i=1}^{|\Delta|} is\_simp(\Delta_i, m);$

$is\_simp(\Delta_i, m) = \begin{cases} 1\ iff\ \Delta_i.type\ is\ "-"\ and\ \Delta_i.pivot\_element\ is\ instanceof\ m \\ 0\ otherwise \end{cases}$

The enrichment by concept metric helps to measure the amount of elements of a certain concept that has been added to the satellite model.

**m7     _Enrichment by concept metric_**

| |
|---|
| The enrichment by concept metric (EC) measures how much a satellite model has been enriched according to a certain concept (m) of the metamodel. $$EC = \frac{sumaddi\ (m)}{|\sigma|}$$ $sumaddi(m) = \sum_{i=1}^{|\Delta|} is\_addi(\Delta_i, m);$ $is\_addi(\Delta_i, m) = \begin{cases} 1\ iff\ \Delta_i.\ type\ is\ "+"\ and\ \Delta_i.\ satellite\_model\ is\ instanceof\ m \\ 0\ otherwise \end{cases}$ |

The adaptation by concept metric is designed in order to measure the amount of modified elements of a certain concept $m$ in the satellite model compared with a pivot model.

**m8     _Adaptation by concept metric_**

| |
|---|
| The adaptation by concept metric (AC) measures how much a satellite model keeps elements of a certain concept $m$. $$AC = \frac{summodi(m)}{|\sigma|}$$ $summodi(m) = \sum_{i=1}^{|\Delta|} is\_modi\Delta_i, m);$ $is\_modi(\Delta_i, m) = \begin{cases} 1\ iff\ \Delta_i.\ type\ is\ "\sim"\ and\ \Delta_i.\ pivot\_model\ is\ instanceof\ m \\ 0\ otherwise \end{cases}$ |

We propose to aggregate the results of the metrics PC, SC, EC and AC in order to get enriched information about the comparison of pivot and satellite models. Below we suggest keys for metrics' results aggregation. The keys that we propose are oriented to analyse business models. We made this decision due to general keys are no meaningful enough to be applied then in practice. To analyse the values of the metrics in a graphical way, we promote the use of the Cartesian plane as is presented for the metrics to measure delta impact (see the metrics for delta impact in the previous section).

## _Modularity_

Modularity of models can be seen as how to analyse business process models when lanes and refinements are enriched. For example if business process models are specified by using the Communication Analysis method, the AC metric (adaptation by concept) can inform about which elements have changed and the if business process under analysis has been rearranged (by analysing the acronym that indicates execution order of communicative events). In addition, it is possible to analyse if modularisations have been performed in satellite models thanks to the analysis of changed acronyms in communicative events.

For BPM, if the amount of simplifications performed in the pivot model regarding to the process element (see the metric m6 plus the amount of enrichment performed in the satellite model for the process element (see the metric m7) is bigger than the amount of enrichments and simplifications performed in the satellite model regarding the lane concept; we propose to evaluate the modularity of the satellite model in order to analyse if refinements in the satellite are convenient. In this case, it is advisable to consider fragmenting the satellite model in various modules.

---

For the concepts of BPM: process metaclass and lane metaclass

*if*

$$SC = \frac{sumsimp(process)}{|\sigma|} + EC = \frac{sumaddi\ (process)}{|\sigma|} > EC = \frac{sumaddi\ (lane)}{|\sigma|} + EC = \frac{sumaddi\ (lane)}{|\sigma|}$$

*then*

Evaluate the modularity of the satellite model in order to analyse if refinements in the satellite are convenient. In this case, it is advisable to consider fragmenting the satellite model in various modules

---

## Specific conservation

Given a certain concept of a metamodel $m$, it is interesting to analyse how the elements of both pivot and satellite models that are instance of $m$ have been conserved. To analyse the conservation by a certain concept, we propose to compare the result of PC against the summation of SC, EC, and AC. The following results could arise:

- PC has a higher value than SC plus EC plus AC. It means that the satellite model conserves the most of the elements instance of $m$ from the pivot model. This can be distinguished in the Cartesian plane because the shape tends to be in the high values of P.
- PC has a lower value than SC plus EC plus AC. This situation happen, when several modifications, simplifications and enrichments or differences for the concept $m$ have been found in the satellite model. This situation is observed in the Cartesian plane because the area of the shape tends to be mostly in the quadrants S - E and E - A.
- PC has a same value as SC plus EC plus AC. In this situation, just a half of the satellite model can be consider as persistent according to the pivot model for the concept $m$. In the Cartesian plane, this is evident because a half of the shape tends to be in the P axis and the rest in the quadrants S - E and E - A.

## Specific consistency

For analysing the consistency of a certain concept $m$, we propose to compare the results of simplifications (SC) against persistent elements (PC). When SC is bigger than PC, it is necessary to check if the satellite model fulfils the requirements and satisfy the demands of the system that it is specifying.

## Specific recreation

When satellite models specify various enrichments and simplifications, possible recreations of pivot models could be contemplated. We propose to analyse the values of simplifications by concepts (SC) against the summation of the values of EC, PC, and AC. If SC is bigger than the aggregation of EC, PC, and AC, it means that a certain satellite model is extremely different according to the pivot model that is compared. In evolution projects, we say the satellite model (or *to-be* model) is recreating the *as-is*. Thus analysts in charge of evolution projects can decide if recreations are intended or it is possible to re-use assets already specified in *as-is* models.

### *Specific Superficiality*

We say the differences between pivot and satellite models are superficial when differences are concentrated in modification of attributes intended to specify elements' descriptions (e.g., the attribute name is commonly used for specifying names of elements).

By analysing the case of business process models, superficiality can happen when modifications in the names of the elements (elements can be processes, lanes, pools, etc.) are bigger than enrichments and simplifications. For example, if we are analysing BPMN like models, we propose to analyse the values of adaptation by concept (AC) for the element process (in activity diagram the analysis can be focused on the tasks; in Communication Analysis the analysis is on the communicative events) against E(lanes) plus S(lanes) plus E(links) plus S(links).

If satellite models presents a huge amount of superficiality, analysts in charge of creating satellite models should justify the superficiality of the models regarding the requirements of evolution projects. In addition, analysts should ensure that satellite model fulfils its purpose.

### *Links*

If the amount of enrichments and simplifications by concept for the BPM element Link (EC) and (SC) are bigger than the amount of enrichments and simplifications by concepts for the elements process and lane; then it is advisable to verify deadlocks, bottlenecks, time performance, etc. In addition, time constraints could be necessary to control the high difference between links and the rest of the elements of BPM.

### *Metrics for situational impact category*

What if we need to know the differences related to the cost of two new brand cars, to decide which one fits a certain budget? Is it possible to establish differences between an enterprise business process models, and a new business strategy, in order to know values of costs, prices, amount of salaries to pay per month, etc.? The questions are highlighting the need to involve <u>external information</u>. Such external or contextual information can be cost estimations, risk assessments, revenues associated to products, etc. When performing comparisons, we propose then to introduce the idea of situational impact measurement as an activity to measure two models in order to know the impact of the differences according to certain situations that need external information to make further decisions.

We call situational impact metrics as the metrics to measure the differences by focusing on certain elements of the pivot and satellite models and it attributes. Fig. 63 presents the situational impact category by the arrow *3. situational impact*; which indicates that the delta of pivot and satellite models are analysed according to certain elements of the models and external information.

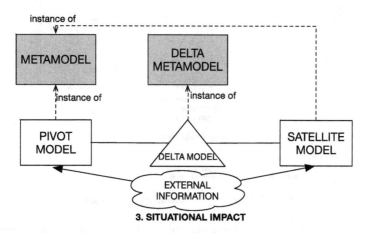

**Fig. 63.** Overview of the situational impact category

By means of delta models, it is possible to calculate the situational impact in terms of persistency, enrichment, simplification and modification (i.e., the four types of delta elements). According to the type of external information required for the situation, metrics will inform then in terms of total cost (if the external information is related to cost of products, salaries or any money type of information), risk assessment, etc.

We propose the following basic metrics for measurement of situational impact. We propose to shape the external information in terms of weights that are related to each element of the pivot and satellite model. Because the external information to relate each element depends on the situation where the models need to be analysed, the term weight is general enough to let the application of the metrics to different situations.

In Fig. 64 we illustrate a pivot, satellite and delta models. The external information is represented in terms of weights by means of rectangles with the letter W: W = #; where the symbol # indicates the value of the weight. For example, the element 7 of the satellite model is of type enrichment and its weight is 8.

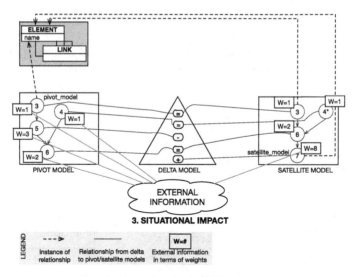

**Fig. 64.** Example of a situational impact case

The inputs of the metrics are delta models, pivot and satellite models with the respective weights for their elements. The results of the metrics provide absolute numbers informing about totals. For example, assume that each element represent a feature of the sound system belong to a special brand of car. If the satellite model represents a configuration of sound systems, the total cost of the sound system is the sum of persistent and added elements' weights of the satellite model.

Below we provide four basic metrics, one for each type of delta element. Further combination of these four metrics can be configured in order to perform different model comparisons based on weights.

The first metric proposed is persistency by weights. With this metric, we provide a support to measure the amount of persistent elements of a satellite model and use the value of the weights of its elements in order to give a total for the model. This total will be interpreted according to the context and the external information that conform the weights.

*m9*      *Persistency by weight*

---

The persistency by weight metric (PW) measures the total of the elements' weights of a satellite model that have related an equal delta element.

$$PW = \frac{sumequal}{|\sigma|}$$

$sumequal = \sum_{i=1}^{|\Delta|} is\_equal(\Delta_i);$

$is\_equal(\Delta_i) = \begin{cases} \Delta_i. \, satellite\_model. \, weight \; iff \; \Delta_i. \, type \; is \; "=" \\ \qquad\qquad 0 \; otherwise \end{cases}$

---

For analysing the total implied in simplifications performed on a certain satellite model, we design the simplification by weight metric. Here we focus on the weights of simplified elements, which can be easily detected by analysing simplification delta elements of delta models.

### m10    *Simplification by weight metric*

The simplification by weight metric (SW) measures the total of the elements' weights of a pivot model that have related a simplification delta element.

$$SW = \frac{sumsimp}{|\sigma|}$$

$$sumsimp = \sum_{i=1}^{|\Delta|} is\_simp(\Delta_i);$$

$$is\_simp(\Delta_i, c) = \begin{cases} \Delta_i. pivot\_model. weight \; iff \; \Delta_i. type \; is \; "\text{-}" \\ 0 \; otherwise \end{cases}$$

When comparing models, it is important to know the impact of "extra" elements that are specified in a satellite model in comparison with a pivot model. To support the measurement of the total weight of additions, we design the enrichment by weight metric presented in the following:

### m11    *Enrichment by weight metric*

The persistency by weight metric (EW) measures the total of the elements' weights of a satellite model that have related an addition delta element.

$$EW = \frac{sumaddi}{|\sigma|}$$

$$sumaddi = \sum_{i=1}^{|\Delta|} is\_addi(\Delta_i);$$

$$is\_addi(\Delta_i) = \begin{cases} \Delta_i. satellite\_model. weight \; iff \; \Delta_i. type \; is \; "\text{+}" \\ 0 \; otherwise \end{cases}$$

If an element is persistent in a model, it could involve a modification on its attributes and its weight can be modified. If a satellite model has modified elements according to a pivot model, the following metric stands for the calculation of the total weight of modified elements in a satellite model.

### m12    *Adaptation by weight metric*

The persistency by weight metric (EW) measures the total of the elements' weights of a satellite model that have related modifications' delta element.

$$AW = \frac{summodi}{|\sigma|}$$

$$summodi = \sum_{i=1}^{|\Delta|} is\_modi\Delta_i);$$

$$is\_modi(\Delta_i) = \begin{cases} \Delta_i. satellite\_model. weight \; iff \; \Delta_i. type \; is \; "\sim" \\ 0 \; otherwise \end{cases}$$

## 4.7.3    Delta models and metrics interpretation report

In this section, we introduce a framework to support the creation of reports for delta models and metrics results. We have two main goals with this framework: a) to facilitate metrics interpretation and understanding by means of templates; and b) to create a repository of interpretations that can be a base of knowledge for interpreting delta models and it measurement.

Fig. 65 illustrates the framework for delta models and metrics interpretation and report. We conceive a framework that has as a core delta models that are specified according to the guidelines for specification of delta models (see the section 4.7.1). After the specification of delta models, they can be measured in order to obtain quantitative information and the tendency of the differences between pivot and satellite models. Metric results together with the delta models are the input for the interpretation template. Interpretation obtained as a result of the analysis of the metrics and delta models are specified interpretation templates. Then, interpretation templates are stored in repositories.

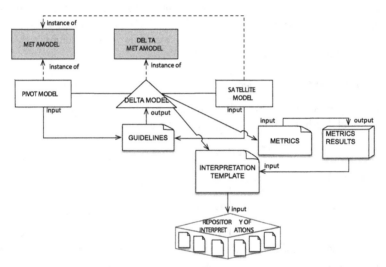

**Fig. 65.** Framework for delta models and metrics interpretation and report

To formalise the framework for delta models and metrics interpretation we design a metamodel for this purpose. Fig. 66 presents the metamodel view for metrics interpretation. The metaclass INTERPRETATION stands for the specification of interpretations and it details. The attribute NAME is for the indication of a short name that summarises the interpretation. The CREATION_DATE attribute is for the registration of the date when the interpretation is performed. The INTERPRETATION_GOAL attribute will describe the objective to perform the comparison of pivot and satellite models; i.e., the interpretation goal could be to analyse the evolution of a certain *to-be* model, the analysis of a model according to a baseline model, etc. The INTERPRETATION_DESCRIPTION attribute is for indicating all the details about the interpretation. Here the authors of the interpretation report describe their perceptions and analysis about the results of the metrics and delta models. The METRIC stands for specifying the metric/metrics that are supporting the ideas that justify a certain interpretation. The KEYWORD is an attribute to specify a set of related or similar words that can describes the interpretation; together with ALIAS they offer additional meaning in order to communicate interpretations. The PROJECT attribute is to specify URL and REFERENCES to link the interpretation with a concrete organisational project. Finally, the template has fields in order to indicate the AUTHOR or authors of interpretations.

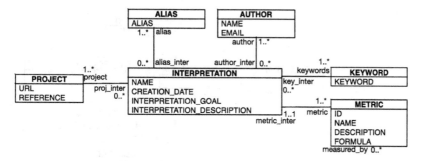

**Fig. 66.** Platform independent metamodel view of the unit 3 of Delta Analysis: Delta models measurement and metrics interpretation

The INTERPRETATION metaclass is instantiated by means of templates that serve for the purpose to collect all the information related with interpretations.

As part of the framework for delta model, we conceive a repository of interpretations. The attributes of the interpretation template like INTERPRETATION_GOAL, METRIC, KEYWORDS, ALIAS, and PROJECT serve as index to search for different kind of interpretations. We envision that this repository of interpretations will serve guidelines to interpret the results of metrics and delta models. With a considerable amount of interpretations templates, generalisations can be established according to certain projects. This field of research is part of the short-term future work for this research project.

In section 5.8 we facilitate the applications of the Delta Analysis technique by making Delta Analysis part of the TraceME method. For the delta models measurement and metrics interpretation unit, we provide the template for its use during interpretations processes. In addition, metrics and guidelines for delta models specification are presented at a glance.

### 4.7.4    Delta analysis metamodel

We follow the Model Driven Architecture (MDA) in order to separate business and application logic from underlying platform technology. Thus, Platform Independent Models (PIM) documents the business functionality and behaviour. We take this concept to a high level of abstraction in order to define Platform Independent Metamodels (PIMm). Fig. 67 presents the PIMm for the Delta Analysis. The objective is to facilitate the implementation of this metamodel by providing this abstract syntax. In the Chapter 7 we describe the details related to the implementation of this PIMm by using Eclipse (http://www.eclipse.org).

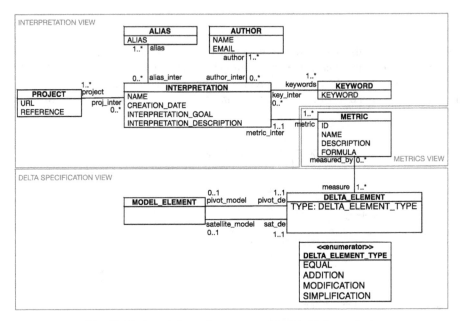

**Fig. 67.** Platform independent metamodel of the Delta analysis

## 4.8 Summary

The design of the TraceME chunks has been inspired by our experience in model-based software engineering. We are aiming at facilitating the chunks industrial transference by providing the support for their implementation.

The *iStar2ca* guidelines and the *evolCA* procedure are two method chunks based on the GoBIS framework. The GoBIS framework specifies how goal and business process perspectives are related and the traceability relationships that can be established. In this way, the *iStar2ca* guidelines supports the forward process from requirements to code by providing guidelines to obtain Communication Analysis models from *i** models.

The *evolCA* procedure guides the evolution of Communication Analysis models from *i** models. Both the *iStar2ca* guidelines and the *evolCA* procedure are exemplified with a running example. By following the *evolCA* procedure, the models involved in a certain evolution process are traced in order to keep pace of changes.

As part of the TraceME's chunks for supporting the forward processes of software development, we develop the *ca2oom* integration framework. This TraceME chunk provides the facilities in order to integrate Communication Analysis and OO-Method. Despite this method can be generalised to integrate any pair of model-based requirements engineering methods, in this research we provide all the design for its application for the integration of Communication Analysis and the OO-Method. As a result of the application of the integration framework, design models are obtained and further transformed in software code. In addition, the traceability among requirements and design models is obtained.

We introduce the Delta Analysis technique as a TraceME chunk to facilitate measurement and delta analysis of two pair of models. Thus, we design a Delta Analysis technique with the objective to support the specification of delta models, delta models' measurement, and delta models' interpretation. Delta Analysis is conceived for supporting measuring analysis in information system evolution scenarios. Nevertheless, Delta Analysis is general enough to be applied for various usages like analysis of baseline or reference models (this case is very common in the establishment of reference models and standards, analysis of two models for educational purposes where a model is compared with a baseline one, methodological reengineering, etc.). As a positive characteristic of Delta Analysis, we want to highlight the establishment of traces among two models and its exploitation by means of metrics.

The four method chunks presented in this chapter are formalised as part of TraceME by following a method engineering effort. The description on how to use each TraceME chunk and how to assemble them is detailed in Chapter 5.

# Chapter 5
## The TraceME method

*"Whether you are flying the Atlantic or selling sausages or building a skyscraper or driving a truck, your greatest power comes from the fact that you want tremendously to do that very thing, and do it well." - Amelia Earhart*

## 5.1    Motivation

This chapter presents TraceME, a traceability-based method that involves model-driven capabilities for conceptual model evolution. TraceME is founded on the idea to help analysts to conduct three kinds of evolution tasks 1) alignment among drivers to evolve conceptual models, 2) conceptual model evolution process, and 3) measurement of changes in order to analyse the evolution value and benefits. The three tasks have been conceived based on our observation performed in collaboration with our industrial partners. In addition, these tasks are contemplated to be vital during evolution processes by Lehman et al. [38].

The nature of TraceME is fragmented because each organisation has its own laws and needs during evolution processes. Then we designed a modular method. This way, TraceME is not a strict set of instructions where everything must be applied. In this way, we make a method engineering effort in order to conceive TraceME as a set of chunks that can be assembled according to certain situations.

Conceptual models are a mean to describe information systems. Different information systems analysis perspectives can be enrolled in an evolution process (business processes, interaction, feature, and communication are some information systems specifications that can be enrolled in an evolution process); which demands a customised support. TraceME do not cover all the possible support for evolving conceptual models belonging to all the existent perspectives. TraceME is abstract enough in order to be applied and extended to different organisational contexts. As a proof of concept, we provide the full support for business process model evolution because these models are widely used in organisational reengineering processes. Also we exemplify how the method can be extended to support the evolution of variability models.

In this chapter, we present a method engineering effort to specify the TraceME method. We provide details of each method chunk, its purpose, how to use it and the organisational roles involved. At the end of this chapter, we present how to assemble the TraceME chunks according to various situations. Some of the possible assembling processes are conceived in order to support different information systems projects; like organisational reengineering, software product line management, methodological reengineering, and model quality evaluation for educational purposes.

## 5.2    TraceME method: the construction

TraceME is a **Trace**ability-based method for conceptual **M**odel **E**volution that helps analysts to support their model evolution tasks. TraceME offers a set of components that can be applied according to analysts needs and requirements demanded for certain situations. The nature of TraceME is fragmented in order to promote several supports in common reengineering tasks.

The way TraceME is described is an adaptation and extension of the method conceptualisation proposed by [105]. Because of the nature of TraceME is fragmented, we undertake the method engineering effort proposed by Ralyté et al. [120] for the construction of TraceME.

Goldkuhl et al. state that methods are conformed by method component; which should be used in different situations i.e., for some situations it is not necessary to use all the method components existent for a certain method. In the TraceME method, we call method components as method chunks in order to emphasise the coherency and autonomy of such method modules according to Ralyte et al. [120].

Following Goldhulk et al., to provide a learnable method description, TraceME should describe the perspective (philosophy) of the method, framework, cooperation principles, and all method chunks. Fig. 68 presents the method notion by Goldhulk et al., and the relationships between perspective, framework, cooperation principles, and method chunks.

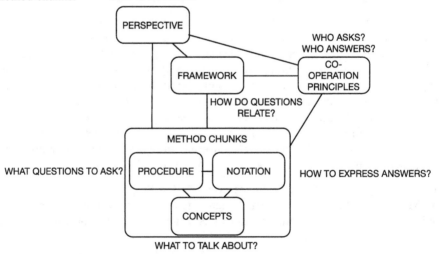

**Fig. 68.** Method notion: relationships between perspective, framework, cooperation principles and method chunks (adapted from [105])

<u>Perspective</u> describes the purpose and preconditions of the TraceME method and the TraceME method chunks.

<u>Framework</u> describes the relationships between method chunks. Also describes which method chunks have to be applied, under what conditions, and recommended sequence to using them. The framework describes an overview of the method chunks.

<u>Cooperation principles</u> are the description of the different roles, skills, and organisational structure for applying the method and each method chunk. They describe how people interact and cooperate when performing the method and/or method chunks.

<u>Method chunks</u> consist of procedures, notations, and concepts that are closely related in order to achieve a certain purpose.

— <u>The procedure</u> describes how to recognise important concepts in a method chunk. It also indicates prerequisites and resources of method chunks.
— <u>The notation</u> specifies how the results of the procedure should be documented.
— <u>The concepts</u> specify what aspects of reality are relevant to be named (and explained if necessary) in method chunks.

To describe TraceME and each method chunk, we will follow the method notion presented above in Fig. 68.

### 5.3    A method engineering effort to construct TraceME

By using the method engineering process model (MEPM) [120], the process model of TraceME is specified as a map with associated guidelines.

<u>A map</u> is a directed labelled graph with nodes and edges called intentions and strategies (see Fig. 69). Maps are conformed by several <u>sections</u> plus start and stop intentions.

STRATEGY

INTENTION

**Fig. 69.** Notation of map graphs

<u>A section</u> is a composition of <*source intention, target intention, strategy*> and has associated a guideline. Guidelines provide advices to fulfil the target intention by following a certain strategy indicated in a section.

The method-engineering map for the construction of TraceME is presented in Fig. 70. Two main intentions are identified: *Specify TraceME requirements* and *construct*

*TraceME*. The latter is the most important intention because it is the creation of the TraceME method[11]. Both intentions are explained below.

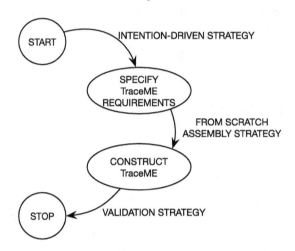

**Fig. 70.** Method engineering map for the construction of TraceME

### *Specify TraceME requirements intention*

The intention *specify TraceME requirements* reflects how the construction of TraceME is requirements-driven. In the case requirements corresponds with the re-search, questions and objectives established for this research project. For that reason, the strategy to specify TraceME requirements is an *intention-driven strategy*. Fig. 71 presents the TraceME requirements map that sum up the TraceME requirements. As we introduce before, sections have associated guidelines. The section <*start, support conceptual model evolution, model-driven development strategy*> has an associated guideline that helps the method engineer to select the most convenient solutions in the model-driven development field (see Fig. 70). To help on the selection of existent model-driven solutions to support conceptual model evolution (the main intention of the requirements map), the strategy *traceability strategy* indicates how to guide the selection. For deep details about the requirements of the TraceME method, goals, and tasks refer to Chapter 1.

The requirements map ends with the *stop* intention after the strategy *completeness strategy* is applied. The completeness is achieved when all the requirements specified are fulfilled.

---

[11] It is important to clarify that TraceME consists in a set of chunks selected according to the requirements established for TraceME. An assembling process of them conform TraceME as a whole. For the application of TraceME we will specify the assembly process for certain situations.

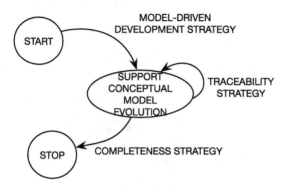

**Fig. 71.** TraceME requirements map

## *Construct TraceME intention*

After requirements specification, the intention *construct TraceME* can be achieved by following a *from scratch assembly strategy* (see Fig. 70). This strategy is selected because TraceME is a new developed brand to satisfy all the requirements previously defined. In this case, neither enhancement nor extensions have been done for establishing TraceME.

Future integration of TraceME with other conceptual model evolution solutions could involve alternative strategies as extension-driven assembly strategy, completeness-driven assembly strategy, and requirements correction strategy. Supports to assemble TraceME with other methods are out of scope of this research. Nevertheless, following method engineering for establishing the method assembly process and solutions in model-driven interoperability like [5] could be applied.

Fig. 72 presents the assembly map of TraceME describing the two main intentions: *select TraceME chunks* and *assemble TraceME chunks*. The selected TraceME chunks are the ones described in Chapter 4. To assemble the TraceME chunks we select an association strategy, which consists in connecting chunks where one chunk produces a product that is the source of other chunk. In TraceME, connections among chunks are in the shape of guidelines and/or traceability relationships. The completeness strategy is verified according to the scope of this research.

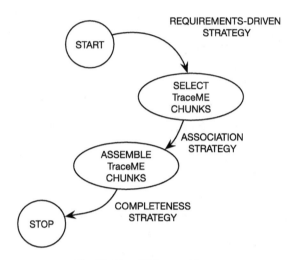

**Fig. 72.** TraceME assembly map

The construction of TraceME finalises with the validation strategy that demonstrate the feasibility of the method and method chunks (see Fig. 70 and Chapter 6 for more details on the validation).

The following sections present the TraceME method and its chunks in a black box representation. We use the method notion presented in Fig. 68 to structure sections' discourse. In the section 5.4 we describe the TraceME method. The perspective of the method (purpose and preconditions to use it) is described in the section 5.4.2. We describe the framework that defines all the method chunks and its relationships (this is an overview of the TraceME chunks). In the section 5.4.3 we introduce the cooperation principles (roles and organisational structures). Each method chunk is described in the sections 5.5, 5.6, 5.7, and 5.8. Validations and laboratory demonstrations that stand for the validation strategy are presented in Chapter 6.

## 5.4    The TraceME Method

### 5.4.1    Introduction

The goal of the TraceME method is to facilitate conceptual model evolution based on the model-driven paradigm. The TraceME method follows the idea that it is possible to automate as much as possible the software development process by means of encouraging the specification of conceptual models. Different information system analysis perspectives must be used in order to cover the specification of information systems requirements. In this context, the concept information system perspective plays an important role. As we defined in the theoretical framework for TraceME (see Chapter 3), information system perspective is the purpose or the point of view from which information systems are analysed.

To establish a clear distinction among information systems perspectives, it is important to apply the most adequate requirements engineering methods. The requirements engineering community has been working on the development of methods to formalise the specification of information systems perspectives. Having in mind that we need to specify different models that corresponds with different perspectives of information systems, traceability relationships become vital in order to have the connection among information systems perspectives.

Fig. 73 presents an example of different specifications to analyse information systems. In this example, goal and process models stand for requirements specification. Also, object models are specified for design purposes. This figure represents a typical model-driven development of software applications that follows a forward process.

Requirements of information systems are specified in goal models, which describe an intentional perspective of information systems. As an example of methods and frameworks for specifying the intentional perspective, the *i** framework has been widely applied [55].

Requirements related to processes and the actors of information systems are commonly specified in process models. For this purpose, modelling notations as BPMN is used in practice [144].

Regarding to the design of information systems; object models and interaction models are used for specifying data and human computer interaction requirements. UML is a notation for specifying design models [145].

For specifying information system requirements and design, we propose a forward development process (a.k.a. waterfall software development process) were different information systems perspectives are specified separately. For this purpose, we have into account goal models, process models, and object models (see Fig. 73). Goal, process, and object models are connected by means of traceability relationships. In this way, we propose to follow a line from requirements to code.

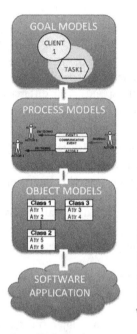

**Fig. 73.** Specification of information systems perspectives to develop software applications

The forward development process gives as main result software applications for supporting information systems. Software applications are used in periods until they need to be up-to-date of changes on the requirements. What happen when information systems change and evolution process must be performed? How to shift the model-driven paradigm to support information systems reengineering? How to support the need to implement round-trip engineering?

By following the model-driven paradigm, TraceME offers two options to evolve information systems that correspond to two situations or possible evolution projects: *evolution by Replacement* and *evolution by Preservation*. After evolution, TraceME offers measurement mechanisms to report on the evolution.

### Evolution by replacement

Evolution by replacement option offers the possibility to **replace** *as-is* systems by *to-be* systems according to the requirements specified for the *to-be* system by applying a forward engineering approach.

*as-is* models commonly are not up-to-date, then, it is a common practice in real projects to specify *to-be* models that involves *as-is* characteristics and the enhancement that motivates the evolution process. To analyse *as-is* models and check if they are up-to-date is time consuming and industry is not interested to spend resources on it [146]. This case is illustrated in Fig. 74, where there is not an explicit evolution of as-is models.

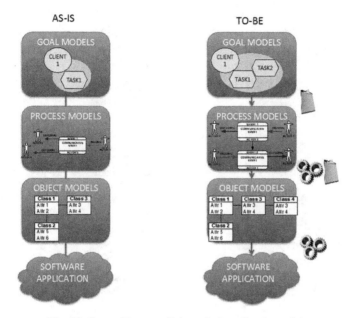

**Fig. 74.** Case without explicit evolution of *as-is* models

In Fig. 74 the *as-is* system is deprecated and a new *to-be* has been created. For this case, it is not interesting to invest effort to evolve *as-is* models and evolutionary requirements are specified in the *to-be*. The TraceME method supports the evolution by replacement projects where *as-is* models are completely replaced by *to-be* models. Desired characteristics of *as-is* system to be preserved in the to-be system are implied in the *to-be* models. Then, TraceME offers a forward support were model-driven techniques are applied in order to derive models from requirements to code.

In evolution by replacement, changes are applied from requirements to code in a waterfall manner. No guided support is given for the evolution process from *as-is* to *to-be* models and, round-trip engineering is not supported, but analysts can freely apply techniques for evolving *as-is* models. For the evolution by replacement in TraceME, we support two cases that depends on the models used for evolution projects: (i) goal models or (ii) business process models. For example, Fig. 75 illustrates an evolution from *as-is* goal models to *to-be* goal models. Then, a forward process is applied to obtain process models, object models and code.

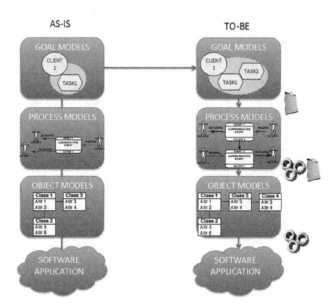

**Fig. 75.** Evolution of information systems by replacement

- (i) Evolution from goal models:
  Evolution projects are performed in order to fulfil new requirements and organisational goals. Advantages of goal models have been proved in industrial real cases. In order to analyse information system requirements and make specifications, we advise to depart from the analysis of goal models. Several approaches have been proposed for goal-oriented requirements engineering (GORE). Goal analysis have attracted a lot of attention in the last decades because of it practical application in information system evolution projects. Horkoff & Yu summarise how to choose the most convenient approach to analyse and evolve goal models [147]. For this reason, TraceME conceive the evolution by replacement option departing from goal models (see 0). In this case, *as-is* goal models are evolved to specify the *to-be* goals. Then, forward model-driven techniques are applied to derive process models, object models, and finally the software application.
- (ii) Evolution from process models:
  In this case, as-is process models are evolved to specify the *to-be* process models. Then, forward model-driven techniques are applied in order to obtain object models and finally the software application. This case is also possible and TraceME is not just designed to departure from goals. Despite organisational goals are vital to trace the road to evolution, sometimes organisations decide to specify their business in terms of organisational rules and work practices; then process models are the focus during evolution projects. TraceME also accept the evolution by replacement departing from process models.

As we already mention, for evolution by replacement the TraceME method does not offer any support for the evolution process of *as-is* models. Decisions about how to evolve *as-is* models and how to specify *to-be* models are out of scope of the evolution by replacement. Despite the strong influence of the forward process in this evolution situation, we consider that this situation is still an evolution of information systems. It is not an explicit evolution because of the replacement nature and no guided support for evolution; but it is led by evolution goals. As a conclusion, in the evolution by replacement situation the TraceME method focuses on the forward process from requirements to code of requirements that specify the desired system.

### *Evolution by preservation*

Information systems specifications do not departure from scratch and characteristics of *as-is* systems sometimes must to be specified in *to-be* systems. With this idea, preservation of *as-is* models arises as a "must have" for evolution projects.

Evolution by preservation option offers a guide to **preserve** characteristics of the *as-is* system in the *to-be* system. The need for preservation departs from the desire to keep things already developed in *as-is* systems.

A common practice is to introduce changes directly into the code of the *as-is* software application to obtain the *to-be* software. These practices (led by the need to quick evolve software applications and agile methodologies) omit the importance of traceability during information system evolution processes.

Despite requirements, specification can be described in goal models, requirements characteristics belonging to processes and design requirements are- by nature- described in processes and design models. A forward development process in evolution scenarios is not enough; round-trip reengineering is necessary to fully support information systems during evolution.

The TraceME method offers a support for evolution by preservation process for various information system perspectives specifications. Introducing an evolution support from *as-is* to *to-be* models and then a way back to support full evolution of all the *as-is* models that specifies information systems perspectives supports round-trip reengineering. The general idea of evolution by preservation is illustrated in Fig. 76.

Evolution by preservation departs from the analysis of *as-is* models of a certain perspective according to evolution requirements. Then, a support (represented by dashed lines) is provided for evolution. For instance, in Fig. 76 the evolution of *as-is* process models is supported (dashed line) having into account what characteristics of the *as-is* system must be preserved and what are the requirements to fulfil specified in the *to-be* goal models. For that reason a dashed line connect the *as-is* process models and the *to-be* goal models. As a result, the *to-be* process models are obtained. In this case, the specification of *as-is* goal models and its evolution is not necessary because it does not add valuable information. To specify the evolution of as-is goal models is dependent on the needs for traceability between *as-is* and *to-be* goal models. Indeed, for practical reasons, it is not necessary to specify formally the evolution of *as-is* goal models. The same example can be applied to the object models and software application.

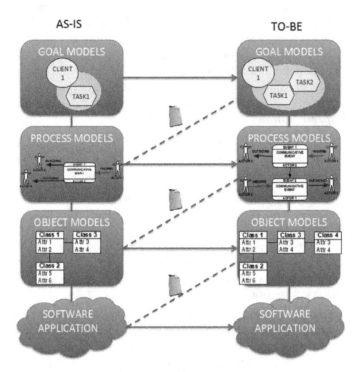

**Fig. 76.** Evolution by preservation: general idea

Based on the idea of evolution by preservation, the TraceME method offers a support to evolve *as-is* process models to *to-be* process models guided by goal models as is presented in Fig. 77. Then, by following a forward software development process, design models (object models) can be automatically derived from process models to get finally software applications.

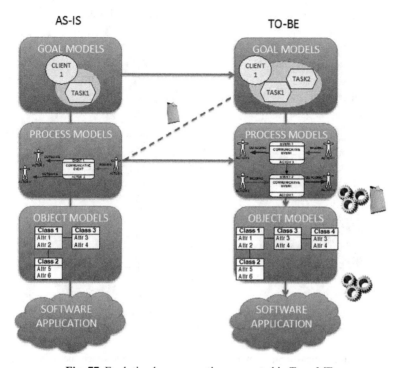

**Fig. 77.** Evolution by preservation supported in TraceME

In contrast with the option of evolution by replacement, here the option to preserve and guide the evolution of as-is models is important to ensure that characteristics of *as-is* systems are preserved and organisational goals are into consideration.

## *Evolution measurement mechanisms*

After information systems evolution, it is important to measure what are the differences between *as-is* and *to-be* models in order to report about the evolution. The TraceME method offers the mechanisms in order to analyse the differences (delta) between two models. Fig. 78 illustrates how the measurements mechanisms can be applied. The rectangle represents differences between two models.

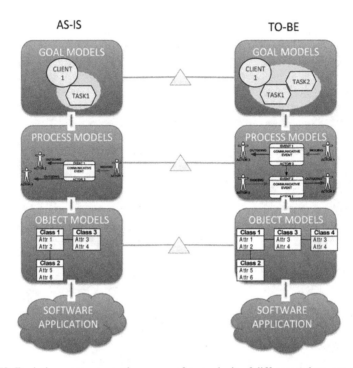

**Fig. 78.** Evolution measurement by means of an analysis of differences between models

Under the light of deltas, it is possible to conclude about several objectives for evolution that are commonly led by the situation of the project. Some examples of objectives can be to inform about organisational reengineering, model quality by comparing with baseline models, decision making in software product lines scenarios (variability), etc. We will develop these ideas in the section that describe the support for evolution measurement.

In short, the TraceME method includes the following method chunks:

- Derivation of business process models from goal models. This method chunk is created to support the forward process. It will be used in situations where evolution by replacement is required.
- Derivation of object models from business process models. This method chunk is created to support the forward process. It will be used in situations where evolution by replacement is required. In addition, this method chunk can be applied in the situation of evolution by preservation.
- Guided evolution of business process models. This method chunk is created to support the evolution process. It will be used in situations where evolution by preservation is required
- Delta analysis. This method chunk can be applied after evolution by replacement and evolution by preservation. It is a transversal chunk that serves as a post-analysis of evolution processes.

### 5.4.2    Perspective

This section briefly describes the purpose of the TraceME method, the TraceME method's chunks, and preconditions for using it.

## *Purpose*

The general purpose of TraceME is to support the evolution of conceptual models as main artefacts to support information systems. By involving traceability-based solutions and model-driven capabilities, TraceME offer chunks that can be configured according to the needs of certain information system evolution projects (i.e., TraceME can be adapted to different situations).

Organisational goals and processes should be captured and specified by means of conceptual models, for their further evolution and/or analysis. TraceME supports mainly the forward development process from requirements to code where goal models specify desired systems. In addition, TraceME supports the evolution of business process models when some guidelines for evolution are provided. A post-evolution analysis measurement is also provided in the TraceME method in order to report on the evolution. By applying TraceME, organisations obtain evolved information systems and reports about evolution.

In short, TraceME was designed for organisational context where TraceME method chunks are configured according to certain organisational needs. Nevertheless, other application contexts have emerged during the development of TraceME. Organisational reengineering and methodological reengineering are possible contexts where the delta analysis method chunk can be applied. The delta analysis method chunk of TraceME can be applied also for academic purposes where model evaluations are performed according to a baseline model. Furthermore, other possible context where TraceME can be applied is the software product line management. Explanation of the use of TraceME for the aforementioned contexts are presented in Section 5.9

## *Preconditions*

The use of the TraceME chunks starts from a number of preconditions:
- The evolution project in which the TraceME method is applied needs to be defined. The method chunks of TraceME are benefit from the definition of the situations to be applied or organisational needs. In order to decide which organisational chunks to apply evolution projects, it is necessary to choose the most convenient whether replace the current information system (evolution by replacement) or preserve characteristics of current information systems (evolution by preservation).
- The models to be measured are defined. If a certain organisation is interested to know about a performed evolution (i.e., apply evolution measurement mechanisms), it is necessary to have the version of the models to be analysed by applying the method chunk for measurement mechanisms.
- If patterns defining evolution of business process models exist (commonly they are specified or can be retrieved from organisational rules and organisational best prac-

tices), these patterns should be known. The chunk for supporting the evolution process allows new pattern definition.

- Models that specify organisational goals for desired system are specified. The method chunks benefit from the desired organisational goals specified by means of conceptual models. Desired organisational goal models define the driver for evolution. If there is none, then these should be specified. If a certain organisation have specified the organisational goal models that describe the current organisational system, it is possible to evolve the current goal models in order to obtain the desired goal models and then reflect the changes over the rest of information systems specifications.

### 5.4.3 Framework

The TraceME method consists of four different method chunks. This section describes which method chunks are included in the method and how they are interrelated:

## *Procedures*

Procedures inform the method users about the actions to be performed as well as its orders. In TraceME, we differentiate four method chunks that consist of guidelines and techniques to be applied to evolution projects. To use TraceME we recommend following two main phases that are described in Fig. 79.

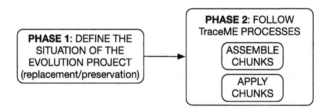

**Fig. 79.** Three main phases of the TraceME method

**Phase 1**: *Define the situation of the evolution project.* The situation in which the TraceME method is applied should be defined. Evolution project requirements as well as replacement or preservation needs should be set.

**Phase 2**: *Follow TraceME processes.* According to the situation defined, forward, evolution and/or measurement processes can be followed. Thus, a certain chunks of the TraceME method should be assembled and applied.

Fig. 80 presents an overview of the TraceME chunks distributed according to the process that TraceME supports: the forward process, the evolution process, and the measurement process. Each method chunk is named with a short name in order to refer to it easily.

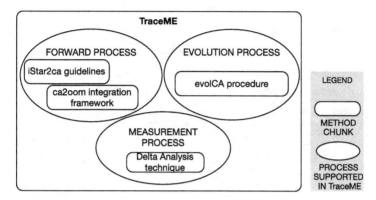

**Fig. 80.** Overview of the TraceME chunks and the processes in which they are involved

Below, we summarise each method chunk; details about each method chunk are presented in the next sections and the design is specified in Chapter 4:

*iStar2ca guidelines*. This method chunk provides a set of guidelines to derive Communication Analysis business process models from *i\** models.

*ca2oom integration framework*. This method chunk provides an integration framework to obtain OO-Method object models from Communication Analysis models.

*EvolCA procedure*. This method chunk provides a set of guidelines in order to evolve Communication Analysis business process models. Facilities to specify new evolution patterns or apply defined ones are also provided.

*Delta Analysis technique*. This method chunk is a technique to measure the difference between two models, which can be *as-is* and *to-be* models. A set of metrics are provided and the facilities to make interpretations and reports on the measurement results.

The *iStar2ca guidelines* chunk, the *ca2oom integration framework* chunk, and the *EvolCA procedure* chunk are the result of a method engineering effort that involve the *i\** language chunk, the Communication Analysis method and the OO-Method. The strategy to create the *iStar2ca* guidelines, the *ca2oom*, and the *evolCA* was chunk assembly by integration; which is detailed in the Chapter 4. We assume that the *i\**, the Communication Analysis and the OO-Method exist as method chunks of TraceME (see Fig. 81)

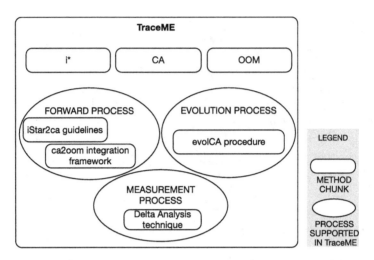

**Fig. 81.** Full specification of the TraceME chunks

In Chapter 4 we present the integration strategies in order to build the *iStar2ca guidelines*, the *ca2oom integration framework* and the *EvolCA procedure* chunks.

We acknowledge that it is possible to provide the integration mechanisms in order to build method chunks "on the fly". For example, it is possible to provide the mechanisms to create the guidelines to obtain Communication Analysis models from i* models when the method engineer need it. Our intention with TraceME is to make it light and free of effort when is used. Thus, due to the *iStar2ca*, *evolCA* and *ca2oom* can be general enough to apply them to different cases and contexts; it is not necessary to carry out the integration strategy if a certain chunk is needed. Then, we make the endeavour to provide the chunks as part of TraceME by following the integration strategy presented in the Chapter 4. For example, we applied ontological analysis in order to assemble the *i*\* language with the CA method; idem for the CA method and the OO-Method.

TraceME consists of several chunks that can be used by method engineers without the need to apply integration strategies. Our purpose is to facilitate method engineer tasks by providing built chunks and reducing the effort to design and apply integration strategies every time s/he needs to apply a certain chunk. The effort of the method engineer will be focused on the association strategies needed for certain evolution projects. The association strategies will be discussed in the further sections.

The assembling processes of TraceME chunks depends on the situation in which the evolution project is developed (situations are established in the phase 1. Each process has a set of chunks to be assembled and applied. To illustrate the sequence of processes for the phase 2, Fig. 82 presents recommended sequence of application of the TraceME processes.

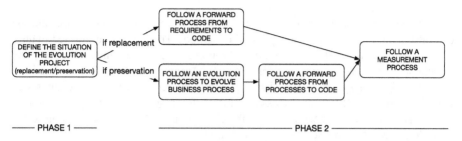

**Fig. 82.** Recommended sequence of TraceME processes

## Concepts

Concepts are the terms included in the phases and chunks introduced above. Most of the concepts used during the explanation of the TraceME method where already introduced in the Chapter 3 (theoretical framework). The concepts for each method chunk are specified in the respective method chunk sections.

## Notation

Notation defines the semantic and symbolic rules for documentation. TraceME chunks use notation as well as tabular forms in order to give to know the results of each chunk. The notation for each method chunk is specified in the respective method chunk sections. As we explained in the procedure of TraceME, three main phases should be followed to apply TraceME. Each phase involves processes and method chunks. All these concepts are abstracted in a metamodel that we present in Fig. 83.

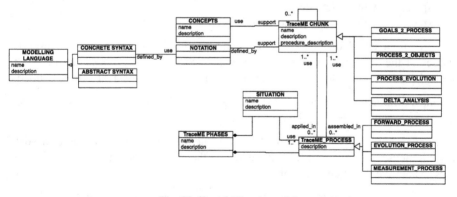

**Fig. 83.** TraceME metamodel

We specify the TraceME metamodel with two main goals: 1) Make explicit the main concepts of the TraceME method and their inter-relations; and 2) facilitate the method implementation by providing the design. The metamodel guides the implementation of TraceME that can be specified in method engineering tools for chunks assembling and method configuration. We provide the details for TraceME implementation in the Chapter 7. In this chapter we focus on the goal 1 of the TraceME metamodel.

The TraceME metamodel helps to understand how the method is conformed and the relationship among the main concepts of the method. TraceME is conformed mainly for TraceME chunks that use notations for reporting and presenting results (see the metaclasses TRACEME_CHUNK and NOTATION). TRACEME_CHUNKS are defined by CONCEPTS that we specify in the Chapter 3 and in the respective method chunks sections. TRACEME_PHASES uses TRACEME_CHUNKS for assembling and application of chunks. The TRACEME_CHUNKS are assembled in TRACEME_PROCESS according to the needs described in the phase 1 of the TraceME phases.

### 5.4.4    Cooperation principles

In this section, we describe the organisational preconditions to be established before to use TraceME. We describe recommendations including both, organisational structures and roles within the team using TraceME, and the enterprise where TraceME is applied.

We recommend the following competences for the use of the TraceME method.
- Skills to manage the concepts involved in the TraceME method. We present these concepts in the Chapter 3.
- Skills in elicitation techniques in order to gather relevant information in respect of the organisational environment.
  Mainly, it is important to be skilful for specifying organisational goal models as a mean to represent motivation of the project and justification about why to use TraceME. It is also important to have analytical skills in order to differentiate models that have change in a line of time; for example: *as-is* and *to-be* models.
- Experience with goal models
- Experience with business process models

We propose a set of roles that have tasks and responsibilities in order to perform the phases of the TraceME method. However, the roles that we propose can be modified/adapted according to the characteristics of the project where TraceME is applied.

*Business Manager*. The Business Manager is the role in charge to establish organisational goals and processes in the organisation.

*Innovation Analyst*. The Innovation Analyst is the role responsible to keep up-to-date organisations, adapt them to fulfil the needs of the environment, as to identify strategies to improve the organisational activities.

*Business Analyst*. The Business Analyst is the role in charge to elicit and specify goal and business process models resulting from the innovation and improvement projects. The Business Analyst works together with the Business Manager and the Innovation Analyst in order to involve changes in organisational contexts.

*Method Engineer*. The Method Engineer is the role expert on the application of the TraceME method. This role is in charge to apply, assemble, and report the results of the application of the TraceME chunks.

In order to apply TraceME, we suggest a roles' assignment (see Table 10). As we mentioned before for the roles proposed, the proposed roles' assignment can be also modified/adapted according to the needs of evolution projects.

Table 10. Assignment of roles to TraceME chunks

| TraceME chunk | Role involved |
|---|---|
| Guidelines goals2process | Business Manager, Innovation Analyst, Business Analyst, Method Engineer |
| Guidelines process2Objects | Business Manager, Innovation Analyst, Business Analyst, Method Engineer |
| Guidelines&Patterns proces-sEvolution | Business Manager, Innovation Analyst, Business Analyst, Method Engineer |
| Delta analysis | Business Analyst, Method Engineer |

The roles assignments will be described in detail in respective method chunks when the *procedure* section is explained.

## 5.5     Method chunk iStar2ca guidelines

The *iStar2ca* guidelines chunk of the TraceME method provides the facilities in order to guide the specification of Communication Analysis models based on *i\** models. Mainly, the *iStar2ca* guidelines are intended for top-down scenarios. These scenarios are widely applied in forward processes. For this reason, this chunk is part of the forward process of the TraceME method.

An overview of the method chunk is given in Fig. 84. The procedure of the iStar2ca guidelines describes the main steps to use the guidelines. The concepts and notation are intended to facilitate understanding and specification of the results of the procedure.

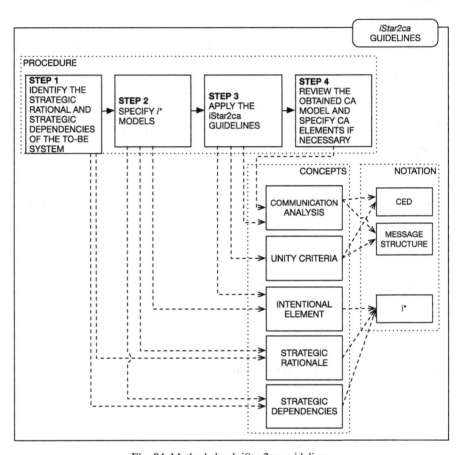

**Fig. 84.** Method chunk iStar2ca guidelines

### 5.5.1 Concepts

The method chunk *istar2ca* guidelines comprises five concepts that are described in Table 11. To illustrate each concept we take our SuperStationery Co. case, which was the running example to describe the design of the istar2ca guidelines in section 4.4.

**Table 11.** Concepts in the *iStar2ca guidelines* chunk

| Concept | Explanation |
|---|---|
| **Communication Analysis** | Requirements engineering method that analyses the communicative interaction between the information system and its environment [66]. |
| | **Example:** The SuperStationery Co. case presented in them section 4.2.2 demonstrates the application of the Communication Analysis method for specifying the business process models with a communicational perspective. |

| Unity criteria | Modularity guidelines for identifying communicative events elements of the Communication Analysis methods [113]. |
|---|---|
| | **Example:** A communicative event of a certain business process model is structured as a sequence of actions that are related to information (acquisition, storage, processing, retrieval, and/or distribution), which are carried out in a complete and uninterrupted way. The communicative event Client places an order of the SuperStationery Co. case fulfils the unity criteria (see section 4.2.2). |
| **Intentional element** | Objective to obtain by an actor (depender) that depends on other actor (dependee). Intentional element is also known as dependum [55]. |
| | Example: In our SuperStationery Co case (see Section 4.2.1), the actor Client depends on the Insurance dept clerk in order to obtain the insurance of acquired products. |
| **Strategic rationale** | Strategic rationale belongs to a certain actor described by mean of intentional elements [55]. |
| | **Example**: In our SuperStationery Co. case (see Section 4.2.1), the strategic rational of the actor Client is specified by means of the intentional elements inside of its boundary. |
| **Strategic dependencies** | Strategic dependencies among actors in order to obtain an objective (intentional element) [55]. |
| | **Example**: In our SuperStationery Co. case (see Section 4.2.1), the actor Client has strategic dependencies with the actors Sales Manager, Insurance dept clerk, Truck driver, and Transport Manager. |

### 5.5.2    Procedure

We describe in this section the different steps performed in the *iStar2ca guidelines* method chunk:

### Step 1. Identify the strategic rationale and strategic dependencies of the to-be system

**Input**

- Organisational information about the requirements and organisational specification of the *to-be* information system, mainly, the specification of the intentional specification of the *to-be* involves the following elements:

  — Organisational actors
  — Intentional elements
  — Dependencies among actors
  — Strategic rationale of actors
  — Constraints

- The *i\** method chunk

**Objective**

Gather information about intentional requirements of a certain organisation. The step 1 is aiming at scoping the requirements elicitation process by focusing on the analysis of intentional requirements. In this way, the intentional perspective of the information system is exploded. To do this, the strategic rationale and the strategic dependencies of the *to-be* information system should be identified.

**Activities**

a) Analyse the documentation that specify intentional requirements of the *to-be* system if any. If there is no intentional requirements specification, move to the activity b.

- Analyse the actors
- Analyse the strategic dependencies among actors
- Analyse the strategic rationale of each actor

b) Start a requirements gathering session with the stakeholders in order to obtain information about the intentional requirements of the *to-be* system.

- Set the requirements gathering session
- Concentrate on business organisational models and information systems are supported
- Discover new goals and challenge to confront by the organisation
- Focus on the actors of the organisation and their roles
- Analyse the strategic dependencies among actors
- Analyse the strategic rationale of each actor

**Output**

A requirements document specifying the intentional requirements of the organisation. It can include sketches or quick drawings.

**Tools**

- Intentional requirements can be specified using common text editors.
- Sketches and quick drawings can be developed by using any diagramming software or digital illustration application.

**Contributors**

Envisioned contributors for the TraceME method. The business analyst is the most important contributor for this step. He should have the skills for the TraceME method (described previously in the section 5.4.4). The business analyst should interact with the business manager and the innovation analyst in order to gather information about the intentional requirements of the *to-be* system. These three roles are working all together in the activities a) and b).

*Step 2. Specify the i\* models*

**Input**
- Requirements document with the specification of the intentional requirements (output of the step 1)
- *i\** method chunk

**Objective**

To specify the *i\** models of a certain organisation. This step identifies meaningful information from requirements documents focusing on intentional requirements.

**Activities**
a)  Select the intentional information to specify in the *i\** models. There are two options: define the strategic rationale (SR) or the strategic dependencies (SD) of information systems. They are not exclusive; it is possible to specify both models (SR and SD) in parallel.
b)  Specify the SR and SD of the information system by using the *i\** language [55].

**Output**

The *i\** models that specifies the intentional requirements of a certain organisation.

**Tools**
- The OpenOME is an open-source requirements engineering tool that provides the modeling environment to specify *i\** models [148].
- Great Process Modeller. It provides a plug-in for *i\** models specification.
- Diagramming software or digital illustration applications with the graphical notation to specify *i\** models.

**Contributors**

Envisioned contributors for the TraceME method. For this step, the main contributor is the business analyst who is the role in charge to specify the *i\** models by using the described tools. The innovation analyst participates validating the *i\** models specified by the business analyst.

### *Step 3. Apply the iStar2ca guidelines*
**Input**
- The *i\** model created in the step 2
- The *iStar2ca guidelines* (see description available in Fig. 85 and Fig. 86)
- The CA method chunk

The TraceME
Method

iStar2ca guidelines

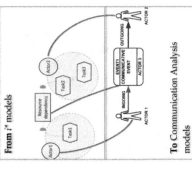

**From i\* models**

**To Communication Analysis models**

Source: M. Ruiz, D. Costal, S. España, X. Franch, and O. Pastor, "Integrating the goal and business process perspectives in information system analysis," presented at the 26th International Conference on Advanced Information Systems Engineering (CAiSE 2014), Thessaloniki, Greece, 2014.

**Authors:**
Marcela Ruiz[1], Dolors Costal[2], Sergio España[1], Xavier Franch[2] and Óscar Pastor[1]

[1]PROS Research Centre, Universitat Politècnica de València (UPV) (opastor, sergio.espana, lruiz)@pros.upv.es

[2]GESSI Research Center, Universitat Politècnica de Catalunya (UPC) (dolors, franch)@essi.upc.edu

COMMENTS

• The number of the guidelines does not indicate a strict order of application.

• A dependency may be connected to SR elements which are not tasks indicating that the task of communicating the resource information is implicit in the i\* model.

• Chained dependencies with the same dependum imply precedences between two mapped communicative events.

• The dependency indicates that the depender expects to receive an information from the dependee, thus a communicative event is needed to allow the dependee communicate that information to the depender.

• The interface actor cannot be determined from the i\*. It may coincide with the primary actor or not. It may even be an actor that does not appear the i\* model at all because it is not strategically relevant.

• Two i\* tasks involved in a dependency maps into a single communicative event.

• Goals, tasks, softgoals and physical resources do not map directly into Message Structures. They may indicate the existence of informational resources not explicit in the i\* model.

• The abstract guideline indicates how to treat implicit informational resources applying the notion of intentional satisfaction.

**Fig. 85.** The *iStar2ca* guidelines at a glance (page 1)

## The iStar2ca guidelines

It main purpose is to guide the mapping from *i\** elements into CA elements. They provide advice to obtain CA elements from explicit *i\** elements and do not explicit ones but which existence can be deduced from the model.

The Communication Analysis method focus on interactions; thus, by applying the iStar2ca guidelines it is possible to identify if an *i\** dependency involves some type of interaction.

***Guideline 1.*** The dependum of a dependency D among two roles maps into a message structure M if this dependum is an informational resource. In that case, D induces a communicative event C such that: (1) C's primary role is D's dependee role; (2) C's receiver role is D's dependee role; (3) C's ingoing and outgoing interactions specify M; (4) if any of the SR elements of D's dependee and dependee roles are tasks, they map into C.

***Abstract guideline.*** The dependum of a dependency D between two roles induces a message structure M the dependee is required to give information to the dependee about the intentional satisfaction of this dependum. In that case, D induces a communicative event C such that: (1) C's primary role is the D's dependee role; (2) C's receiver role is the D's dependee role; (3) C's ingoing and outgoing interactions specify M; (4) if any SR elements of D's dependee and dependee roles are tasks, those tasks map into C.

***Guideline 2.*** When the dependum is a goal, the

notion of intentional satisfaction of the abstract guideline refines into attainment of this goal.

***Guideline 3.*** When the dependum is a task, the notion of intentional satisfaction of the abstract guideline refines into accomplishment of this task.

***Guideline 4.*** When the dependum is a softgoal, the notion of intentional satisfaction of the abstract guideline refines into level of satisfaction of this softgoal.

***Guideline 5.*** When the dependum is a physical resource, the notion of intentional satisfaction of the abstract guideline refines into the provision of this physical resource.

***Guideline 6.*** An actor about which relevant information must be registered in the IS indicates that a communicative event and its corresponding message structure must be specified in order to register the actor information.

***Guideline 7.*** Two dependencies (D1 and D2), mapping into two communicative events (C1 and C2), indicate that C1 precedes C2 in the communicative event diagram if:

(1)   D1 and D2 have the same dependum
(2)   the dependee of D1 is the dependee of D2

***Guideline 8.*** Two dependencies, (D1 and D2), mapping into two communicative events (C1 and C2), indicate that C1 and C2 can be merged into a single communicative event C in the communicative event diagram if:

(1)   D1 and D2 have the same dependum
(2)   D1 and D2 have the same dependee

***Guideline 9.*** Assume a dependency D that induces a communicative event C such that C's primary and receiver actors are P and R respectively; and assume C's message structure is M. The recommended names for C, P, R, and M are determined as follows:

- C is based on the name of D's dependee + the name of the SR related element of the dependee+ the name of D's dependum (optional)
- P is based on the name of D's dependee role
- R is based on the name of D's dependee role
- M is based on the name of D's dependum if D's dependum is an informational resource; otherwise M is based on the name of the intentional satisfaction that corresponds to D's dependum.

**Fig. 86.** The *iStar2ca* guidelines at a glance (page 2)

## Objective

The objective of this step is the specification of CA models from *i\** models. The idea is to connect intentional requirements with the business process models for organisational support. Thus, by applying the iStar2ca guidelines it is possible to derive a first "light" version of the CA models. The strategy is to follow the *iStar2ca* guidelines which will ensure the vertical traceability among *i\** and CA model elements. The *iStar2ca* guidelines promote to follow good practices to transform models that are belong to different information systems specification perspectives.

## Activities

a)  Be familiarised with the input *i\** model. Analyse the actors, strategic dependency and strategic rationale models

b)  Apply the iStar2ca guidelines (see 0 and 0)

## Output

- CA business process models
- Traceability relationships among *i\** and CA models elements

## Tools

- GREAT Process Modeller to specify the CA models obtained from *i\** models
- GREAT Process Modeller to specify the vertical traceability among *i\** and CA model elements
- Diagramming software or digital illustration applications with the graphical notation to specify CA models.

## Contributors

The method engineering that has the skills for applying the TraceME method and to use the *iStar2ca* guidelines method chunk. S/he is the role in charge to analyse the *i\** model and apply the *iStar2ca* guidelines method chunk.

## *Step 4. Review the obtained CA model and specify elements if necessary*

### Input

- A CA model obtained as a result of the step 3
- CA method chunk

## Objective

In order to ensure that the resulting CA models of the step 3 specify the business requirements for a certain organisation, a review of the obtained CA models must be performed. Because of the revision step, could be necessary to add new elements to resulting CA models as to make some modifications on them. This review is necessary because the nature of the *i\** models is intentional-oriented, not business process-oriented. Thus, from an *i\** model it is not possible to derive all the business specification of an organisation.

## Activities

a)  Analyse the resulting CA models of the step 3

- Review if the organisational actors are properly specified. Check if the communicative event are depicted and with the ingoing and outgoing communicative interactions. Review if the precedences among communicative events are specified.
- Review the business requirements of the organisation and analyse if all of the requirements are specified in the CA models. If there are some requirements that are missing in the CA models, continue with activity b.

b) Review the requirements that are not specified in the CA model. Specify the CA elements in the CA model in order to make this model compliant with the organisational needs.

**Output**

An improved CA business process model

**Tools**

Use the tool that was selected in the step 3

**Contributors**

The business analyst that knows all the requirements of the organisation is the role in charge to make the modifications on the resulting CA model. To do this, he should use the CA method chunk in order to specify missing elements. The innovation analyst should validate the CA model resulting of this step. Both the business and innovation analysts should iterate in order to find the most appropriated business process specification for the organisation.

### 5.5.3   Notation

The iStar2ca guidelines method chunk uses three notations that are listed and summarised as follows:

*i**

The *i** framework is a goal-and agent-oriented requirements engineering method [55]. The *i** framework proposes two models: the Strategic Dependency model (SD) to specify the intentional level, and the Strategic Rationale model (SR) to specify the rationale level.

Organisational actors can be specialised into agents, roles and positions. Agents are actors with a concrete physical manifestation. Roles are abstract characterisation of the behaviour of a social actor within a context. A position covers roles. Further information about the *i** framework can be found in the *i** wiki available at http://istarwiki.org/

For the *iStar2ca* guidelines, the *i** language is applied to model the intentions and goals of the *to-be* information systems. *i** models are used as inputs for the *iStar2ca* guidelines in order to generate CA models.

## Communicative event diagrams

The communicative event diagram (CED) is a modelling technique of the Communication Analysis method to specify business process from a communicational perspective. Communicative event diagrams are consisted of communicative events, which is an organisational action that answers a change in the world. Communicative events can be identified by a set of guidelines defined by the unity criteria [113]. Communicative events are triggered by primary roles that provide input information. Actors that need to be informed about the occurrence of an event are named receiver roles. From the interaction perspective, the interface roles are in charge to edit and enter information. The interactions between primary and receiver roles with communicative events are represented by means of ingoing and outgoing interactions. Communicative event sequence can be specified by means of precedences relationships.

By applying the *iStar2ca* guidelines to a certain i* model CED are obtained. For more information about CED notation check [149].

## Message structures

The message structures is a technique of the Communication Analysis method for specifying new meaningful information that is conveyed to the information system in a certain event [113].

After the application of the iStar2ca guidelines to a certain i* model, the resulting CED make explicit the need to specify its corresponding message structures. For more information about message structure specification check [149].

Table 12 summarises the notations with the steps and activities they are applied in.

**Table 12.** Notations for iStar2ca guidelines method chunk

| Notation | Step | Activity |
|----------|------|----------|
| i* | Identify the strategic rationale and dependencies | All activities |
| | Specify *i*\* models | All activities |
| | Apply the *iStar2ca* guidelines | Be familiarised with the input *i*\* model |
| Communicative event diagrams | Apply the *iStar2ca* guidelines | Apply the *iStar2ca* guidelines |
| | Review obtained CA model | All activities |
| Message structure | Apply the *iStar2ca* guidelines | Apply the *iStar2ca* guidelines |
| | Review obtained CA model | All activities |

### 5.6    Method chunk ca2oom integration framework

The *ca2oom integration framework* chunk is intended to support the forward process to obtain object models of the OO-Method from business process models of the Communication Analysis. This TraceME chunk is applied in order to obtain the de-

sign of the information system based information systems requirements specifications.

It is important to mention how the *ca2oom* integration framework is applied in practice. The integration framework promotes the application of MDA techniques in order
to design implementation-oriented solutions for methods integration. As a practical
case, we apply the integration framework to integrate the Communication Analysis
and the OO-Method. In practical conditions, analysts use the artefacts resulting from
the integration framework; such artefacts are diagramming tools to allow combined
modelling together with transformation engines for automatic transformations. In this
sense, the *ca2oom* integration framework as a method chunk of TraceME offers the
diagramming tool and transformation engine for combined modelling of Communication Analysis and OO-Method.

This method chunk is very valuable when an evolution of information systems is performed; this is due to the facilities to obtain the object models automatically. We give
an overview of the chunk in Fig. 87.

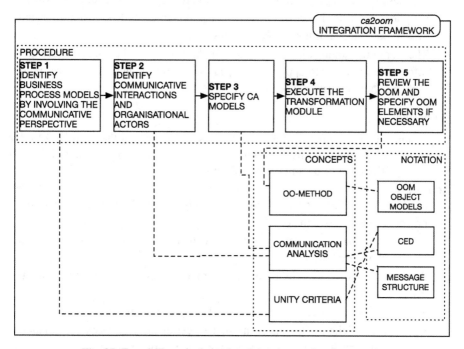

**Fig. 87.** TraceME method chunk ca2oom integration framework

**5.6.1    Concepts**

| Concept | Explanation |
|---------|-------------|
| OO-Method | OO-Method is a model-driven software development method, whose conceptual models are supported by Integranova, a models compiler that allows the code-automatic generation. |
| | Example: The OO-Method object models of the SuperStationery Co. case specified in [138] |

**5.6.2    Procedure**

The five steps to be performed in order to apply this method chunk are described in the following:

*Step1. Identify business process models by involving the communicative perspective*

**Input**

- Business process specification of the information system. It could be textual descriptions with the information system requirements, models of the information system, knowledge of the business analysts, etc.
- The Communication Analysis method chunk. This method chunk provides all the information in order to apply the method to identify the business process models with the communicational perspective.

**Objective**

Step 1 aims at establishing the business process by identifying the meaningful information of information systems. To do this, it is advisable to apply the unity criteria to help the identification of communicative events.

**Activities**

a) Analyse the business process models, if there is any. If there are not business process models, move to activity b.
   - Review that each process correspond with a communicative event by following the unity criteria.
b) Analyse the textual description of the information system and identify communicative events.
   - Follow the unity criteria in order to identify communicative events.
   - Prepare elicitation meetings in order to get all the necessary information in order to specify the business process of the information system.

**Output**

- A document with the information about the identified communicative events. The document could be drafts of business process models, drafts of textual specification of communicative events, drafts of communicative events diagrams.

**Tools**
- GREAT Process Modeller for the specification of communicative events.
- Diagraming tools for business process specification.
- Textual editors if the analyst just wants to write a draft with the detected communicative event.

**Contributors**
- The Business analyst contributes with the identification and specification of the business process models.
- Method engineer participate in all the activities.

## *Step2. Identify communicative interactions and organisational actors*
**Input**
- Output from the step before
- Organisational information regarding actors and roles
- The communication Analysis method chunk

**Objective**

To identify organisational actors and the meaningful information that is communicated. To identify the structure of the information interchanged by the organisational actors.

**Activities**
a) To relate the organisational actors with the communicative events identified in the step 1, if there are any. If the actors are not identified, move to step b.
- To relate the organisational actors with the communicative events
- To identify the structure of the information exchanged in each communicative event.
b) To identify the organisational actors and the structure of the information exchanged in each communicative event.
- To have elicitation meetings in order to identify the actors and the structure of the information.
- To review current templates, software and documents in order to elicit the information's structure of the information system.
- To analyse the hierarchical chart to identify organisational roles.

**Output**
- A document with the information about the identified organisational roles and the structure of the exchanged information among the communicative roles. The document could be drafts of business process models, drafts of textual specification of communicative events, drafts of communicative events diagrams.

**Tools**
- GREAT Process Modeller for the specification of organisational roles and message structures.
- Diagraming tools for business process specification.
- Textual editors if the analyst just wants to write a draft with the detected communicative roles and the structure of the information that is conveyed in the information system under analysis.

**Contributors**
- The business analyst who is in charge of the identification of the business process models.
- The method engineer participates all the time during the execution of the activities.

## Step 3. Specify CA models
**Input**
- Outputs of the steps 1 and 2
- The *ca2oom* integration method chunk (see description available in in Fig. 88 and Fig. 89). This integration method chunk indicates how to use the diagramming tool to specify Communication Analysis models.
- The Communication Analysis method chunk to review the notation and method guidelines if necessary.

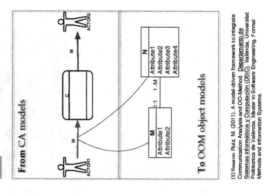

**Authors:**
Marcela Ruiz, Sergio España, and Óscar Pastor

PROS Research Centre, Universitat Politècnica de València (UPV)
{lruiz, sergio.espana, urueda, opastorj@pros.upv.es

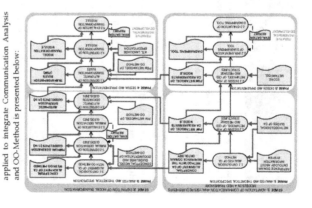

**Fig. 88.** The *ca2oom* integration framework at a glance (page 1)

## ca2oom integration framework

An integrated environment for Communication Analysis and OO-Method is implemented in the GREAT Process Modeller: a Global Reengineering Environment for Automated model Transformations. Mainly, GREAT offers facilities in order to a) model the Communication Analysis models (communicative event diagrams and message structures); and b) transform Communication Analysis models into OO-Method object models.

### 1. Download GREAT Process Modeller

The tool is **global**, covering the whole software development process (from system analysis and requirements specifications to code production and maintenance). It supports **reengineering** projects helping them in the adaptation of existing software assets to new environment needs. And, it supports agile development through **automated transformations** inside a model-driven methodology for software development.

Business architects, Software analysts, and all software development/maintenance concerned parties interested in the production and maintenance of quality software are the expected users of the tool.

The GREAT Process Modeller manual with technical details can be found at
http://arxiv.org/abs/1502.07693

To download GREAT Process Modeller, drop an email to Marcela Ruiz: lruiz@pros.upv.es

### 2. Specify communicative event diagrams

To specify the communicative event diagrams, GREAT provides a graphical modelling editor in order to specify the communicative events, communicative subevents, organisational actors, communicative interactions, precedences and logical gates.

By following the GREAT user manual and examples presented in [1], specify communicative event diagrams by using the facilities of the project explorer, modelling space and tool palette.

### 3. Specify message structures

GREAT facilitates the specification of message structures by means of tree-view structures associated with communicative event diagrams. The tree-view allows the specification of complex substructures, substructures, fields, data field and reference fields.

Specify the message structures using the tree-view of the communicative event diagram. Review the GREAT user manual and the examples presented in [1] for further details and illustrations.

### 4. Apply the ca2oom transformation module

The ca2oom transformation module implements the rules published in [2]. The transformation module offers an automated environment that takes as input Communication Analysis models and as output generates the OO-Method object models.

To obtain the object models just find the generation button in the GREAT menu or the tool bar. The generation button automatically takes the Communication Analysis models, apply the transformation rules and generate the object models that can be found in the project explorer. The OO-Method object models in GREAT implements the notation of class diagrams of UML. Afterwards, the generated object model can be edited by using the facilities of the GREAT platform.

GREAT PROCESS MODELLER

eclipse

PROS

UNIVERSITAT POLITÈCNICA DE VALÈNCIA

[2] Gonzalez, A., et al. (2011). Systematic derivation of class diagrams from communication-oriented business process models. 12th edition of the Business Process Modeling, Development, and Support (BPMDS) in conjunction with CAiSE'11. London, Uk.

**Fig. 89.** The *ca2oom* integration framework at a glance (page 2)

**Objective**

To specify the Communication Analysis models in the GREAT Process Modeller. The specification of the business process models helps on the formalisation of the organisational processes for it further support.

**Activities**

a) Review the outputs of the steps 1 and 2

b) Apply the ca2oom integration method chunk

**Output**

- The Communication Analysis models specified in the GREAT process modeller

**Tools**

- GREAT process modeller

**Contributors**

- The method engineer and the business analyst can cooperate in order to specify the models in the GREAT Process Modeller

### Step 4. Execute the transformation module

**Input**

- The output of the step 3
- The ca2oom integration framework method chunk. This method chunk indicates how to apply the transformation engine.
- The OO-Method chunk

**Objective**

Obtain object models of information systems. By executing the transformation engine of GREAT Process Modeller, object models of information systems can be obtained.

**Activities**

a) Execute the transformation engine of GREAT Process Modeller in order to obtain OO-Method object models

b) Review if the model is generated and stored in its corresponding project folder.

**Output**

The OO-Method object models

**Tools**

The GREAT Process Modeller

**Contributors**

Either the business analyst or the method engineer can execute the transformation engine of GREAT.

### Step 5. Review the obtained object model OOM and specify OOM elements if necessary

**Input**

- The output of the step 4
- The OO-Method chunk

**Objective**

Arrange and review the obtained object model after the execution of GREAT's transformation module. The objective is to arrange the elements of the obtained model and review if all the important elements of a certain information system are specified.

**Activities**

a) Review the arrangement of the generated model and dispose the elements in an appropriate manner.
b) Review design requirements of the information system and analyse if important elements are specified.

  — If elements are missing, it is advisable to review the Communication Analysis models and discover if the missing elements corresponds with the analysis of the information system from the communicational perspective. In this case, complete the Communication Analysis models and execute the transformation module (see steps 3 and 4).
  — If elements are missing but they do not correspond with the communicational perspective, use the tool palette in order to specify the missing elements in the object model.

**Output**

A validated object model

**Tools**

GREAT Process Modeller

**Contributors**

Either the business analyst or the method engineer can contribute to the execution of this step.


### 5.6.3 Notation

The *ca2oom integration framework* chunk uses three notations: the communicative event diagrams, the message structures and the object models of OO-Method. Below we describe the OO-Method object models. Communicative event diagrams and message structures are described in the method chunk istar2ca guidelines (see 5.5.3)

### *OO-Method Object models*

The notation of the object model of the OO-Method is to graphically describe structures of information systems in terms of classes and relationships. Mainly, the object model notation facilitates the specification of classes that make up the information systems and structural relationships; provides internal structures for classes in terms of their properties like attributes, services and integrity constraints; supports agents specification in order to model authorisations and service activation [67].

**Integranova** is the suite that implements the OO-Method. The object model, together with the dynamic model, the functional model and the presentation model are the input in order to obtain full-equipped software applications that can be deployed in different technological platforms. Further details can be founded in http://www.integranova.com/.

Table 13 comprises the notations with the steps and activities they are applied.

**Table 13.** Notations for *ca2oom integration framework* TraceME chunk

| Notation | Step | Activity |
|---|---|---|
| OOM object models | Review the OOM | n/a |
| CED | Identify business process models | - Analyse business process models.<br>- Analyse textual description of information systems |
| | Identify communicative interactions | - To relate organisational actors<br>- To identify organisational actors |
| | Specify CA models | Review outputs of steps 1 and 2 |
| Message Structures | Identify communicative interactions | - To relate organisational actors<br>- To identify organisational actors |
| | Specify CA models | Review outputs of steps 1 and 2 |

## 5.7 Method chunk evolCA procedure

The *evolCA procedure* is a TraceME method chunk for guiding evolution of Communication Analysis models based on *i** models that specifies desired information systems (intentional specification of *to-be* information systems). The *evolCA procedure* is a method chunk that supports CA evolution models by following the model-based paradigm. To apply the method chunk for evolving CA models 4 steps should be performed (see Fig. 90). As it is presented in the section 4.5, the CA models for the *as-is* system are marked with the index $_{AS-IS}$ as $CA_{AS-IS}$, as well as the CA models for the *to-be* system are named as $CA_{TO-BE}$. The same index are applied to the *i** models.

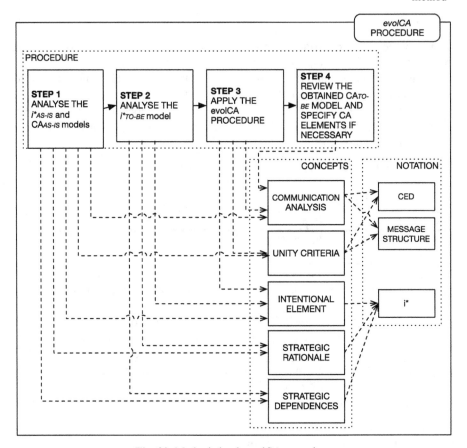

**Fig. 90.** Method chunk evolCA procedure

### 5.7.1 Concepts

Mainly, the concepts of Communication Analysis method and the *i\** language are required to properly apply the *evolCA procedure.* The Communication Analysis and the *s* concepts were introduced in the *iStar2ca guidelines* TraceME chunk (see section 5.5). In addition, the concepts related to model evolution like *as-is* and *to-be* specifications for information systems are detailed in the Chapter 3.

### 5.7.2 Procedure

#### *Step 1. Analyse the i\*AS-IS and CAAS-IS models*

As a first step, we advise to review the *i\** and CA *as-is* models in order to guarantee that both models represents the as-is system. We encourage to the TraceME's users to perform this step due to the importance to have a wide knowledge about the *as-is* system before to apply the *iStar2ca* guidelines.

**Input**

- The $i*_{AS\text{-}IS}$. We advise to have review the $i*_{AS\text{-}IS}$ in order to clarify the objectives of the *as-is* system and make further comparisons with $i*_{TO\text{-}BE}$. This input is not mandatory.
- The $CA_{AS\text{-}IS}$. The model to evolve.
- The CA TraceME chunk
- The $i*$ TraceME chunk

**Objective**

Collect and understand the *as-is* models of the information system to evolve. This step is mainly designed to promote the analysis and interpretation of *as-is* models to facilitate it evolution.

**Activities**

a) Review the $i*_{AS\text{-}IS}$ and $CA_{AS\text{-}IS}$. Understand the communicative events of the CA model and how they are related with the intentional elements of the $i*$ model. If there are not $i*$ and CA models, move to activity b.

b) Review the *as-is* system and make a reverse engineering effort in order to obtain the $CA_{AS\text{-}IS}$ models. If necessary, specify the $i*_{AS\text{-}IS}$ models.

**Outputs**

Depending on the organisational situation (e.g., existence or not of the $CA_{AS\text{-}IS}$ and/or $i*_{AS\text{-}IS}$) various outputs can be obtained:

- $i*_{AS\text{-}IS}$ and $CA_{AS\text{-}IS}$ models together with meaningful information about the *as-is* models.

**Tools**

- Diagraming tools for $i*$ and CA models specification and analysis. We recommend using GREAT Process Modeller.
- Textual editors to describe meaningful information related to the *as-is* models.

**Contributors**

The business analysis and the innovation analyst are the envisioned contributors for this step. They are the organisational roles in charge to specify and analyse the organisational business process and design the strategies for implementing reengineering and innovation projects.

## Step 2. Analyse the i*TO-BE model

We advice to review the $i*_{TO\text{-}BE}$ model in order to guarantee that all the intentional aspects to be supported in the *to-be* system are already specified.

**Input**

- The $i*_{TO\text{-}BE}$ model that specifies the intentional characteristics of the *to-be* information system.
- The $i*$ TraceME chunk.

**Objective**

Review the $i^*_{TO-BE}$ model to ensure that its specify intentions and goals of the *to-be* information systems.

**Activities**

a)  Review the $i^*_{TO-BE}$ model and check if the requirements conceived for the to-be system are specified. If there is no $i^*_{TO-BE}$ model move to activity b.

   - By comparing the desired to-be system and the $i^*_{TO-BE}$ model it is possible to identify if they are perfectly aligned. It means that the $i^*_{TO-BE}$ model specifies the intentional perspective of the *to-be* in a complete manner. If the $i^*_{TO-BE}$ model and the to-be system are not aligned, add/remove elements of the $i^*_{TO-BE}$ model until get a stable version of the $i^*_{TO-BE}$ model.
   - If there are textual information about the to-be, specify it by using textual editors that can be a supplement of the $i^*_{TO-BE}$ model.

b)  Perform elicitation sessions with the business analyst and the innovation analyst in order to gather the requirements of the *to-be* system.

   - Specify the intentional requirements of the organisation by using the $i^*$ language. Compare the $i^*_{TO-BE}$ model with the requirements of the *to-be* system in order to identify missing or over specification of elements in the $i^*_{TO-BE}$ model. Make the corresponding actions in order to get both the $i^*_{TO-BE}$ model and the *to-be* aligned.
   - If there are textual information about the to-be, specify it by using textual editors that can be a supplement of the $i^*_{TO-BE}$ model.

**Outputs**

A reviewed version of the $i^*_{TO-BE}$ model.

**Tools**

- Diagraming tools for $i^*$ and CA models specification and analysis. We recommend using GREAT Process Modeller.
- Textual editors to describe meaningful information related to the *to-be* models.

**Contributors**

The contributors for this chunk are the business manager, the innovation analysis and the business analyst. Business manager and innovation analyst are mainly in charge of the validation of the $i^*$ models. The business analysis help on the tasks to compare the $i^*$ models with the to-be information systems and make $i^*$ model specifications.

### Step 3. Apply the evolCA procedure

In this step the *evolCA* procedure is applied in order to obtain the $CA_{TO-BE}$ models.

**Input**

- The outputs of the steps 1 and 2

- The *evolCA* procedure method chunk (see description available in Fig. 91 and Fig. 92).
- The *i\** language method chunk and the Communication Analysis method chunk

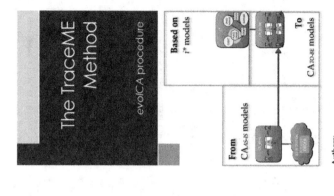

**The TraceME Method**

*evolCA procedure*

From CA_AS-IS models → Based on i* models → To CA_TO-BE models

models and traceability support. For the former purposes we advice to do the following:
(1) Find the most appropriated pattern according to the pattern description in the pattern repository. Thus, apply the pattern
(2) Create an instance of the delta metamodel for establishing the traceability relationships.

**Table 1.** Business activities behavior and their corresponding evolution patterns

*Exception in internal treatments:* A business activity that involves an authorization can demand an exceptional behaviour related to approvals or decision making.

*Deviations from optimist assumptions:* A business activity related to carry out orders of resources can lead saturation of resources and it can affect mediator objects that are responsible of a specific management places, over booking, supplies, etc.). As a result, deviation from optimist assumptions can affect basic business activities and it can demand exceptional behaviour related to approvals in order to maintain resource balance.

*Exceptions in external treatments:* Exceptions in business activities outside the range of action of organisational system or environment. This case is related to a business activity that depends of feedback from a business activity outside range of action of organisational system. These exceptions in external treatments can imply a decision taking in order to offer different alternative.

*Issuance audit:* Business activities related to issue specific documents can demand an audited output. Consequently, business activities related to issuance can lead exceptional behaviour in order to issuance.

*Reception audit:* As before business activity, reception audit is related to confirm reception of information. Thus, business activities related to reception of information can lead exceptional

behaviour in order to ensure reception.

*Audit of occurrence:* A business activity needs the occurrence of other business activity. It can demand an exceptional behaviour related to ensure the occurrence of a specific business activity.

*Audit of information content:* A business activity affected by indicators of the business rules can demand an exceptional behaviour related to decision taking.

*Audit of normative events:* Business activities related to normative sequence of events defined in the business rules. It can demand an exceptional behaviour where business activities should be reordered in order to fulfil the business rules.

*Guideline 9.* Assume an organisation that has a set of organisational rules and best practices for evolve their business process models. They want to establish their best practices and evolution rules as patterns for their business processes and benefit of traceability support. For the former purposes we advice to do the following:
(1) Create an instance of the pattern evolution metamodel and specify the new pattern to be stored in the pattern repository
(2) Apply the pattern to the certain cases that derived its creation
(3) Create an instance of the delta metamodel for establishing the traceability relationships.

**Authors:**
Marcela Ruiz[1], Dolors Costal[2], Sergio España[1], Xavier Franch[2] and Óscar Pastor[1]
[1]PROS Research Centre, Universitat Politècnica de València (UPV)
{opastor, sergio.espana, lruiz}@pros.upv.es
[2]GESSI Research Center, Universitat Politècnica de Catalunya (UPC)
{dolors, franch}@essi.upc.edu

**Fig. 91.** The *evolCA* procedure at a glance (page 1)

## The evolCA procedure

The *evolCA* procedure facilitates obtaining an evolved CA model and establishing the traces identified at a metamodel level. As depicted in the following figure, the procedure has as input a given CA model that requires to be evolved (we call it $CA_{AS-IS}$) and a given i* model that specifies the strategic conditions to be supported in the desired CA model (called $CA_{TO-BE}$).

The procedure of evolution is divided in four main steps: (1) Analysis of elements supported in the *as-is* system; (2) Analysis of elements not supported in the *as-is* system; (3) Analysis of elements that should be kept; and (4) Application and/or creation of evolution patterns. The guidelines for each step are described in the following:

**Guidelines for the step (1)**
*Guideline 1.* The dependum of a dependency D that is an informational resource is equivalent to a message structure of a $CA_{AS-IS}$ model ($M_{ASS}$) if both represent the same information in an *as-is* information system. In that case the $CA_{TO-BE}$ model should contain the $M_{ASS}$ such that: (1) the $M_{ASS}$'s communicative event ($C_{ASS}$) is specified in the $CA_{TO-BE}$ as $C_{TOBE}$; (2) the $C_{ASS}$'s primary role is specified in the $CA_{TO-BE}$ as $C_{TOBE}$'s primary role; (3) the $C_{ASS}$'s receiver role is specified in the $CA_{TO-BE}$ as $C_{TOBE}$'s receiver role; (4) $C_{ASS}$'s ingoing and outgoing interactions are specified in the $CA_{TO-BE}$ as $M_{TOBE}$; (5) if any SR element of D's dependee and depender roles are tasks, those tasks are traced with $C_{TOBE}$.

*Abstract guideline.* The dependum of a dependency D is equivalent to a message structure of a $CA_{AS-IS}$ model ($M_{ASS}$) if both represent the same information in an *as-is* information system. If the D and $M_{ASS}$ are equivalent and D's dependee is required to give information to the D's dependee about the *intentional satisfaction* of this dependum, the $CA_{TO-BE}$ model should contain the $M_{ASS}$ such that: (1) the $M_{ASS}$'s communicative event ($C_{ASS}$) is specified in the $CA_{TO-BE}$ as $C_{TOBE}$; (2) the $C_{ASS}$'s primary role is specified in the $CA_{TO-BE}$ as $C_{TOBE}$'s primary role; (3) the $C_{ASS}$'s receiver role is specified in the $CA_{TO-BE}$ as $C_{TOBE}$'s receiver role; (4) $C_{ASS}$'s ingoing and outgoing interactions are specified in the $CA_{TO-BE}$ as $M_{TOBE}$; (5) if any SR element of D's dependee and depender roles are tasks, those tasks are traced with $C_{TOBE}$.

*Guideline 2.* When the dependum is a goal, the notion of intentional satisfaction of the abstract guideline refines into the attainment of this goal.
*Guideline 3.* When the dependum is a task, the notion of intentional satisfaction of the abstract guideline refines into accomplishment of this task.
*Guideline 4.* When the dependum is a softgoal, the notion of intentional satisfaction of the abstract guideline refines into level of satisfaction of this softgoal.
*Guideline 5.* When the dependum is a physical resource, the notion of intentional satisfaction of the abstract guideline refines into the provision of this physical resource.

**Guidelines for the step (2)**
*Guideline 6.* When the dependum of a dependency D does not specify the information of an *as-is* system, consequently D is not equivalent to a message structure of a $CA_{AS-IS}$ model ($M_{ASS}$). Thus, D represents new requirements to be supported in the $CA_{TO-BE}$ model. In this case, apply the *iStar2ca guidelines* 2.0 to create the new elements in the $CA_{TO-BE}$ corresponding to D.

**Guidelines for the step (3)**
*Guideline 7.* When the elements of the $CA_{ASIS}$ are not equivalent with elements in the i* model, they can be specified in the $CA_{TO-BE}$ if (1) they corresponds to elements that cannot be traced with i* models because of their business process nature; or (2) they do not corresponds with dynamic goals but are strategically important to be kept in the $CA_{TO-BE}$. For each possibility do the following:
For (1):
a) Review the precedences of the $CA_{ASIS}$ and specify all of them in the $CA_{TO-BE}$ if necessary for the *to-be* system.
b) Review the precedences and relationships with other processes of the $CA_{ASIS}$; then specify all of them in the $CA_{TO-BE}$ if necessary for the *to-be* system.
For (2):
a) Review the communicative events, the primary and receiver actors of the $CA_{ASIS}$; then specify all of them in the $CA_{TO-BE}$ if necessary for the *to-be* system.

**Guidelines for the step (4)**
*Guideline 8.* Assume an organisation that wants to reuse existent patterns defined in the pattern repository for evolving business process models (see table 1). They want to benefit from common best practices when evolving business process

**Fig. 92.** The *evolCA* procedure at a glance (page 2)

## Objective

To apply the *evolCA* procedure in order to obtain the $CA_{TO-BE}$ models.

## Activities

To apply the *evolCA* procedure

**Outputs**

- The CA$_{TO-BE}$ models
- The horizontal traceability relationships between CA$_{AS-IS}$ and CA$_{TO-BE}$ together with the vertical traceability relationships between the $i*_{TO-BE}$ and the CA$_{TO-BE}$ models.

**Tools**

- Diagraming tools for $i*$ and CA models specification and analysis. We suggest using GREAT Process Modeller.
- Textual editors to describe meaningful information related to the evolution procedure, *as-is* and *to-be* models.

**Contributors**

The method engineer is the person in charge to apply the *evolCA* procedure method chunk. If necessary, the business analyst can participate in this step by helping in the application process of the chunk.

### Step 4. Review the obtained CATO-BE model and specify CA elements if necessary

This step is to review the obtained CA$_{TO-BE}$ model add elements if necessary according with the *to-be* information system.

**Input**

- The output of the step 3
- The $i*$ language chunk
- The Communication Analysis method chunk

**Objective**

To validate the obtained CA$_{TO-BE}$ model and ensures that its specify the communicational and business perspective of the *to-be* system.

**Activities**

a) Analyse the CA$_{TO-BE}$ model and check its alignment with the to-be information system.
   - Review if the communication and process requirements of the *to-be* system are specified in the CA$_{TO-BE}$ model. If there are missed or over specification of elements the CA$_{TO-BE}$ model should be adapted in order to achieve an alignment with the to-be information system.
b) The elements of the CA$_{TO-BE}$ model should be properly described, which is ensured by the *evolCA* procedure. If Communication Analysis elements are added, deleted or modified as a result of a, it is necessary to validate that they fulfil the Communication Analysis method.

**Outputs**

The CA$_{TO-BE}$ model reviewed and a report ensuring that it is aligned properly with the *to-be* information systems.

**Tools**

- Diagraming tools for *i\** and CA models specification and analysis. We suggest using GREAT Process Modeller.
- Textual editors to describe meaningful information related revision process of the $CA_{TO-BE}$.

**Contributors**

The method engineer and the business analyst collaborate to review the $CA_{TO-BE}$ model and specify or modify elements of the $CA_{TO-BE}$ model if necessary.

### 5.7.3    Notation

The notations to use in this method chunk are the concrete syntaxes specified for the *i\** language and the Communication Analysis method. The *evolCA* procedure has as an input for guiding evolution *i\** models. Thus, contributors use the *i\** notation for analysing and reviewing *i\** models, when applying the steps 1, 2 and 3.

The Communication Analysis notation is used when the steps 1, 3 and 4 are applied. The evolCA procedure ensures a correct use of the notation and the concepts of Communication Analysis. Nevertheless, contributors can modify CA as-is and to-be models to make them aligned with their corresponding information systems. For the former alignments, notation provided by the CA is used.

### 5.8    Method chunk Delta Analysis

The Delta Analysis technique serves on the purpose to analyse the delta of two information systems. Delta Analysis is model-based, thus the comparison or delta is performed between pair of models that specify information systems. Below we present the details of this method chunk. Fig. 93 presents an overview of the Delta Analysis TraceME chunk.

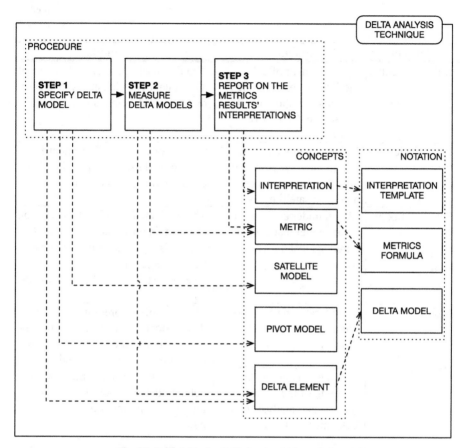

**Fig. 93.** TraceME chunk Delta Analysis technique

## 5.8.1    Concepts

Concepts of Delta Analysis are fully detailed in the section 4.7 and the Chapter 3.

| Concept | Explanation | Example |
|---|---|---|
| Delta element | Basic element of delta models for representing information about comparisons between two models. | The first basic delta element is equal. The equal delta element is to specify that two model elements are alike. |
| Pivot model | Reference models, baseline models, *as-is* models, etc., that is compared against a satellite model. | A reference model of a standard is a pivot model to be compared with a certain model of an organisation. |
| Satellite model | Model under analysis or to-be model that is compared against a pivot model. | The model that specify the evolution of a certain business process (*to-be model*) is a satellite model that can be compared with the *as-is* to analyse the feasibility to be implemented |
| Metric | Set of mathematical formulas to measure delta models. | The symbol $\Delta$ represent a certain delta model. $|\Delta|$ is a basic mathematical formula that calculate the number of elements of delta models. |
| Interpretation | Abstraction and understanding of the results of metrics and analysis of delta models for understanding. | Based on the results of metrics and delta models it is possible to make interpretations about the satellite model. |

### 5.8.2    Procedure

#### *Step 1. Specify delta model*
**Input**
- Models to compare. This input can be conformed by a pivot model and a satellite model; or it can be conformed by a pivot model and the requirements to specify a satellite model in an incremental way based on the pivot model.
- Guidelines to specify delta models (see description available in Fig. 94 and Fig. 95). These guidelines specify how to obtain delta models having as input pivot and satellite models. In addition, the guidelines specify how to obtain delta models while incrementally specifying satellite models.

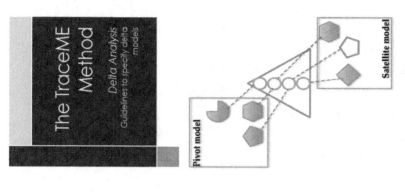

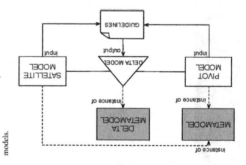

**Fig. 94.** Guidelines to specify delta models at a glance (page 1)

# Guidelines to specify delta models

A delta model specifies the differences and similarities of one pivot model (reference model, baseline model, *as-is* model, etc.) and one satellite model (model under analysis, *to-be* model, etc.). Both pivot and satellite models are instance of the same metamodel. Delta models are conformed by delta elements.

For example, the delta d(A,B) presented in the following figure specifies the differences and similarities of the models A and B; or how model A is turned into model B. The delta elements are represented by means of rounded rectangles.

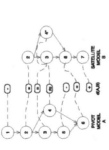

Figure 1. Delta model d(A,B)

## Guidelines for incremental creation of delta models

*Input*: a pivot model (A). *Output*: a satellite model (B) and a delta model d(A,B).

The following guideline stands when an element specified in the model A needs to be kept in the model B. This situation occurs when the requirements of the model B rule the specification of elements belong to the model B.

*Guideline 1.* Assume that an element e that is part of A (eA) needs to be kept in the model B. In that case, specify the element e in the model B (eB) and create an equal element (=) in the delta model that link both eA and eB.

The following guideline stands when an element specified in the model A needs to be kept in the model B. This situation occurs when the requirements of the model B rule the specification of elements belong to the model A by making some variations.

*Guideline 2.* Assume that an element e that is part of A (eA) needs to be kept in the model B with some variations in its attributes. In that case, specify the element e with variations (e') in the model B (e'B) and create a modification element (≈) in the delta model that link both eA and e'B.

When the requirements for the model B demand the creation of elements that are not specified in A. The guideline 3 indicates how to proceed in this situation.

*Guideline 3.* Assume that the requirements for the model B demand the creation of an element e that is not specified in the model A. In this case, specify the element e in the model B (eB) and create an addition element (+) in the delta model linking to the element eB.

If the model A has elements that are not required to be specified in the model B, such models should not be kept for the model A. Thus, the delta model will represent this situation with a simplification element (-). The following guideline presents the steps to treat this situation.

*Guideline 4.* Assume that an element e that is part of A (eA) should not be kept in the model B. In that case, do not specify the element e in the model B and create a simplification element (-) in the delta model linking to the element eA.

## Guidelines for creation of delta models

*Input*: a pivot model (A) and a satellite model (B). *Output*: a delta model d(A,B).

*Guideline 1.* Given two elements eA and eB that are specified in the models A and B respectively. If eA and eB are the same elements, then create an equal element (=) in the delta model that links both eA and eB.

E.g., In Figure 1 the element 2 of the model A is also specified as an element 2 in model B; which induces the creation of an equal element (=) in the delta model d(A, B) that links 2 of model A and 2 of model B.

*Guideline 2.* Given one element eB that is specified in the models B. If eB is not specified in the model A, then create an addition element (+) in de delta model for the eB element.

E.g., In Figure 1 the element 7 of model B is not specified in model A; which induces the creation of an addition element (+) in the delta model d(A, B) for the 7 element.

*Guideline 3.* Given one element eA that is specified in the models A. If eA is not specified in the model B, then create a simplification element (-) in de delta model for the eA element.

E.g., In Figure 1 the element 5 of model A is not specified in model B; which induces the creation of a simplification element (-) in the delta model d(A, B) for the 5 element.

*Guideline 4.* Given one element eA that is specified in the models A. If eA is also specified in the model B (e'B) but with some variations in its attributes, then create a modification element (≈) in de delta model that links both eA and e'B.

E.g., In Figure 1 the element 4 of model A is also specified in model B with some variations on its attributes (the variation is indicated by means of the "≈"); which induces the creation of a modification element (≈) in the delta model d(A, B) that links both 4 and 4".

**Fig. 95.** Guidelines to specify delta models at a glance (page 2)

**Objective**

To obtain delta models from two input pivot and satellite models.

**Activities**

a) Because of there are two possible set of guidelines to apply (incremental creation of delta models and directly specify them by having as input a given pivot and satellite models), it is necessary to identify which guidelines are the most appropriate to apply:

- Apply the guidelines for incremental creation of delta models when as input is given the pivot model and the requirements to turn the pivot model in a satellite model. The delta model is created in an incremental manner based on the changes performed in the pivot model.
- Apply the guidelines for creation of delta models when pivot and satellite models are given as input.

**Output**

Delta models

**Tools**

- Eclipse plug-in for automatic specification of delta models.
- Diagraming and modeling tools that allows the specification of delta models.

**Contributors**

The business analyst and the method engineer are the roles in charge to collaborate in order to perform this step.

*Step 2. Measure delta model*

**Input**

- Delta model (output of the step 1)
- Metrics for delta model measurement (see description available in Fig. 96, Fig. 97, Fig. 98, Fig. 99, Fig. 100, and Fig. 101)

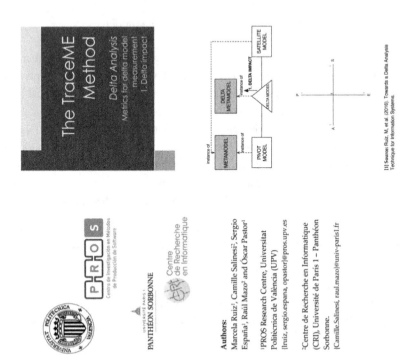

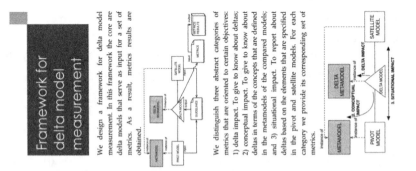

**Fig. 96.** Delta Impact: metrics for delta models measurement at a glance (page 1)

**Metrics**
**1. Delta impact**

**General statements for the metrics**
The following statements are used through the specification of the metrics.

**Statements for delta models**
Let $\Delta$ represent a delta model; $\Delta_i$ represents an element belong to $\Delta$;
$|\Delta|$ represents the number of elements of $\Delta$;
$\Delta_i.type$ represents types of delta elements: $\Delta_i.type \begin{cases} = \\ + \\ - \end{cases}_{\approx}$

**Statements for pivot models**
Let $\sigma$ represents a pivot model; $\sigma_i$ represents an element belong to $\sigma$;
$|\sigma|$ represents the number of elements of $\sigma$;

**Statements for satellite models**
Let $\lambda$ represents a satellite model; $\lambda_i$ represents an element belong to $\lambda$;
$|\lambda|$ represents the number of elements of $\lambda$;

**Statements for metamodels that define pivot and satellite models**
Let $M$ represents a metamodel that defines both pivot and satellite models; $M_i$ represents a metaclass belong to $M$;
$|M|$ represents the number of metaclasses of $M$;

**Delta impact metrics**

**m1) *Persistency metric***
The persistency metric (P) measures how much a satellite model specifies elements that are part of a pivot model.

$$P = \frac{sumequal}{|\sigma|}$$

$$sumequal = \sum_{i=1}^{|\Delta|} is\_equal(\Delta_i);$$

$$is\_equal(\Delta_i) = \begin{cases} 1 \ iff \ \Delta_i.type \ is" = " \\ 0 \ otherwise \end{cases}$$

**m2) *Simplification metric***
The simplification metric (S) measures how much a satellite model is simplified according to elements specified in a pivot model.

$$S = \frac{sumsimp}{|\sigma|}$$

$$sumsimp = \sum_{i=1}^{|\Delta|} is\_simp(\Delta_i);$$

$$is\_simp(\Delta_i) = \begin{cases} 1 \ iff \ \Delta_i.type \ is" - " \\ 0 \ otherwise \end{cases}$$

**m3) *Enrichment metric***
The enrichment metric (E) measures how much a satellite model is enriched with elements that are not specified in a pivot model.

$$E = \frac{sumaddi}{|\Delta|}$$

$$sumaddi = \sum_{i=1}^{|\Delta|} is\_addi(\Delta_i);$$

$$is\_addi(\Delta_i) = \begin{cases} 1 \ iff \ \Delta_i.type \ is" + " \\ 0 \ otherwise \end{cases}$$

**m4) *Adaptation metric***
The adaptation metric (A) measures how much elements of a satellite are modified according to a pivot model.

$$A = \frac{summodi}{|\sigma|}$$

$$summodi = \sum_{i=1}^{|\Delta|} is\_modi(\Delta_i);$$

$$is\_modi(\Delta_i) = \begin{cases} 1 \ iff \ \Delta_i.type \ is" \approx " \\ 0 \ otherwise \end{cases}$$

**Delta impact keys**

The values of the former metrics are specified in axes that meet in the origin or point 0 (e.g., for the metric persistency (P), the axis to specify its values is P). The figure of the Cartesian plane presented in the page 1 stands for the former four metrics.

The following keys help on the analysis of tendencies that can be analysed in Cartesian planes.

*Global conservation:* Tendency of P against S, E, and A. Three situations can happen:

• P has a higher value than S plus E plus A. It means that the satellite model conserves the most of the pivot model. This can be distinguished in the Cartesian plane because the shape tends to be in the high values of P. Check if it is necessary to keep everything. Are there some elements in the satellite model that need to be kept according to the system requirements?

• P has a lower value than S plus E plus A. This situation happen when several modifications or differences have been found in the satellite model. This situation is observed in the Cartesian plane because the area of the shape tends to be mostly in the quadrants S - E and E - A. Review what has changed. Evaluate the main purpose of the process, is the process aligned with it purpose? Review dependencies and the requirements of the system in order to ensure that the satellite model fulfil with this requirements.

• P has a same value as S plus E plus A. In this situation, just a half of the satellite model can be consider as persistent according to the pivot model. In the Cartesian plane this is evident because a half of the shape tends to be in the P axis and the rest in the quadrants S - E and E - A.

*Consistency:* The consistency tendency (C) indicates how much a satellite model still "good enough" according to its purpose or mandatory requirements. Consistency is the tendency of S against P. When the tendency is to S. It is necessary to check the conformity of the satellite model with it purpose.

*Enrichment:* The enrichment tendency (E) invites to review if it is possible to find reusable assets in the as-is models.

*Recreation:* The recreation tendency (R) indicates how much a satellite model incorporates new components or simply recreates everything. The key is to analyse the value of S and E against P and A.

*Superficial:* The superficial tendency (SU) indicates how to analyse a satellite model when changes are related on modifications on elements' names. We say that the tendency shows a superficial delta when A has a greater value than P plus S plus E.

**Fig. 97.** Delta Impact: metrics for delta models measurement at a glance (page 2)

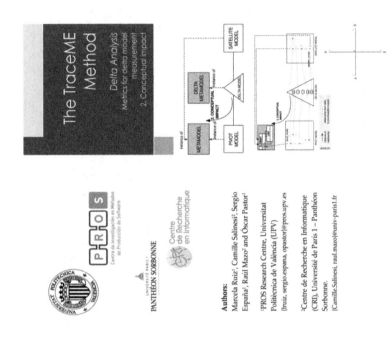

# The TraceME Method

**Delta Analysis**
Metrics for delta model measurement
2. Conceptual impact

**Authors:**

Marcela Ruiz[1], Camille Salinesi[2], Sergio España[1], Raúl Mazo[2] and Oscar Pastor[1]

[1]PROS Research Centre, Universitat Politècnica de València (UPV)
[lruiz, sergio.espana, opastor]@pros.upv.es

[2]Centre de Recherche en Informatique (CRI), Université de Paris 1 – Panthéon Sorbonne.
[Camille.Salinesi, raul.mazo]@univ-paris1.fr

[1] Source: Ruiz, M, et al. (2016). Towards a Delta Analysis Technique for Information Systems.

*Specific recreation:* Recreation can be indeed analysed by a certain concept of the metamodels. To do this, we propose to analyse the values of SC against the summation of the values of EC, PC, and AC. If SC is bigger than the aggregation of the other values, it means that the satellite model is extremely different according to the pivot model. In this case, we say that the satellite model is recreating because several elements of the pivot model are no specified in the satellite model.

*Specific Superficiality:* We say that the differences between pivot and satellite models are superficial when differences are concentrated in modification of the names of the elements. For specific superficiality, this situation is analysed for a certain concept c.

By analysing the case of business process models, superficiality can happen when differences of the names of the elements are bigger than differences according to enrichment and simplification of links, compositions (lanes and pools), and elements. For example, if we are analysing BPMN like models, we propose to analyse the values of AC for the element process (in activity diagram the analysis can be focused on the tasks; in Communication Analysis the analysis is on the communicative events) against E(lanes) plus S(lanes) plus E(links) plus S(links).

To make conclusions, the differences should be justified. In addition, if the differences are just superficial and this is valid of a certain case, the modifications should be checked in order to ensure that the differences are correct and the satellite model fulfils it purpose.

*Links:* If the results of E(link) and S(link) (EC and SC for the concept link) of business process models are bigger than the values of E (process) plus S(process) plus E(lane) plus S(lane); then it is advisable to verify deadlocks, bottlenecks, time performance, etc. In addition, time constraints could be necessary to control the high difference between links and the rest of the elements of BPM.

**Fig. 98.** Conceptual impact: metrics for delta models measurement at a glance (page 1)

## Metrics
## 2. Conceptual impact

**General statements for the metrics**
The following statements are used through the specification of the metrics.

Statements for delta models
Let $\Delta$ represent a delta model; $\Delta_i$ represents an element belong to $\Delta$;
$|\Delta|$ represents the number of elements of $\Delta$;

$\Delta_i.type$ represents types of delta elements: $\Delta_i.type \in \left\{ \begin{array}{c} + \\ - \end{array} \right\}$

Statements for pivot models
Let $\sigma$ represents a pivot model; $\sigma_i$ represents an element belong to $\sigma$;
$|\sigma|$ represents the number of elements of $\sigma$;

Statements for satellite models
Let $\lambda$ represents a satellite model; $\lambda_i$ represents an element belong to $\lambda$;
$|\lambda|$ represents the number of elements of $\lambda$;

Statements for metamodels that define pivot and satellite models
Let $M$ represents a metamodel that defines both pivot and satellite models; $M_i$ represents a metaclass belong to $M$;
$|M|$ represents the number of metaclasses of $M$;

**Conceptual impact metrics**

m1) *Persistency by concept metric*
The persistency by concept metric (PC) measures how much a satellite and models keeps elements of a certain concept c of the metamodel.

$$PC = \frac{sumequal(c)}{|\sigma|}$$

$sumequal(c) = \sum_{i=1}^{|\Delta|} is\_equal(\Delta_i, c);$

$is\_equal(\Delta_i, c) = \begin{cases} 1 & iff\ \Delta_i.type\ is\ "="\ and\ \Delta_i.pivot\_model\ is\ instance\_of \\ 0 & otherwise \end{cases}$

m2) *Simplification by concept metric*

much a satellite model has been simplified according to a certain concept c of the metamodel.

$$SC = \frac{sumsimp(c)}{|\sigma|}$$

$sumsimp(c) = \sum_{i=1}^{|\Delta|} is\_simp(\Delta_i, c)$

$is\_simp(\Delta_i, c) = \begin{cases} 1 & iff\ \Delta_i.type\ is\ "-"\ and\ \Delta_i.pivot\_element\ is\ instanceof \\ 0 & otherwise \end{cases}$

m3) *Enrichment by concept metric*
The enrichment by concept metric (EC) measures how much a satellite model has been enriched according to a certain concept c of the metamodel.

$$EC = \frac{sumadd(c)}{|\sigma|}$$

$sumadd(c) = \sum_{i=1}^{|\Delta|} is\_add(\Delta_i, c);$

$is\_add(\Delta_i, c) = \begin{cases} 1 & iff\ \Delta_i.type\ is\ "+"\ and\ \Delta_i.satellite\_model\ is\ instance \\ 0 & otherwise \end{cases}$

m4) *Adaptation by concept metric*
The adaptation by concept metric (AC) measures how much a satellite model keeps elements of a certain concept c.

$$AC = \frac{summodi(c)}{|\sigma|}$$

$summodi(c) = \sum_{i=1}^{|\Delta|} is\_modi(\Delta_i, c);$

$is\_modi(\Delta_i, c) = \begin{cases} 1 & iff\ \Delta_i.type\ is\ "\sim"\ and\ \Delta_i.pivot\_model\ is\ instanceof \\ 0 & otherwise \end{cases}$

**Conceptual impact keys**

To analyse the values of the metrics in a graphical way, we promote the use of the Cartesian plane (see the page 1).

**Modularity:** Modularity of models can be seen as how to analyse business process models when lanes and refinements are enriched. For example if the business process models are specified using the Communication (adaptation by concept) focusing on the acronyms of the concept communicative event. Base on the acronyms, check they have e changed and the business process under analysis has been rearranged. Based on the results of AC, we can conclude about if the satellite model is more modular than the pivot model and the percentage of this comparison.

For BPM, if the value of S(process) plus E(process) (E(process)) is the adaptation by concept (AC) for the concept process) is bigger than E(lane) plus S(lane); we propose to evaluate the modularity of the satellite model in order to analyse if refinements in the satellite are convenient. As a result, it is advisable to consider fragmenting the satellite model in several pieces.

**Specific conservation:** According to a certain concept c, it is interesting to analyse how the elements of both pivot and satellite models that are instance of a certain concept c have been conserved. To analyse the conservation by a certain concept, we propose to compare the result of PC against the summation of SC, EC and AC. The following situations can happen:

• P has a higher value than SC plus EC plus AC. It means that the satellite model conserves the most of the elements instance of c of the pivot model. This can be distinguished in the Cartesian plane because the shape tends to be in the high values of P.

• P has a lower value than SC plus EC plus AC. This situation happen when several modifications or differences for the concept c have been found in the satellite model. This situation is observed in the Cartesian plane because the area of the shape tends to be mostly in the quadrants S - E and E - A.

• P has a same value as SC plus EC plus AC. In this situation, just a half of the satellite model can be consider as persistent according to the pivot model for the concept c. In the Cartesian plane this is evident because a half of the shape tends to be in the P axis and the rest in the quadrants S - E and E - A.

**Specific consistency:** For analysing the consistency of a certain concept c, we propose to compare the results of SC against PC. When the SC is bigger than PC, it is necessary to check if the satellite model fulfills the requirements and satisfy the demands of the system that it is specifying.

**Fig. 99.** Conceptual impact: metrics for delta models measurement at a glance (page 2)

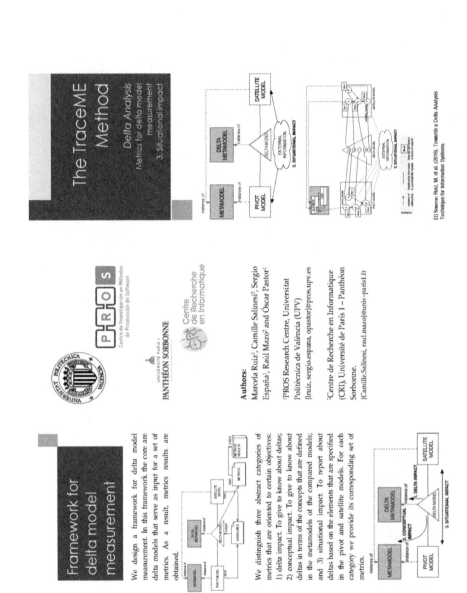

**Fig. 100.** Situational impact: metrics for delta models measurement at a glance (page 1)

**Metrics**
**3. Situational impact**

The first metric of this category is persistency by weight. With this metric we provide a support to measure the amount of persistent elements of a satellite model and use the value of the weights of its elements in order to give a total for the model. This total will be interpreted according to the context and the external information that conform the weights.

**Situational impact metrics**

*m1) Persistency by weight*
The persistency by weight metric (PW) measures the total of the elements' weights of a satellite model that have related an equal delta element.

$$PW = \frac{sumequal}{|\sigma|}$$

$$sumequal = \sum_{i=1}^{|\Delta|} is\_equal(\Delta_i):$$

$is\_equal(\Delta_i)$
$= \begin{cases} \Delta_i.satellite\_model.weight & iff\ \Delta_i.type\ is\ "=" \\ 0\ otherwise \end{cases}$

For analysing the total of elements implied in simplifications performed on a certain satellite model, we design the simplification by weight metric. Here we focus on the weights of simplified elements, which can be easily detected by analysing the simplification delta elements of the delta model.

*m2) Simplification by weight metric*
The simplification by weight metric (SW) measures the total of the elements' weights of a pivot model that have related a simplification delta element.

$$SW = \frac{sumsimp}{|\sigma|}$$

$$sumsimp = \sum_{i=1}^{|\Delta|} is\_simp(\Delta_i):$$

$is\_simp(\Delta_i, c)$
$= \begin{cases} \Delta_i.pivot\_model.weight & iff\ \Delta_i.type\ is\ "-" \\ 0\ otherwise \end{cases}$

When comparing models, it is important to know the impact of "extra" elements that are specified in a satellite model in comparison with a pivot model. To support the measurement of the total weight of additions, we design the enrichment by weight metric presented in the following:

*m3) Enrichment by weight metric*
The persistency by weight metric (EW) measures the total of the elements' weights of a satellite model that have related an addition delta element.

$$EW = \frac{sumaddi}{|\sigma|}$$

$$sumaddi = \sum_{i=1}^{|\Delta|} is\_addi(\Delta_i):$$

$is\_addi(\Delta_i)$
$= \begin{cases} \Delta_i.satellite\_model.weight & iff\ \Delta_i.type\ is\ "+" \\ 0\ otherwise \end{cases}$

If an element is persistent in a model, it could involve a modification on its attributes and also its weight can be modified. If a satellite model has modified elements according to a pivot model, the following metric stands for the calculation of the total weight of modified elements in a satellite model.

*m4) Adaptation by weight metric*
The persistency by weight metric (EW) measures the total of the elements' weights of a satellite model that have related modifications' delta element.

$$AW = \frac{summodi}{|\sigma|}$$

$$summodi = \sum_{i=1}^{|\Delta|} is\_modi(\Delta_i):$$

$is\_modi(\Delta_i)$
$= \begin{cases} \Delta_i.satellite\_model.weight & iff\ \Delta_i.type\ is\ "\sim" \\ 0\ otherwise \end{cases}$

**Notes:**

It is the role of the business analyst to gather the information related to the context. Based on this information, the weights of the element belongs o pivot and satellite models are assigned.

**Fig. 101.** Situational impact: metrics for delta models measurement at a glance (page 2)

**Objective**

Make measurements of delta models in order to obtain quantitative information from them.

**Activities**

a)  Establish the objective for measurement and select the most convenient category of metrics. The categories are established be to measure delta impact, conceptual impact or situational impact.

b)  Based on the objective for measurement, apply the metrics designed for each category.

**Output**

- Quantitative information of delta models
- Graphical specification of quantitative information

**Tools**

- Eclipse plug-in with the implementation of the metrics.
- Excel template with the metrics and the fields to specify the pivot, satellite and delta models.

**Contributors**

The business analyst and the method engineer collaborate to perform this step by deciding the objective for measurement and applying the metrics.

## *Step 3. Report on the metrics results' interpretations*

**Input**

- Output of the steps 1 and 2
- Template for specifying interpretations (see description available in Fig. 102 and Fig. 103).

The framework has as a core delta models that are specified according to the guidelines for specification of delta models. After the specification of delta models, they can be measured in order to obtain quantitative information and the tendency of the differences between pivot and satellite models. Metrics' results together with delta models are the input for the interpretation template. Interpretation obtained as a result of the analysis of the metrics and delta models are specified in interpretation templates. Then, interpretation templates are stored in repositories.

**Authors:**

Marcela Ruiz[1], Camille Salinesi[2], Sergio España[1], Raúl Mazo[2] and Óscar Pastor[1]

[1]PROS Research Centre, Universitat Politècnica de València (UPV)
{lruiz, sergio.espana, opastor}@pros.upv.es

[2]Centre de Recherche en Informatique (CRI), Université de Paris 1 – Panthéon Sorbonne.
{Camille.Salinesi, raul.mazo}@univ-paris1.fr

**Fig. 102.** Template for the specification of interpretations (page 1)

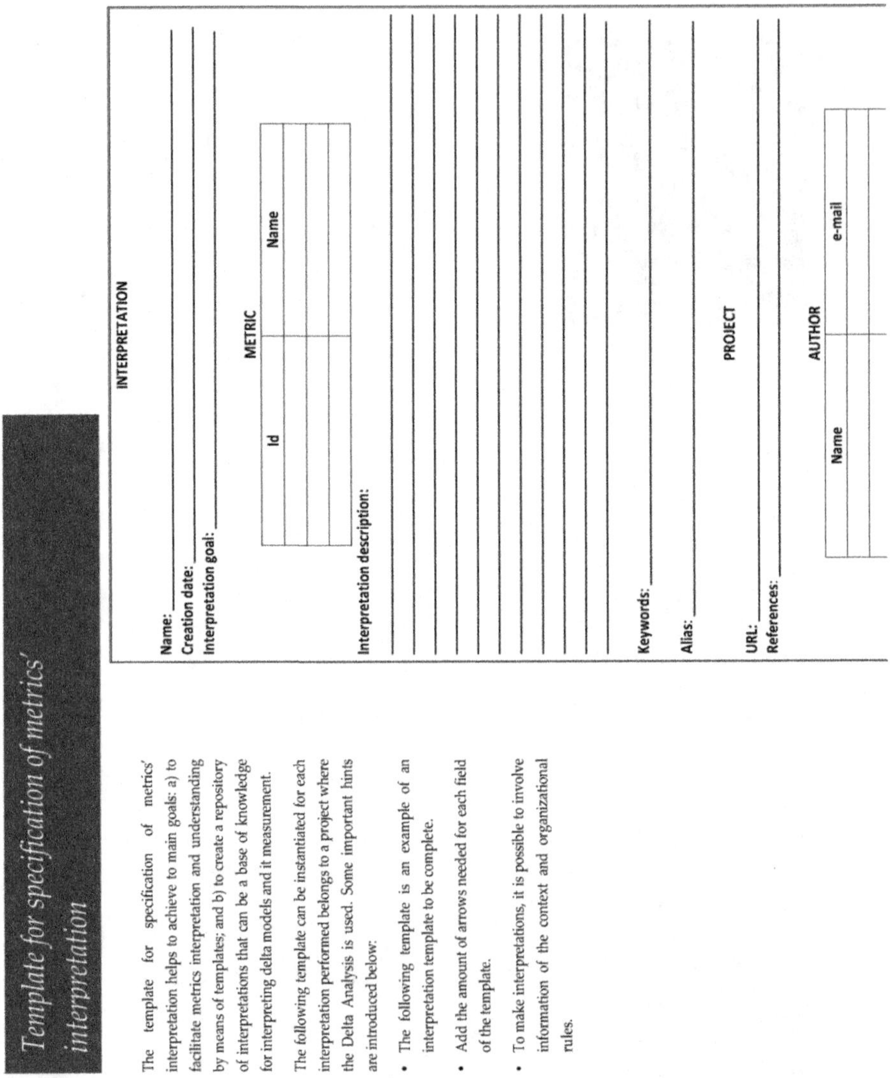

*Template for specification of metrics' interpretation*

The template for specification of metrics' interpretation helps to achieve to main goals: a) to facilitate metrics interpretation and understanding by means of templates; and b) to create a repository of interpretations that can be a base of knowledge for interpreting delta models and it measurement.

The following template can be instantiated for each interpretation performed belongs to a project where the Delta Analysis is used. Some important hints are introduced below:

- The following template is an example of an interpretation template to be complete.

- Add the amount of arrows needed for each field of the template.

- To make interpretations, it is possible to involve information of the context and organizational rules.

**INTERPRETATION**

Name:
Creation date:
Interpretation goal:

**METRIC**

| Id | Name |
|----|------|
|    |      |
|    |      |

Interpretation description:

Keywords:
Alias:

**PROJECT**

URL:
References:

**AUTHOR**

| Name | e-mail |
|------|--------|
|      |        |
|      |        |

**Fig. 103.** Template for the specification of interpretations (page 2)

## Objective

Make interpretations based on metrics' results and delta models.

## Activities

a) Analyse the results of the metrics and delta models

b) Make interpretations and register them by using the template for specification of interpretations

- If there is information that cannot be specified in the interpretation's template, report such interpretations as an attachment of the interpretation template. If the information seems to be a pattern, it means that an extension of the template should be reconsider. For this situation, evaluate the possibility to adapt the template and consult it feasibility with the authors of this method chunk.

c) Store the interpretations in the repository of interpretations for it further usage

**Output**
- Interpretations of delta models and metrics' results structured in a template.
- Attachments of the interpretations' template that report on the analysis of metrics and delta models.

**Tools**

Text processors and spread sheet for specifying interpretations of metrics and delta models.

**Contributors**

The business manager, the innovation analyst and the business analyst are the roles in charge to analyse the result of the metrics, delta models and make interpretations on this outcomes. They collaborate to fill the interpretation's template and make appropriate decisions according with the results.

### 5.8.3 Notation

We design a metamodel for Delta Analysis aiming at offering different graphical and textual notation for the technique. The current notation for Delta Analysis technique involve three main supports:

**Interpretation template:** For the interpretation template we apply a textual notation. We propose to specify the information related with interpretations by using the shape of a form. Each field of the template is predefined together with the option to indicate the information required for each one. Nevertheless, we recognise that it is possible to provide a graphical notation in order to specify interpretations. Further research should be performed in this line together with field study in order to know the preferences of TraceME's users.

**Metrics formulas:** We propose a textual notation for specification of the metrics to measure delta models. The metrics are based on formulas for model management, set theory and subsets.

**Delta model:** We propose a graphical notation for delta models as it is presented in the section for delta models. This notation can be adapted according with the desires of TraceME' users.

## 5.9 Situational-oriented assembling of the TraceME chunks

Table 14 summarises various situations where the TraceME chunks have been applied. We indicate which TraceME chunks need to be used for the assembling process and it purpose in each case.

**Table 14.** Samples of certain situations and the corresponding application of the TraceME chunks

| Situations / TraceME chunks | iStar2ca guidelines | ca2ooom integration framework | evolCA procedure | Delta Analysis | i* | CA | OOM |
|---|---|---|---|---|---|---|---|
| Organisational reengineering | | | | | | | |
| Replacement strategy | To obtain business process models | To obtain design models | | To evaluate the changes and keep trace of the evolution | To specify evolution and business goals | To specify business process models | To specify object models |
| Preservation strategy | | To obtain design models | To preserve elements of the *as-is* | To evaluate the changes and keep trace of the evolution | To specify evolution and business goals | To specify business process models | To specify object models |
| Software product line management | | | | To analyse product line configurations | | | |
| Model quality evaluation with baseline models | | | | To evaluate models according to a baseline | | | |

## 5.10    Summary

In this chapter, we present the TraceME method. We specify TraceME by following the assembly process model for method engineering of Ralyté et al [120]; and we report each TraceME chunk using the method notion of [105].

We assume that *i*\* language, the Communication Analysis method and the OO-Method are method chunks that are part of TraceME. Based on that method chunks, we performed a method integration strategy based on ontologies in order to specify the *iStar2ca* guidelines and the *evolCA* procedure. The *iStar2ca* guidelines and the *evolCA* procedure part of the GoBIS framework that establish integration of the Communication Analysis method and the *i*\* language. To build GoBIS we also follow method engineering. With GoBIS we provide the integration rationale and how to build guidelines for scenario dependant application and we make the effort to build the guidelines. We recognise that it is also possible to provide the rationale for integration and guidelines configuration. It means that the method engineering effort can be applied to configure the *iStar2ca* guidelines and *evolCA* procedure when the method engineer needs them. But, if we make the effort to provide the outputs of method engineering efforts (in this case, the *iStar2ca* guidelines and the *evolCA* procedure), it facilitates the chunks application and their implementation.

The *oom2ca* integration framework follows the MDA architecture in order to provide an implementation-oriented integration framework. To integrate Communication Analysis and OO-Method, an ontological approach is also applied [68] [7]. The *ca2oom* integration framework is implemented in GREAT Process modeller, a modelling tool that facilitates combined modelling or Communication Analysis and OO-Method; as well as it provides a transformation engine for automatic model transformations. For TraceME, method engineers use GREAT in order to get the benefits of the integrated framework.

The *evolCA* procedure support evolution processes and the *iStar2ca* guidelines together with the *oom2ca* integration framework support forward processes. Those method chunks can support two possible evolution projects: evolution by replacement (*to-be* models are defined and forward engineering processes are applied to obtain *to-be* desired system) and evolution by preservation (*as-is* models are evolved to *to-be* models, forward process are applied together with round-trip engineering for supporting the evolution of various information systems specifications).

As part of the support for the evolution process, we have developed a Delta Analysis technique in order to facilitate delta analysis of models. This technique provides the support to specify delta models, measure, and guide interpretation of differences. We envision the application of Delta Analysis as an important measurement activity for organisational evolution analysis.

Finally, we propose association strategies to assemble the TraceME chunks. The assemble process is motivated by various situational applications of the TraceME method. In this way, we say that TraceME is situational-oriented. It means that organisations can use TraceME chunks and create their own assemble processes according with their needs. With this philosophy we provide a conceptual model evolution framework that can be adapted to different circumstances. We envision that the TraceME method will grow in order to include more chunks to broad its organisational evolution support.

# Chapter 6    TraceME validation

*Facts are stubborn things; and whatever may be our wishes, our inclinations, or the dictates of our passions, they cannot alter the state of facts and evidence. - John Adams*

## 6.1    Introduction

The next step in our engineering cycle to develop the TraceME method is the design validation. Our main objective is to validate the TraceME chunks in certain contexts to analyse the effects on their application.

The TraceME method involves seven method chunks: 1) the *i\** language, 2) the Communication Analysis method, 3) the OO-Method, 4) the *iStar2ca* guidelines, 5) the *evolCA* procedure, 6) the *oom2ca* integration framework and 7) the Delta Analysis technique. The chunks 1, 2, and 3 exist before the design of TraceME. We perform ontological integration strategies in order to provide a combined use of intentional and business process models together with the design models of OO-Method. As a result, we design the method chunks 4, 5, 6 and 7.

In this chapter we present validations for the TraceME chunks 4, 5, 6, and 7, because they are original results of this research. Strong validations for the chunks 1, 2, and 3 have been performed and reported in several research documents.

For the *iStar2ca* guidelines we perform a comparative experiment. The experiment was lunched with students of the official master in Software Engineering, Formal Methods, and Information Systems of the Universitat Politècnica de València. In this experiment we evaluate the performance and subjects' perceptions when they analysed information systems with the *iStar2ca* guidelines and when they apply their own criteria. As a result, from the quantitative and qualitative point of view, the *iStar2ca* guidelines helps on the specification of business process models aligned with intentional models.

For the *evolCA* procedure, we have performed a laboratory demonstration. We evaluate the feasibility of the *evolCA* procedure by applying it the elections for department board case; a fictional case that conceptualise the elections process in the Universitat Politècnica de Catanlunya. As a result, the application of the *evolCA* procedure in the elections case is feasible and we design an experiment to be performed with subjects in order to analyse their perceptions.

For the *oom2ca* integration framework we have performed a sensitivity analysis with the students of the Information Systems Engineering course of the official master in Software Engineering, Formal Methods and Information Systems of the Universitat Politècnica de València. In this experiment we analyse the application of the *oom2ca* integration framework module of GREAT Process Modeller.

© Springer International Publishing AG, part of Springer Nature 2018
M. Ruiz: TraceME, LNBIP 312, pp. 207–270, 2018.
https://doi.org/10.1007/978-3-319-89716-5_6

For the Delta Analysis technique we got in contact with real practitioners and performed an action research protocol. For the action research, the Delta Analysis technique was applied to two real cases of the everis, a Spanish consultancy company. As
a result, the everis' analysts evaluated the Delta Analysis as a very useful technique
for analysing information systems evolution. They recognise the importance of the
delta models and the metrics as a way to make interpretations about the evolution and
how the organisations get several benefits of the performed reengineering process.

In the following sections we present the validation for each TraceME chunk. We describe the evaluation protocol, the design, the procedure, conclusions, and lessons
learnt. We apply various empirical software engineering protocols for each validation.
As a result, we improved the TraceME chunks and the latest version of each are presented in the Chapter 5. We believe that the empirical results make the TraceME
chunks strong and attractive to be further transferred to industry.

## 6.2    Validation of the iStar2ca guidelines – a laboratory demonstration and comparative experiment

We present the *iStar2ca* guidelines v2.0 which are intended for a top-down modelling
scenario and are an evolution of the *iStar2ca* guidelines v1.0 reported in [127] (see
the evolution time-line in Fig. 104).

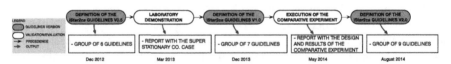

**Fig. 104.** Evolution time-line for the *iStar2ca* guidelines

In this section we present the two validations performed as part of our research: the
first one is a laboratory demonstration performed to demonstrate the feasibility of the
*iStar2ca* guidelines V1.0; and the second one is a comparative experiment to evaluate
the practitioners' performance and perceptions when they apply the *iStar2ca* guidelines 1.0 for obtaining CA models from *i\** models.

### 6.2.1    Laboratory demonstration

The laboratory demonstration (a.k.a., lab-demo) was an iterative process to demonstrate the feasibility of the *iStar2ca* guidelines. In this lab-demo we evaluated the
*iStar2ca* guidelines V0.5 (conception of the guidelines), this version was evolving
until achieved a stable version: the *iStar2ca* guidelines V1.0. The *iStar2ca* guidelines
V0.5 were a set of 6 guidelines, which were not exemplified, they were not structured
to facilitate their application, and they didn't include information to help CA model
elements' obtaining.

### *Design and procedure*

The lab-demo was performed by the authors of this paper (from now on, the research-ers) in a controlled environment using the SuperStationery Co. case (see 0). The lab-demo was run as an iterative process; approximately we did 13 iterations during one year (from December 2012 to December 2013). The objective was to demonstrate the feasibility of the *iStar2ca* guidelines application; also it exemplifies such guidelines for training usage.

The researchers were divided in two teams according to their expertise: (1) the CA experts' team formed by the first author, the third one and the fifth one; and (2) the *i*\* experts' team formed by the second author and the fourth one. The lab-demo was performed in a controlled laboratory environment where the SuperStationery Co. case was analysed and specified using Microsoft Office tools as Microsoft Word (for tex-tual requirements specification) and Microsoft Visio (for modelling tasks). To model the *i*\* models we used the OpenOme tool [150].

Fig. 105 illustrates the *k*-th iteration of the lab-demo. As inputs, the *i*\* model for the SuperStationery Co. case, a textual requirements specification of the case, the meta-model integration (see section 4.3.4), and the version V0.*k* of the *iStar2ca* guidelines were provided. Each team applied the *iStar2ca* guidelines V0.*k*. As a result, each team obtained the corresponding CA models. Then, all researchers met for decision-making with two main objectives: 1) Consolidate one resulting CA model for the Super-Stationery Co. case. Regarding to this, the researchers focused on avoiding solutions biased towards the expertise of each team. 2) Evaluate the *iStar2ca* guidelines to pre-pare a renewed version that included the emerging improvements.

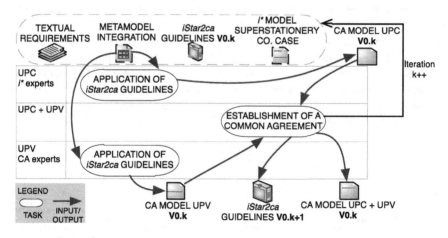

**Fig. 105.** Iteration *k* of the lab-demo applying the *iStar2ca* guidelines V0.*k*

The last iteration of the lab-demo was used to exemplify the *iStar2ca* guidelines V1.0 [127]. The feasibility to apply the *iStar2ca* guidelines V1.0 (guideline 1 to guideline 7) is demonstrated by means of this lab-demo. Section 4.4 presents the models of the SuperStationery Co. case (full details about the case are described at [138]) and illus-trates the guidelines application.

### Conclusions and changes on the guidelines

The lab-demo let us to demonstrate the feasibility of the *iStar2ca* guidelines V1.0. Some of the main changes applied to the guidelines are: Structure of the guidelines according to the type of dependency, the creation of the abstract guideline for the dependencies that are not informational resources, the creation of the guideline 7 for identifying precedence relationships in the CED, each guideline includes information to help communicative events' identification, and all guidelines are exemplified using the case of SuperStationery Co (see section 4.4 guidelines 1 to 7).

#### 6.2.2    Comparative experiment

The following is a description of the comparative experiment to evaluate the *iStar2ca* guidelines V1.0 published in [127]. This guidelines' version 1.0 did not include neither the guideline 8 to merge communicative events nor the naming guideline 9 to help visual model traceability (see section 4.4 guidelines 1 to 7). The experimentation was carried out in 2014 (from March to May) in the context of a master course in information systems at the Universitat Politècnica de València in Spain. This experiment has been designed according to Wholin et al. [151], and it is reported according to Jedlitschka & Pfahl [152] and Juristo & Moreno [153].

### Research goal

The experiment is motivated by the need to investigate the benefits and drawbacks of the *iStar2ca* guidelines; that is, we intend to compare the performance and perception of the subjects when they use their own criteria (the current, common practice) or the *iStar2ca* guidelines (the novel proposal) to create CA models from *i\** models, in top-down scenarios. The experiment goal, according to the Goal/Question/Metric (GQM) template [154] is to **analyse** *the resulting CA models* **for the purpose** of *evaluation* **with respect to** their *performance and perception* **from the point of view of** *the researchers and practitioners* **in the context of** a master *course*. Fig. 106 shows the decomposition of this goal into research questions and the necessary variables (metrics, according to GQM).

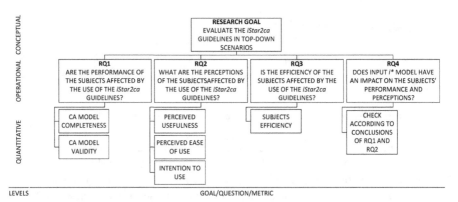

**Fig. 106.** GQM model of the evaluation of the *iStar2ca* guidelines

## Context

The experimental context is the Information System Engineering (ISE) last-year, master course[12] in the Universitat Politènica de València (UPV), Spain. The students of the ISE course have a background in software engineering and information system analysis methods and techniques. In addition, some of them have experience in industry. As part of the usual ISE course, the students are trained in the CA method and, thus, they are appropriate subjects for this experiment. The course content and planning were updated in order to incorporate the experimental setup (e.g. they were trained in *i\**), still maintaining the original course objectives. They executed the experimental task as part of the course assignments and received grades for it.

## Research questions

**RQ1.** When the subjects are creating CA models from *i\** models, is their performance affected by the use of the *iStar2ca* guidelines? To answer this question, the subjects create CA models from *i\** models in top-down scenarios. We evaluate the completeness and validity of the resulting CA models; and we compare the results when the subjects apply the *iStar2ca* guidelines to when they apply their own criteria.

**RQ2.** When the subjects are creating CA models from *i\** models, is their efficiency affected by the use of the *iStar2ca* guidelines? To answer this question, the subjects create CA models from *i\** models; and we compare their efficiency when they apply the *iStar2ca* guidelines to when they apply their own criteria.

**RQ3.** Does the use of the *iStar2ca* guidelines have an impact on the perception of subjects when they attempt to create CA models from *i\** models? To answer this question we measure the perceived usefulness, perceived ease of use and their intention to use the *iStar2ca* guidelines in the future.

**RQ4.** Does the input of *i\** model have an impact on the performance and perceptions of the subjects when they attempt to create CA models from *i\** models? To answer this question, we check the conclusions of RQ1, RQ2 and RQ3 in order to evaluate the influence of input *i\** cases.

## Variables

We have adapted the method evaluation model [155] to structure the variables of this experiment (see Fig. 107). Effectiveness has been decomposed into CA model completeness and CA model validity, according to the model quality framework by [156].

---

[12] http://www.upv.es/titulaciones/MUISMFSI/indexi.html

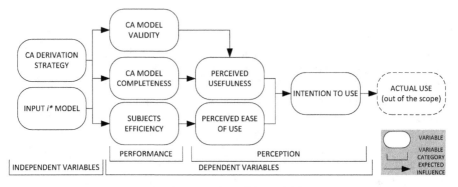

Fig. 107. Overview of the variables

### Independent variables

We consider two independent variables (a.k.a. factors [153]):

- **CA derivation strategy.** The strategy to obtain CA models from *i*\* models in top-down scenarios. This variable can have two values (a.k.a. treatments [153]):
  - **Users apply their own criteria** in order to obtain CA models from *i*\* models. When coding the name of dependent variables depending on the CA derivation strategy (e.g. see hypotheses formulation), we represent this value as C.
  - **Users apply the *iStar2ca* guidelines V1.0** as defined in [127]. We represent this value as G.
- **Input *i*\* model:** The *i*\* model that specifies the goals of an organisation; which needs an information system specified by means of CA models. We used two different cases to increase the external validity:
  - **Case A** has 5 actors and 11 dependencies (4 task dependencies and 7 resource dependencies). We represent this value as A.
  - **Case B** has 4 actors and 8 dependencies (1 goal dependency, 1 softgoal dependency and 6 resource dependencies). We represent this value as B.

### Dependent variables

We consider the following dependent variables (a.k.a. response variables [153]), which are expected to be influenced to some extent by the independent variables.

- **CA model completeness:** The completeness of a model is the degree to which all the model elements that should appear in the model (because they represent relevant phenomena of the domain) are actually contained in the model. To facilitate this calculation, the researchers take into account a reference model containing the minimum, indispensable elements. The term for this variable is CA_model_completeness and its values are percentages. We performed a more detailed analysis of completeness by modelling primitive:

- o **Completeness of communicative events:** The degree to which all relevant communicative events are included in the subject's model. The name of this variable is CA_model_completeness_ComEve.
- o **Completeness of primary actors:** Idem, for primary actors. We name it CA_model_completeness_PrimAct.
- o **Completeness of receiver actors:** Idem, for receiver actors. We name it CA_model_completeness_RecAct.
- **CA model validity:** The validity of a model is the degree to which all the model elements contained in the model should actually appear in the model in the right way (e.g. an element representing phenomena that does not occur in the domain is invalid). The reviewers identified candidate invalid elements based on a reference model, and then discussed until they agreed on the veredict. The term for this variable is CA_model_validity and its values are percentages. We also carry a more detailed analysis by type of invalidity (as done before in [80]):
  - o **Aggregation errors:** An aggregation error is the result of modelling two or more communicative events for a part of the domain which, according to the given modularity criteria [113], should have been modelled as only one communicative event. The term for this variable is CA_model_validity_agg and its values are positive integer numbers.
  - o **Fragmentation errors:** A fragmentation error is the result of modelling certain part of the domain as one communicative event when, according to the modularity criteria [113], the phenomena should be modelled using two or more communicative events. The term for this variable is CA_model_validity_fra and its values are positive integer numbers.
  - o **Invalid elements:** Any other invalidity caused by including incorrect elements to the model (e.g. modelling that a certain message is received by an organisational actor who should not be aware of that information). The term for this variable is CA_model_validity_ele and its values are positive integer numbers.
- **Subject efficiency:** The efficiency is the degree of success during the application of a derivation strategy of CA models according to the time consumed (CA model completeness divided by time consumed). The term for this variable is Subjects_efficiency.
- **Perceived usefulness:** The degree to which the subject considers that a CA derivation strategy is effective in achieving its intended objectives. This variable is measured using a 5-point Likert scale format to obtain users' perception. The term for this variable is PU.
- **Perceived ease of use:** The degree to which a subject considers that using a CA derivation strategy is free of effort. This variable is measured using a 5-point

Likert scale format to obtain users' perception. The term for this variable is PEOU.

- **Intention to use:** This variable will be measured using a 5-point Likert scale format to obtain users' perception. The term for this variable is ITU.

## *Hypotheses*

We define null hypotheses that correspond with impact absence from the independent variables to the dependent variables (represented by a 0 in the subscript) and alternative hypotheses that suppose the existence of such impact (represented by a 1 in the subscript) and correspond to our expectations. As mentioned above, we append the values of the independent variables to the name of the dependent variables. The hypotheses are summarised in Table 15.

**Table 15.** Hypotheses specification

| Null Hypothesis | Statement: The CA derivation strategy from *i\** models does not influence... | Formalization |
|---|---|---|
| **$H1_0$** | ... the completeness of the resulting CA models | CA_model_completeness_C = CA_model_completeness_G |
| **$H2_0$** | ... the validity of the resulting CA models according to incorrect elements | CA_model_validity_fra_C = CA_model_validity_fra_G |
| **$H3_0$** | ...the efficiency of the subjects | Subjects_efficiency_C = Subjects_efficiency_G |
| **$H4_0$** | ...the perceived usefulness | PU_C = PU_G |
| **$H5_0$** | ...the perceived ease of use | ITU_C = ITU_G |
| **$H6_0$** | ... the perceived intention to use | ITU_C = ITU_G |

We have expectations that the *iStar2ca* guidelines will have a positive impact on the dependent variables, so each null hypothesis has an associated alternative hypothesis (e.g. $H1_1$ is the alternative hypothesis to $H1_0$) but we have omitted their formulation for the sake of brevity (full description can be reviewed at [157]).

## *Design*

Properly speaking, we have performed a quasi-experiment because the subjects have not been sampled randomly across the population [158], but this is typical in experiments with students

The independent variable CA derivation strategy has two possible values (there are two strategies) and we also have two objects (the two cases). The proper design, according to [151] is a "blocked subject-object study" (a.k.a. "paired design blocked by experimental objects" [153]).

**Table 16.** Experimental design

| | CA model derivation strategy | Input i* model (i.e. object) | |
|---|---|---|---|
| | | Group 1 | Group 2 |
| Session 1 | Users apply their own criteria (C) | Case A1 | Case B1 |
| Session 2 | Users apply the iStar2ca guidelines (G) | Case B2 | Case A2 |

Also, the standard design type of our experiment is <u>two factors</u>; because we have two variables (two independent variables) each with two values, we have a <u>2*2 factorial design</u>.

In order to keep the equality treatment to the subjects, they applied both CA derivation strategies. During the first experimental task session, they applied their own criteria; half of the group applied it to Case A and the other half to Case B. During the second session, they applied the *iStar2ca* guidelines and the cases are swapped. Splitting the group of subjects into two groups was done randomly. As explained below, to avoid cheating and plagiarism (students of group 1 passing the case to those of group 2 and viceversa), we told them that there were four different cases, when we simply mapped all concepts appearing in A1 (and B1) by its counterpart in a different domain (e.g., the concept course was substituted by expedition) to obtain the case A2 (and B2).

According to this design, we take two measurements on the same subject, one before and one after the introduction of the *iStar2ca* guidelines. As a consequence, for statistical analysis we can apply the Paired-Samples T Test to analyse the collected data and, for the data that does not fulfil the T Test assumptions, we apply the Wilcoxon signed-ranked non-parametric test.

See a discussion on the rationale for selecting this experimental design and discarding others in the discussion about the threats on the validity.

### *Experimental Subjects*

The study participants are master's students with some professional experience. They are the practitioners who had been trained in the CA method, the *i** language and the *iStar2ca* guidelines. We recruited 20 students with information systems background, but few of them knew previously the CA method and the *i** language. None of them had been in contact with the *iStar2ca* guidelines.

In order to characterise the population of subjects, register their background and skills; we performed a demographic questionnaire[13]. Questionnaires were filled before running the experiment. Information about demographic questionnaire is summarised in Table 17.

**Table 17.** Previous experience of subjects

| Experience on: | No | Yes |
|---|---|---|
| 1. IS modeling with the *i*\* language | 92,9% | 7,1% |
| 2. IS modeling with the CA method | 28,6% | 71,4% |
| 3. Professional experience regarding requirements engineering or conceptual modeling | 78,6% | 21,4% |

The first question focuses on explore previous experiences of the subjects in the use of *i*\* language. Because of just one of the subjects has a little experience on it, we accounted these results to put emphasis in the *i*\* language training for the experimental design. On the contrary, the most of the subjects had experience modelling business process models with the CA method (see the results of the second question in 0). Nevertheless, we consider an exhaustive training in the CA method in order to equilibrate the knowledge of the subjects. The third question is aiming at to explore previous professional experience regarding requirements engineering and conceptual modelling. Just the 21,4% have experience in real projects with it. Because of this course is about information systems engineering, the students were trained in order to obtain the capabilities to manage the vocabulary and the most important concepts of information systems engineering. Regarding to the subjects' knowledge and experience, we notice a uniform background. They did not have any experience with i\* and CA and their practical experience was mostly limited to solve cases in class room. The results are summarised in [157]. According to the demographic questionnaire, only 7,1% of the subjects (just 1 of them) have an understanding of English that is moderately low. To minimise this lack of language competences, we were available to solve doubts during the experimental task.

### Experimental objects

As mentioned above, we have two cases (A and B) but two equivalent versions of each (A1, A2, B1 and B2):

- **Case A:** The domain of case A1 is the *elections for department board*. The Universitat Politècnica de Catalunya organises elections for department board regularly. The Academic department Clerk is in charge to arrange the elections and coordinate the activities in order to guarantee the success of the entire process. The actors that are part of this case are: The University General Clerk, the Academic Department Clerk, the Voter, the Candidate, and

---

[13] The material for the demographic questionnaire can be found at 157.          Ruiz, M., et al. *Validation of the iStar2ca guidelines: variables, hypotheses, instrumentation and statistical results.* 2015; Available from: http://upcommons.upc.edu/handle/2117/27746.

the Polling table. The case A1 was converted into a *Literary competition* to create case A2.

- **Case B:** The domain of case B1 is the *National language academy*. The National language academy receives language course proposals each year. The idea is to increase the offer of courses to the community. The director is the main actor who manages the courses and is interested in to ensure a good number of enrolments. The actors that are part of this case are: The Director, the Teacher, the Secretary and the Student. The case B1 was converted into an *International mountaineering federation* to create the case B2.

## *Instrumentation*

We design a set of instruments in order to train the subjects, collect data from the experimental task and also facilitate the subsequent data analysis. For the training in the both methods (*i\** and CA) and the guidelines, we provide textual material as cheat sheet and technical reports. We notice that the provision of the cheat sheets for *i\**, CA and *iStar2ca* guidelines was a very good motivation for learning. For the experimental task we design templates to collect data about subjects' behaviour as time and decision-making. Further information about the instrumentation can be consulted at [157].

## *Experimental procedure*

We design a set of task to carry out the experiment according to the design described above. Fig. 108 presents an overview of the experimental procedure.

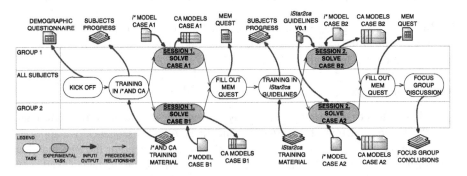

**Fig. 108.** Experimental procedure

During the training sessions the subjects solved some exercises and they received feedback on their performance. To randomly allocate subjects into groups we used the webpage http://www.random.org/. Fig. 109 presents one of the subjects reviewing the *iStar2ca* guidelines while performing the experimental task.

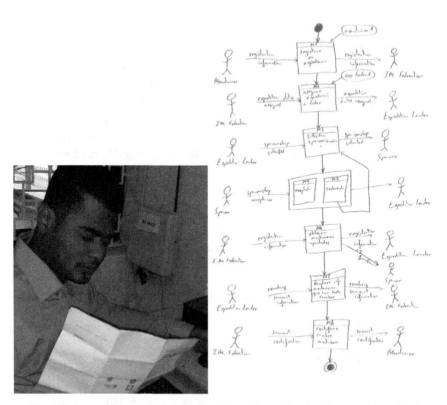

**Fig. 109.** One subject reviewing the *iStar2ca* while performing the experimental task

Finally, in the focus group session we presented a summary of the sessions and preliminary results of the experimental task (in the following sections we further explain the details about the focus group session).

## *Analysis of results*

According to this design, we take two measurements for each subject, one before and one after the introduction of the *iStar2ca* guidelines. As a consequence, we apply the Paired Sample T-Test to statistically analyse the collected data. For the data that does not fulfil the T-Test assumptions, we apply the Wilcoxon signed-ranked non-parametric test. A summary of the results is presented below (further details can be found in [159] ).

## CA model completeness with respect to a reference model

The results of descriptive statistics show an average completeness of 58% when the subjects apply their own criteria versus 79% when they apply the *iStar2ca* guidelines. A Paired Sample T-Test was applied to verify the null hypotheses $H1_0$. A **significant** difference ($p<0,05$) between the applications of the subjects' criteria against the *iStar2ca* guidelines is demonstrated. Thus, the null hypothesis $H1_0$ is rejected and the alternative hypothesis $H1_1$ is corroborated, demonstrating that the application of iStar2ca guidelines as CA derivation strategy yields greater completeness in resulting CA models. This analysis contributes to answering RQ1.

Regarding the RQ4, the results show that the input i* model case influences the application of the guidelines in respect to the performance; we will have this results into account for further replications of this experiment.

**CA model validity with respect to a reference model**

The results of descriptive statistics show an average of 4% of validity errors per model when the subjects applied their subjective criteria versus 3,4% when they applied the iStar2ca guidelines. By applying the Paired Sample T-Test, we observe there is **no significant difference** (p=0,582) between the application of the iStar2ca guidelines and the subjects' criteria. Therefore, H2$_1$ is not corroborated, and we conclude that the application of the derivation strategy does not influence the validity of the resulting CA models. In any case, the descriptive statistics indicate favourable results for the iStar2ca guidelines. This analysis contributes to answering RQ1.

**Subject efficiency**

To measure the subjects' efficiency, we recorded the time (in minutes) that each subject spent during the experimental task. The results of the descriptive statistics show that applying the iStar2ca guidelines took longer than applying subjective criteria. A possible explanation for these results is related to the forms that the subjects had to fill out in to indicate the reasoning steps while applying the guidelines. During the focus group session, the subjects expressed that they spent a lot of time filling out these forms and, conversely, the application of the guidelines was agile and easy for them. Nevertheless, there are no significant results to corroborate the alternative hypothesis according to the results of the Paired Sample T-Test (p>0,05). As a result, H3$_1$ was not corroborated, and we conclude that the CA derivation strategy does not influence the subjects' efficiency. This analysis contributes to answering RQ2.

**Subject perceptions**

Subject perceptions were collected by means of the MEM questionnaire [155], containing 5-point Likert scale questions (the questionnaires can be found in [157]). Each variable has several questions, whose answers are aggregated as an average value. For **perceived usefulness**, the averages obtained from the descriptive statistics indicate that the PU of the iStar2ca guidelines (a value of 3,8) is higher than the PU of their own subjective criteria (3,5). For **perceived ease of use**, we found that the subjects found the iStar2ca guidelines easier to apply (3,7) than their own criteria (3,5). For **intention to use**, the results were positive for the application of the iStar2ca guidelines (3,6 versus 3,3). However, the results of the Paired Sample T-Test indicate that such differences are not significant (p>0,05). Thus, H4$_1$, H5$_1$ and H6$_1$ are not corroborated, and we conclude that there is no influence of the subjects' perceptions on the CA derivation guidelines. This analysis answers RQ3.

*Focus group session*

This section presents the focus group session protocol, its results and a discussion based on them.

## Protocol

The participants in the focus group session were students of the ISE course that had been subjects of the experiment described in previous section. The number of participants was 17. The two first authors of the paper (one expert in CA, the other in $i*$) conducted the session.

The steps of the focus group session were the following:

1.  Introduction and motivation for discussion. The objective was to motivate the subjects with some ideas to discuss during the focus group session. Time dedicated: 20 minutes.

2.  9 empty post-its were delivered to each participant: 3 for guideline positive aspects, 3 for guideline negative aspects and 3 for guideline improvements.

    Time was given to fill in the post-its. It was not mandatory to fill all them. Time dedicated: 25 minutes.

3.  Each participant (in random order) presented his/her post-its and sticked them in a white board. Discussion among participants about the content of each post-it was encouraged and each post-it was classified according to its category (see point 2 above). Other categories emerged. Time dedicated: 75 minutes.

## Set-up

The focus group session was carried out in a big room and it took two hours. The subjects were placed in a round table distribution in order to see each other all the time. During the focus group session the subjects had available water, juice and some snacks. The idea was to promote a comfortable environment for discussion and a friendly communication with the researchers.

## Results

As a result of the focus group session, a set of 92 post-its from 17 participants and an initial categorization for them were obtained (see Fig. 110). Most of the post-its fell into the predefined three categories (see point 2). A subset did not match any category and had to be classified into emerging ones: *training* (for comments on the training received on the guidelines application), *languages* (for comments on the $i*$ and CA languages) and *experimental tasks* (for comments on the design of the experimental tasks and material provided to develop them). These emerging categories are out of the scope of the focus group but it must be noted those on the training and experimental tasks have been useful to detect possible threats to validity of the experiment.

**Fig. 110.** Picture of the whiteboard with the post-it classification at the end of the focus group
session

The initial categorization of post-its performed during the focus group session had
been done based on first impressions and was not a product of a careful reflection so
as not to compromise the session flow and progress. Thus, it was revised with the
purpose of solving possible misclassifications. The re-categorization was performed
jointly by two of the authors of this paper and conflicting cases were discussed till a
consensus was reached. As a result of it, 13 (out of 92) changed category and 5 where
discarded for being ambiguous or non-clear, leaving a final set of 87 non-discarded
post-its. Table 18 depicts the number of post-its finally assigned to each category.

**Table 18.** Final categorization of post-its

| Category | Number of post-its |
|---|---|
| Guidelines positive aspects | 29 |
| Guidelines negative aspects | 16 |
| Guidelines suggested improvements | 13 |
| Training | 4 |
| Languages | 11 |
| Experimental tasks | 14 |
| Total | 87 |

In order to facilitate the analysis of results a clustering of post-its was performed for
each of the relevant categories (i.e. guideline positive aspects, negative aspects and
suggested improvements). Miles and Huberman [160] state that clustering is a tactic
that can be applied at many levels to qualitative data and, in all instances, its goal is to
understand a phenomenon better by grouping and then conceptualizing objects that
have similar patterns or characteristics. Post-its expressing similar contributions were
grouped. The clustering was performed by one author and revised by the other. Since
each post-it was expected to provide a single contribution, all of them fell into a single cluster except for one post-it which fell into two clusters.

## *Discussion*

Some key observations can be drawn from the focus group results. They are organised in three groups: guideline perceived usefulness, guideline perceived ease of use and suggested improvements. Observations in the first and second group are related to RQ2. The suggested improvements have been influential in the revision of the *iStar2ca* guidelines V1.0 to obtain V2.0.

## *Guideline perceived usefulness*

*1- Improvement of the resulting CED.* Considering cluster P1 (15 post-its) we can observe some participants' perception that the guidelines contribute to achieve an improved CED compared with the case of using their own criteria. The aspects mentioned are: the correctness of the result, its completeness and, finally, the perception that the guidelines contribute to obtain CEDs less dependent on the subject performing the task. Remarkably, this homogeneity in the resulting CEDs was considered a positive aspect in 9 post-its. An explanation can be that it increases the participants' confidence on the quality of the resulting CEDs.

*2- Non-ability of obtaining the whole CED by the guidelines application only.* A fact that appeared to be frustrating for some participants according to post-its in cluster N1 (7 post-its) is that the guidelines did not allow to derive all the elements of the final CED. Although this should not be surprising for participants since the purposes of a *i\** model and a CA model are complementary and, thus, not all CA elements can possibly be obtained from *i\** elements, this fact appears to damage the perceived usefulness of the guidelines. Note that this perception is not contradictory with the perception mentioned previously about the guidelines contributing to the completeness of the result since they may contribute to obtain all elements derivable from *i\** while not obtaining the whole CEDs.

*3- Systematization vs. creativity.* According to cluster P2 (9 post-its) an improvement of the mapping process is perceived by some participants due to the systematization provided by the guidelines. However, from cluster N3 (4 post-its), we can also observe the perception that the mapping process loses creativity when using them. These two perceptions, while contradictory at first-sight, may be complementary (actually, two of the participants in the focus group contributed post-its both to cluster P2 and N3). The guidelines systematization is mentioned useful for organizing the mapping task, simplifying it and making it quicker while, at the same time, this systematization is perceived to lessen the creativity of the process.

## *Guideline perceived ease of use*

*4- Guideline description.* A good description of the guidelines contributes to their ease of use. Positive and negative perceptions can be observed on this matter. Cluster P3 (4 post-its) gathers positive comments and cluster N2 (3 post-its) gathers negative ones. Positive comments mention simplicity, clarity and memorability of the guideline description. Regarding negative comments, two of them are somewhat contradictory: one stating that guidelines refining the abstract guideline are not needed since they give too much details and the other stating that the abstract guideline is not clear enough. Another post-it mentions the lack of details on exceptions to each guideline. The explanation to this diversity may be that different subjects may have different perceptions on the level of detail needed for an easy to use description of the guidelines and, then, a good strategy could be to provide different versions. The plausibility of this explanation is reinforced in observation 6.

5- *Intuitiveness.* Intuitiveness of the guidelines is a relevant property since it will probably make their application easier. Although there is a single post-it dealing with intuitiveness (classified in cluster P4), it shows a positive perception on it and qualifies the guidelines as intuitive because they reinforce individual perceptions on the mapping process.

## *Suggested improvements for the guidelines*

6- *Guideline description: more detailed vs. less detailed.* Consistently with observation 4, contradictory improvements were suggested on the level of detail adequate for the guidelines description. Cluster I2.1 (3 post-its) advocates for more details while cluster I2.2 (3 post-its, too) proposes to lessen it. Therefore, the above mentioned idea of providing different versions of the guidelines description with different level of detail is strengthened. As a consequence we evaluate positively to maintain the abstract guideline in the description because it can serve seen as a short version of guidelines 2 to 5 and we consider an interesting line of further work to develop those different versions of the guidelines.

7- *Additional guidelines.* Cluster I1 gathers 4 post-its that propose to develop additional guidelines. All post-its except one mention the purpose of the guidelines that should be added: guidelines for merging events (2 post-its), 1 post-it requires guidelines for ordering events (besides guideline 7) and 1 post-it requires guidelines for deciding event variants. We have analyzed these cases and we have been able to formulate an additional guideline (guideline 8 incorporated to version 2.0) for merging events. On the other hand, we have not identified guidelines for more cases of event merging, event ordering or for deciding event variants since they would require input knowledge which is usually not deducible from $i^*$ diagrams due to its goal-oriented rather than process-oriented nature. Acknowledging that these aspects cannot be deduced from the $i^*$ diagrams only, opens a new line that must be considered for our future work, i.e. a complementary set of guidelines could be developed in order to help designers to elicit the adequate requirements from the stakeholders to decide on them and, thus, obtain a whole CED. This complementary set of guidelines would probably contribute to mitigate the negative perception mentioned in observation 2 above. Another approach to facilitate the definition of additional guidelines would be to extend $i^*$ expressivity so as to allow it to represent additional knowledge about event ordering, event merging and event variants needed in CA models but we discard it because it would be rather contradictory with the purpose of our general framework i.e. the joint use of the two languages so that they complement each other in expressivity.

*8- Automatic application.* The (semi-)automatic application of the guidelines is a relevant suggestion that must be considered when deciding our future work. It was suggested by a single post-it classified in cluster I3.

## Discussion on the threats to validity
### Regarding the comparative experiment

In order to discuss the experiment threats to validity, we follow the categories proposed by [151].

### Internal validity

#### *Threat due to maturation*

The subjects react differently as time passes. For instance, between the two experimental tasks (i.e. the derivation of a CA model using their own criteria –T3- and the derivation of a CA model applying the *iStar2ca* guidelines –T5-) the subjects increase their competence in both i* and CA. The training on the *iStar2ca* guidelines –T4- contributes to this maturity. The threat is that this maturity may be in part responsible for the differences in performance. It is expected to have a positive effect. We could mitigate this threat with the experimental design presented in Fig. 111.

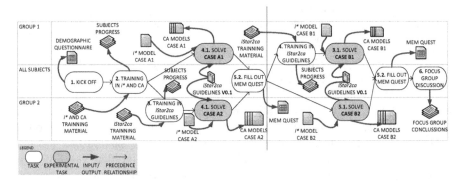

**Fig. 111.** Alternative, discarded experimental design

The subjects are randomly allocated in two groups. In the first experimental task, the subjects in group 1 solve the case by using their own criteria whereas the subjects of group 2 are trained in the *iStar2ca* guidelines and solve the case by applying the guidelines. Then the subjects in group 1 are trained in the guidelines. In the second experimental task, all subjects now apply the guidelines to solve a case. This design would allow partially mitigating the effect of maturity when comparing the effect of the two treatments in experimental task 1. This design would allow assessing the effect of maturity by comparing the increase in the performance of subjects of group 2 between the first and the second experimental tasks.

However, this design only mitigates the threat partially, since training the subjects of group 2 in the guidelines would imply an advantage with respect to those in group 1, by increasing their competence in *i\** and CA. Moreover, this design conveys a new risk that we have observed in the past: *resentful demoralization*. The students of group 1 would have the impression that they have a disadvantage during experimental task 1. This usually affects their motivation and has an (often negative) effect in their performance. Lastly, the setting of the ISE course makes this design difficult to implement. We discarded this design for all these reasons.

### *Testing*

We had initially planned to have the subjects evaluate their models after each experimental task. However, evaluating their models after the first experimental task (i.e. after task 3) would not only make them more aware of their errors, but also aware of how we are carrying out the measurements of the dependent variables. This would influence their performance and perceptions during the execution of the next experimental task (5), both due to the effect of *testing* (students would put a strong emphasis in obtaining good grades by focusing on the specific quality criteria that we are measuring) and *maturation* (the self-evaluation collaterally increases their competence in creating CA models). Therefore, we have planned the evaluation of both models after the second experimental task, as part of a preparation for the focus group discussion (T6.1).

### External validity

### *Threat due to the use of students instead of real practitioners*

The students do not have the same competence in CA as the real practitioners of the method. However, according to [161], students are often good surrogates for real practitioners. Also, we intend to further mitigate this threat by means of providing a training that is enough to create middle-sized CA models. Also, in order to identify possible outliers (some of our master students have industrial experience in requirements engineering), we will establish the profile of each subject by means of the demographic questionnaire.

### *Threat due to using a limited amount of i\* models*

The *i\** models used in this experiment are not able to represent all possible *i\** models found in industrial practice. We have narrowed the scope of the experiment to information system development, which is the scope of the tested guidelines, so our conclusions cannot be generalised to other developments (e.g. real-time enhanced-reality surgery assistance systems). Also, instead of just one, we have used two distinct *i\** models that are representative of the type of developments in which the guidelines can be used. Of course, replications of this experiment with other *i\** models are recommended. With regards to the characteristics of the *i\** models, see the discussion of construct validity.

## Construct validity

### *Inadequate preoperational explication of constructs*

Measuring perception is complex and the questionnaire could be inappropriate. We chose MEM, which is a validated questionnaire. Even in that case, the questions have to be adapted to the experiment, so the questions could be difficult to understand. The characteristics of the $i$* model used as input for the experimental task (e.g. cardinality, types of dependencies) can have an effect in the performance of subjects (i.e. in the quality of the resulting CA models). We limit the size but we use two different models to mitigate the threat. The characteristics of the $i$* model used as input for the experimental task (e.g. cardinality, types of dependencies) can have an effect in the performance of subjects (i.e. in the quality of the resulting CA models). With regards to cardinality, we have limited the experiment to middle-sized $i$* models (as opposed to real models appearing in industrial projects, which can be bigger); otherwise, the experimental task would take too long to allow its execution in a single session. However, the cardinality of the models is only expected to affect the number of times the subjects have to apply the guidelines, so we hypothesise that the result can scale up, but generalising the results of the experiments to real projects should be done with caution. With regards to the types of dependencies, we have included this as an independent variable and considered two treatments that correspond to two different styles of $i$* modelling.

### *Inadequate comparison of treatments*

Currently, analysts that obtain CA models from $i$* models use their own criteria. We will compare this current situation with the situation where analysts have the *iStar2ca* guidelines in order to guide the derivation task. The threat is the demonstration that the guidelines will be a better manner to guide derivation tasks from $i$* to CA models instead of to carry out without methodological guides. Nevertheless, we want to discover in which cases the guidelines are valuable. In conclusion, the idea is to compare our proposal with the current manner to perform the derivation tasks from $i$* to CA models.

## Regarding the focus group

A threat to validity of the focus group session results is that the participants were students of the ISE master course and the session was part of the course. The students could be biased towards formulating positive comments on the guidelines if they felt that this could help them to obtain a better mark in the course.

In order to mitigate this, post-its both for positive and negative comments on the guidelines were provided to the participants making explicit that both types of comments were expected. Post-its for suggesting improvements on the guidelines were also provided so as giving an additional way to express negative aspects that were susceptible of being enhanced. Finally, a comfortable and friendly environment was promoted by the set up of the session to encourage communication.

### *Conclusions on the comparative experiment, focus group session and changes on the guidelines*

The results of the comparative experiment and the focus group session let us to demonstrate evidence on how the *iStar2ca* guidelines V1.0 improve information systems analysis task of real practitioners. Some of the main changes applied to the *iStar2ca* guidelines V1.0 are the creation of the guideline 8 (with the purpose of identifying situations where the merging of events is needed) and guideline 9 (with the purpose of naming the obtained CA elements from *i\** elements in order to make explicit the traceability between models). Concretely, guideline 8 was motivated by the results of the focus group session, and guideline 9 was motivated regarding the model evaluation that we performed over the resulting CA models after the guidelines application. We noticed that some naming advices were needed in order to facilitate visual analysis for traceability purposes. These guidelines were motivated by empirical results and led the creation of the new version of the guidelines: the *iStar2ca* guidelines V2.0.

### 6.3 Validation of the Delta Analysis technique: Action research experience in everis Spain

Our main motivation is to validate the delta analysis in real-world conditions. We want to bridge the gap between the idealisations made when we designed the delta analysis and the concrete conditions of practice that occur in real-world problems. Delta analysis were conceived and evaluated in "an ivory tower", where just laboratory demonstrations (lab-demo) have been performed.

To bridge the gap, we validate the delta analysis applying it in practice in the context of the Spanish consulting company everis. everis has designed a new version of their current business process models in order to support new requirements. By applying the delta analysis, it is possible to perform a deeply analysis on the business process model evolution. Thus, the everis' case is a real-world environment where the delta analysis can be applied.

The research exercise to apply the delta analysis to the everis' case is not purely observational (i.e., exploratory, descriptive or explanatory); it involves an implication of the researchers[14] and an organisational improvement because of the application of delta analysis. Thus, we decided to use technical action research (TAR) as a research method.

*The objective is to validate the delta analysis in real-world conditions.* During the validation process (the technical action research) we want to know how delta analysis can help on the analysis of information systems evolution. In addition, we aim at discovering what kind of practical interpretations can be obtained from industry practitioners.

---

[14] The researchers are Marcela Ruiz (the author of this book), Sergio España, Camille Salinesi, Raul Mazo, and Óscar Pastor.

Primary object of this action research is based on an improvement approach. By applying the delta analysis to the everis' case, the everis' analysts will be more aware about its business processes model evolution. Also, reports and findings resulting from the delta analysis will serve as a basis for future decision-making in the everis organisation. Data collected from the action research experience will serve to validate the application of delta analysis in real-world experiences. Qualitative data will be analysed using categorisations or sorting techniques. The research process is characterised as a flexible design because it will be adjusted to the findings during the course of the research.

As a result of the action research experience, we are going to collect many kind of evidence: words, figures, statements, documents, pictures, etc. Evidence will be linked together to support a strong and relevant conclusion on the application of delta analysis.

### Research method

Following the research method prescribed by the technical action research [162], we structured our research in two engineering cycles (EC1 for the design of the delta analysis, and EC2 for the application of delta analysis in the everis' case) and one research cycle (RC1 for the validation of delta analysis in the everis' case). Fig. 112 presents an overview of the technical action research applied for the everis' case.

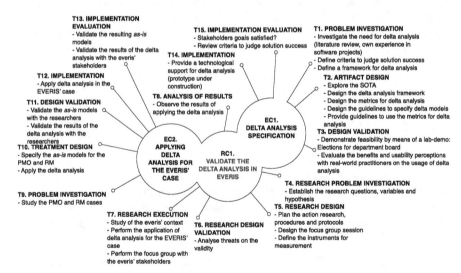

**Fig. 112.** Overview of the technical action research method for the validation of the delta analysis for the everis' case

The action research is performed in everis, a multinational firm offering business consulting, as well as development, maintenance and improvement of IT. everis is performing an evolution project to improve a service-oriented architecture (SOA) platform for e-government. By applying the delta analysis in the everis case, we are going to analyse the evolution of two reengineering projects: the project management office and the module registration. Taking the delta analysis as the object of study, we want to analyse the application of delta analysis in real-world conditions.

## *Background on method evaluations*

The foundations of this action research is supported by means of the establishment of a theoretical framework, which allows the definition of the research questions, propositions and their measures.

Moody proposed the Method Evaluation Model (MEM) to relate stakeholders' performance, perceptions and intentions [155] (see Fig. 113). The arrows represent influence relationships among the constructs.

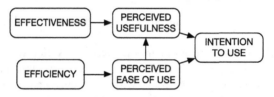

**Fig. 113.** MEM (adapted from [155])

The constructs of the MEM are presented below:
- **Effectiveness:** The degree to which the method achieves its objectives.
- **Efficiency:** The effort required to apply a method.
- **Perceived usefulness:** The degree to which stakeholders consider that a method is effective in achieving its intended objectives.
- **Perceived ease of use:** The degree to which stakeholders consider that using a particular method would be free of effort.
- **Intention to use:** The degree to which stakeholders intend to adopt a method.

We use this framework to evaluate the performance and perceptions of everis stakeholders when interpreting delta models and metrics results.

Card et al. proposed the GOMS model to support the analysis of observable behaviours, by reducing interactions to their most basic concepts [163]:
- **Goals:** What the stakeholder intends to accomplish.
- **Operators:** Actions that are performed to reach the goal.
- **Methods:** Sequences of operators to accomplish a goal.
- **Selection rules:** The decision making process to select a method when several are possible.

We use this framework to analyse the procedural knowledge by which the everis' stakeholders interpret the delta models and the metrics results.

## 6.3.1    Design of the action research in everis

This action research has deductive characteristics because it starts with the existent theory that the delta analysis is useful in real-world practices. According to this theory, research questions are going to be established and later they will be confirmed or rejected.

## Research questions

In the following, we formulate the research questions (RQ) and briefly describe how we plan to gather the data to answer the question. The overall approach is based on interviews with everis stakeholders and observing their behaviour while interpreting delta models and metric values. However, applying additional methods of data collection we will be able to make triangulation.

RQ1. To what extent does delta analysis facilitate the understanding of information systems evolution?

Besides collecting evidence from interviews and observation we plan to assess the effectiveness by counting the number of delta analysis metrics that have a meaningful interpretation for everis analysts. Also, we will assess everis analysts' perceived usefulness by means of the MEM questionnaire (MEM questionnaire is a 5-point likert scale questionnaire created based on the MEM of Moody).

RQ2. To what extent is interpreting delta models and metrics results free of effort?

Besides collecting evidence from interviews and observation we plan to assess the efficiency by calculating the times spent in each step of the delta analysis interpreting process. Also, we will assess everis analysts' perceived ease of use by means of the MEM questionnaire.

RQ3. How do the interpretations of the delta analysis metrics come about?

Interpreting the values of the delta analysis metrics is a cognitively complex process that may require formulating hypotheses and verifying them by reading several models (e.g. as-is, to-be and delta models), discussing with other analysts, consulting additional documentation, etc. To investigate this process we will apply GOMS analysis.

RQ4. What kind of practical applications within everis projects do analysts envision for delta analysis?

We, the researchers acting as method engineers, consider that delta analysis can be useful in the context of everis as a method to facilitate the understanding of how the models of an information system have evolved. However, everis analysts may envision additional purposes for the method. To investigate this, we will conduct a brainstorming session with everis analysts.

## The everis' case and units of analysis

The research action company is everis, a multinational firm offering business consulting, as well as development, maintenance and improvement of IT. Within the public administration sector, everis has wide experience in projects related to modernization of public procurement management, education, e-government, health, justice, etc.

everis is performing an evolution project to improve a service-oriented architecture (SOA) platform for e-government. It aligns with the Spanish administration goal of sharing human resources, software and hardware to support e-government.

The most valuable feature of the SOA platform is offering electronic services provided by municipalities to citizens and companies. By the end of 2013, the platform provided a service catalogue of around 200 services (e.g. marriage registration application, public pool booking, taxes). Approximately 50 of them are in active use in 250 municipalities. As a result, over 1 million Spanish citizens benefit from using the SOA platform. We selected this project because the platform context is complex and volatile; for instance, each municipality has a distinct profile, citizens have different interests, and laws and regulations change frequently. everis has to adapt the electronic services when the platform is deployed for a new municipality and whenever the context changes. For the time being, service customisation is done at code level. The main challenges are (i) to perform organisational actions tailored for a specific municipality in a given moment in time (i.e. taking into account the period of the year, real-time usage indicators, calendar events, or most requested services in a certain period of time), and (ii) to automate the adaptation of the supporting IT.

By means of applying Capability Driven Development method and tools [164], everis intends to adapt its way of working and to evolve the SOA platform into a context-aware, self-adaptive platform. In this first attempt to apply CDD, everis set up the following team:

- A Public Sector and R&D Manager, has over 12 years of experience in the IT sector for public administrations and that has led several innovation projects. This role has a mixture of knowledge about the SOA platform, the CDD method, and of the results expected by public administrations.
- A Business Consultant, with concrete expertise in the CDD method. She is willing to apply the CDD paradigm to several projects, and with little initial knowledge of the use case domain (i.e. the SOA platform).
- Two Technological Consultants, with concrete expertise in the SOA Platform, whose responsibility is improving the services provided by the SOA platform, but with no initial knowledge about the CDD Approach.

This team had the support of academic partners that are part of the CaaS consortium (http://caas-project.eu).

For this action research, we take two units of analysis that are part of the SOA platform: the Registration Module (RM) and the project management office (PMO).

This action research can be characterised as a single embedded study, with an overall case (everis), and two units of analysis.

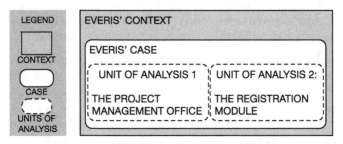

**Fig. 114.** Desing of single embedded case study for the everis case

### Unit of analysis 1: the registration module (RM)

Registration module allows Spanish citizens to register in several municipal activities offered by municipalities. The activities will require documentation and/or payment, which can be an online or a face payment.

The registration module is supported by means of a software tool. Two main users are considered for the RM tool: user and municipality manager. Users can be registered in activities offered by municipalities. Municipality managers are in charge of managing activities' enrolments; waiting lists; create, modify or drop activities; and validate activities' registration.

Currently the RM supports activities as cooking workshops, sewing workshops, marriage management, public pool booking, etc. everis wants to improve the RM by means of supporting the management of activities that involve context information. From the point of view of everis, the main goal of the project is to improve service usage in the SOA platform; one of the mechanisms to achieve this is by service promotion. The purpose is to highlight services in the municipality homepage in case this service is highly used in municipalities with similar profile (e.g. number of citizens, location -coast or inland-) or if the context is favourable (e.g. hot weather increases pool booking, marriage applications increase on the week of Valentine's day).

One main factor of the RM is the variability and the existence of different facilities provided by a municipality (e.g. public pool, marriage registration institution), the characteristics of the facilities (e.g. pool size, opening hours), and the legislation affecting the services. The identification and modelling of variability is key to CDD. To avoid manual customization of the RM, everis intends to apply CDD so as to identify the variability in the context and, in design time, define solution patterns that deal with such variability. Following the CDD vision, at run-time, a context platform will enable the SOA platform to be context-aware and automatically select the patterns that suit the context. Variability brings challenges to CDD that need further investigation. As a result, the RM is changed in order to incorporate the CDD method.

### *Unit of analysis 2: the project management office (PMO)*

A PMO is the department or group of designated people in charge of defining the best practices and standards for project management in the portfolio of projects of an organisation or collaborative environment. A PMO is established in everis in order to train civil servants, design integration with existing solutions from different providers and evaluate the best way to optimise resources on the use of the eGoveris platform. eGoveris was created aiming at delivering an eGoverment solution for municipalities based on a SOA paradigm.

The PMO is responsible of facilitating to the Project Managers and the rest of personnel involved their task to keep the project under control and establish a fluent communication between stakeholders.

As such, the PMO can use and establish several tools, depending on the nature of the environment and the type of projects. In this action research we are focused on the incident management process of the PMO. Incidents emerge when the eGoveris' users have problems using the platform.

The PMO offers several services to their customers and wants to improve them when context changes are produced through CDD, but it does not know how. It does not have enough technical knowledge to accomplish this, so it needs an external CDD provider. Several companies would interact with the PMO because a contract procedure defined by the end customer. This implies that a change in the service provider, according to different context conditions, influences in the value delivered to customers, activities and service provisioning.

In case the PMO have technicians with technical knowledge regarding CaaS, it would be the external CDD provider also. Otherwise, it needs to hire the services of an external CDD provider in order to supply the lack of technical knowledge. In this case, everis is the external CDD provider who defines the better way to apply CaaS according to the requirements specified by the PMO. As a result, the PMO is modified in order to incorporate the CDD method.

### Methods for data collection

**To collect *as-is* and *to-be* models for the PMO and RM:** The everis' stakeholders provided us with the *to-be* models for the PMO and RM. The *as-is* models are specified by the researchers by means of reviewing existent documentation and the *as-is* software implementations. The final version of the *as-is* models are corroborated with the current software and the everis' stakeholders.

**To collect stakeholders' perceptions and interpretations on the evolution:** The method selected to collect data is the focus group. We are going to gather information using questionnaires, free expression of perceptions and interpretation using a blackboard.

We selected this method because it is very useful in qualitative research, to discover new insights accounting the different background of each everis' stakeholder, facilitates discussion in order to confirm or reject facts, cost-efficiency because the everis' stakeholders are interviewed at the same time, depth discussions thanks to the nature of the focus group meeting and the relaxed environment, and business benefit to the participants because they are able to compare their point of views with the other participants and increase their perspectives about the discussed topics.

### Adaptation of MEM to the everis' case and information gathering

We apply the MEM framework to answer the **RQ1** and **RQ2** by establishing the following:

**Effectiveness and perceived usefulness:** The researchers will register the stakeholders' perceived usefulness by means of a 5-point Likert scale questionnaire based on the MEM framework. In addition, to evaluate the effectiveness we will review if all the metrics were interpreted (completeness of the task by using the results of the metrics).

**Efficiency and Perceived ease of use:** The researchers will analyse the stakeholders' perceived ease of use by means of a 5-point Likert scale questionnaire based on the MEM framework. For efficiency we are going to register time consumed using chronometers when the everis' stakeholders are analysing delta models and metrics results. In addition we will ask to the everis' stakeholders if they perceive that delta models and metrics are efficient for evolution analysis.

### Adaptation of GOMS to the everis' case and information gathering

We apply GOMS to answer the **RQ3** by establishing the following:

**Goal:** The everis stakeholders' goal is to interpret the derived delta model and the results of the metrics for the everis' case.

The researchers prepare a PowerPoint presentation to show the delta models and metrics' results for the everis' case evolution. Then, to accomplish the goal, a discussion around the interpretation of each metric will start following the PowerPoint presentation. The everis' stakeholders will be provided with papers and pens in order to take notes if it is necessary. The session will be recorded by using a recording machine to register metrics interpretation. The researchers will be provided by templates in order to take notes during each metric interpretation.

**Operators**: The everis stakeholders' actions to accomplish the interpretation of delta analysis

The researchers are provided with a template to register all the actions taken by the everis' stakeholders: discussions, information gathering from organisational documentation, questions to external people (for example, during the focus group, it is possible that the everis' stakeholders want to call other everis' people to make questions…etc.), internet searching, etc. In addition, the session will be recorded. To register operators a template will be provided.

**Method**: Sequence of operators and subgoals

The researchers are provided with a template to register the sequence of operators performed by the everis' stakeholders to analyse the results of each metric and the delta models (i.e., sequence of operators to accomplish the goal). Methods will be identified after the focus group session.

**Selection rules:** Different methods to accomplish a goal. Is a pair of method plus the knowledge of everis' analysts.

The researchers are provided with a template to identify possible methods to accomplish the same goal and the previous knowledge that the everis' analysts have in order to select each method. The selection rules will be stored in an excel form for classification. We will ask to the everis' analysts why they select each method to accomplish the goals. Possible answers can be: previous experience in this kind of analysis meetings, training, organisational protocol, etc. Selection rules will be identified after the focus group session.

## *Information gathering for discovering practical applications of delta analysis*

We design a brainstorming session to answer the **RQ4** by establishing the following: The researchers will perform a brainstorming session where the everis' analysts will specify three possible practical applications of the delta analysis (as a whole), three for delta models, and three for each metric. Practical applications will be specified in post-it to facilitate a discussion in the blackboard. During the discussion, a first classification of post-it will be applied according to Fig. 115. The objective is to discover if the post-it are related to the results of the delta analysis as a whole, if they are related to a certain metric, or if they are related to other sources (in order to identify possible interpretation that where no obtained from the delta analysis. in addition, this is an opportunity to identify new metrics).

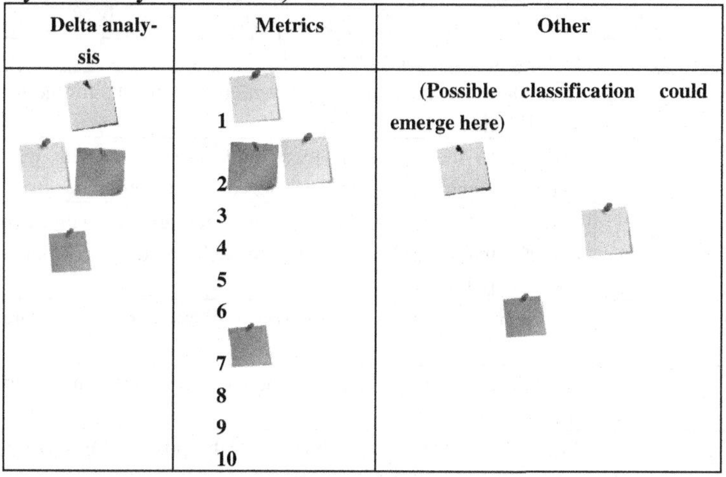

| Delta analysis | Metrics | Other |
|---|---|---|
| | 1 | (Possible classification could emerge here) |
| | 2 | |
| | 3 | |
| | 4 | |
| | 5 | |
| | 6 | |
| | 7 | |
| | 8 | |
| | 9 | |
| | 10 | |

**Fig. 115.** Initial classification of post-it during the brainstorming session

## *Procedure of the action research in everis*

Fig. 116 summarises the procedure for data collection.

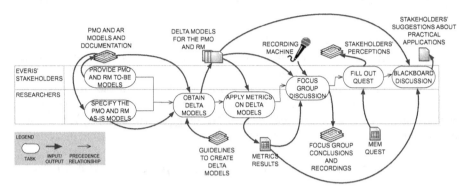

**Fig. 116.** Procedure for data collection

**Details of the activities during the focus group session**

The session will be performed in a meeting room in the Universitat Politècnica de València or in the everis' offices. The researchers will set up a relaxed environment by providing some snacks and colourful material for motivating discussion. A detail of the activities during the session is specified in the following:

| Activity code | Description |
|---|---|
| A 1 | Presentation of the focus group session. The objective is to describe the activities that to be performed during the session. |
| A 2 | Demographic questionnaire |
| A 3 | Presentation of the delta models and metrics results for the PMO and RM cases |
| A 4 | Provide to the everis' analysts and researchers with textual material specifying the delta models and the metrics' results |
| A 5 | Provide to the everis' analysts and researchers with textual material that describe guidelines for delta model derivation and metrics application |
| A 6 | For each metric the everis' analysts will express their interpretations |
| A 7 | Provide to the researchers with the templates to take note during the session |
| A 8 | Provide to the everis' analysts with the post-its for specifying practical application of delta analysis |
| A 9 | everis' analysts fill out the MEM questionnaire |

*Analysis of the validity and ethical issues*

In order to increase precision and strengthen the validity of this action research, we are going to take into account four types of triangulations (multiple perspectives towards the action research for providing a broader picture of the everis' case):

- Data source triangulation: three analysts of everis will be part of the action research.
- Observer triangulation: All the researchers will be involved in the action research (design, execution and data analysis).
- Methodological triangulation: we are going to combine different types of data qualitative and quantitative collection methods.
- Theory triangulation: we are going to have into account different hypotheses, which include alternative theories to conclude on the everis' case.

To highlight the transparency of this action research with everis, we are going to provide a replication package with two main goals: 1) provide the instruments for replications that can be carried out by the researchers, or by other researchers that want to confirm or contrast our findings; and 2) demonstrate a trustworthy research plan.

Four kinds of threats were addressed in the research project; they respectively impair: internal validity, external validity, construct validity and conclusion validity.

**Conclusion Validity**

Threats to the conclusion validity are concerned with issues that affect the ability to draw the correct conclusion about relations between the treatment and the outcome of an experiment.

Threats to the validity of conclusions are typically due to poor use of the statistical tool. This is for instance the case when assumptions behind statistical tests are violated or when the statistical power is actually low. As the method used in this research project is purely qualitative, we consider that this kind of threat does not apply here. As a result, we avoid making any conclusion resulting from a generalisation that would be made by inference from the observation made during the research.

Avoiding "Fishing" for results is of course a more serious concern. We address this issue first by a careful statement of hypotheses that balance all possible answers to the research questions (including nullity f the questions themselves), at least with respect to state of the art literature. The second action taken to mitigate this threat is triangulation. Answers that are not consistently shown from the three different angles cannot be considered fully valid. This of course does not demonstrate that answers are valid when triangulation shows consistent results.

**Construct validity**

Construct validity concerns the generalization of the result of the experiment to the concept or theory behind the experiment. Some of the threats presented below relate to the design of the experiment, others to social factors.

- *Inadequate preoperational explication of constructs:* we check that the constructs of our experiment are sufficiently well defined (that is, the measures or treatments are sufficiently clear) by asking a group of senior and junior researchers to tell us after a presentation of the project if they feel the research questions, hypotheses and measures are (a) ambiguous (b) underspecified (c) over-specified (d) inconsistent or (e) incomplete.

- *Mono-method bias:* Using a single type of measures or observations involves a risk that if this measure or observation gives a measurement bias; therefore, our experiment involves two types of measures and observations that can be cross-checked against each other. In particular, we design a focus group session to collect audio recordings when the everis' analysts analyse Delta Analysis' results. In addition, everis' analyst filled out questionnaires asking about their perceptions about Delta Analysis.
- *Restricted generalizability across constructs:* in order to prevent that our treatment unintentionally affects other constructs negatively, which constitutes a threat for the generalization of the experiment's results, the potential constructs to be affected will also be observed and measured. The analysis of the results obtained from our experiment will take into account not just the results of the main treatment but also their unintended side effects.
- *Experimenter expectancies:* this effect is about a form of reactivity in which a researcher's cognitive bias causes them to unconsciously influence the participants of an experiment. Due to the fact that it is not possible to use in our experiment a double-blind experimental design, we reduce the threat by involving different people that have no -or different- expectations from the experiment.

**Internal validity**

Because this is an action research, we are highly concerned about the effects of conducting the experiment on the actual results of the experiment. We have in particular in mind the Pygmalion effect (self realizing prophecy), and the Hawthorne effect (people who participate to the experiment tend to satisfy or deceive the expectations of the researchers to please them or to disappoint them). The following measures are taken to address these issues.

- *Group threats*: participants of this experiment are allocated to groups randomly.
- *Time threats*: with time, events may occur and produce changes in the behaviour of participants. This experiment is carried out in a short period of time in order to reduce the probability that such change of behaviour alters the experiment.
- *History*: as indicated earlier, this experiment is conducted in Spain. We know by experience that people in Spain are less concerned with work during certain celebrations such as the San José Fallas Celebration in Valencia, Christmas and during certain periods like summer. Thus, this experiment is executed during a normal working period, "sufficiently" outside these celebration days.
- *Reactivity and experimenter effect*: we are aware and concerned that measuring a person's work may affect their behavior and that participants often respond to the "demand characteristics" of an experiment [165] in order to please (or annoy) the experimenter. Therefore, we decided not to communicate the experimental hypothesis to the participants. We also explained to the participants that this experiment is not a test with the aim to avoid the "evaluation apprehension" behavior [166].

**External validity**

External validity refers to the fact that the results of the research can be applied to the external environment, and improved through replication of the study in other places, with different people, at another time. This study follows the indications for conducting research studies in software engineering proposed by (ref to Experimentation in software engineering). By using a real case and involving all the engineers of the company concerned with the topic rather than using a frame random sample, we avoided problems like the fact that some members of the population are excluded or the fact that non-members of the population are included. Due to the fact that, by construction, our experiment involves only one very specific group of participants (an action research can only be one of a kind), the members of the subject population cannot be surveyed more than once.

As European model-driven software firms of similar sizes are also similar in technological infrastructure and development processes, it could be argued that the results from this study may be replicated in, or generalised to the context of small and medium European software companies where software development process is driven by software models. However, the context, time, participants, problem will be different, and most likely be different. We feel it would be more interesting to conduct a statistical analysis or explore different questions than try to replicate this study *stricto sensu*.

## *Legal, ethical and professional issues*

In this research projects, the following steps are taken to address ethical concerns. First, the working session and questionnaires were organised on a voluntary basis so as to not breach the respondent's right to privacy and freedom to participate or not in the research experiment. The respondents' rights in regard to confidentiality were recognised and made explicit before the project, and they were implemented by a careful design and execution of the research. The data collected from the working session and the questionnaires were carefully checked by everis, and accurately preprocessed by the research team to track any violation of these constraints. Besides, we used observer triangulation to ensure that they were reported objectively by all the researchers. Last, researchers signed an agreement whereby they guaranteed that any non disclose information or data will be kept confidential and will be used for academic purpose only.

## *Answers to research questions*

To answer the research questions we establish a set of preliminary hypotheses. The hypotheses are funded in our previous experience with the application of Delta Analysis for a master's student project. In this project, an information system evolution was performed, thus the Delta Analysis was applied to analyse the differences between the *as-is* and *to-be* systems. Table 19 presents the research questions related with its corresponding hypotheses.

Generally speaking, for the RQ1 and RQ2 we establish hypotheses in order to distinguish if there are some positive, negative or not influence at all when Delta Analysis is applied. For RQ3 and RQ4 we do not establish hypotheses due to our intention is to make an exploratory exercise.

**Table 19.** Research questions and hypotheses

| Research questions | RQ1. To what extent does delta analysis facilitate understanding of IS evolution? | RQ2. To what extent is interpreting delta models and metrics results free of effort? | RQ3. How do interpretations of Delta Analysis metrics come about? | RQ4. What kind of practical applications within everis' projects do analysts envision for Delta Analysis? |
|---|---|---|---|---|
| **Hypotheses** | $H_{10}$ Delta Analysis technique does not influence positively of negatively analysts' understanding of information systems evolution | $H_{20}$ Interpreting delta models and metrics results is an activity that does not reduce or increment the effort of analysts when analysing information systems evolution | Exploratory | Exploratory |
| | $H_{11}$ Delta Analysis technique facilitates analysts' understanding of information systems evolution | $H_{21}$ Interpreting delta models and metrics results is an activity free of effort for the analysts when analysing information systems evolution | Exploratory | Exploratory |
| | $H_{12}$ Delta Analysis technique does not facilitate analysts' understanding of information systems evolution | $H_{22}$ Interpreting delta models and metrics results is an activity that increments the effort of analysts when analysing information systems evolution | Exploratory | Exploratory |

Since the most of the information gathered from the focus group session is qualitative information, we have explored tools for the organisation and structuration of elicited data. We have chosen NVivo[15] software for qualitative data analysis. We use NVivo for both the analysis of the recording gathered from the focus group session and the questionnaires.

---

[15] http://www.qsrinternational.com/product

We propose a set of tags in order to identify meaningful information recorded during the focus group session in everis. The tags are grouped in clusters and are motivated by the research questions. Some open clusters have emerged during the focus group session and the analysis of the recording.

We designed two taxonomies to use for tagging: explicit tagging to be used while analysing the recording, if an analyst says a positive comment related to the effectiveness of the metrics, this comment is tagged as a positive comment for effectiveness mainly using the leaves of the taxonomy, depicted in Fig. 117; and orthogonal tagging to be using while analysing the recording, if an analyst says a positive comment related to the effectiveness of the metrics, this comment is tagged with three tags (e.g., positive, effectiveness, metrics) mainly using three leaves of the taxonomy presented in Fig. 118.

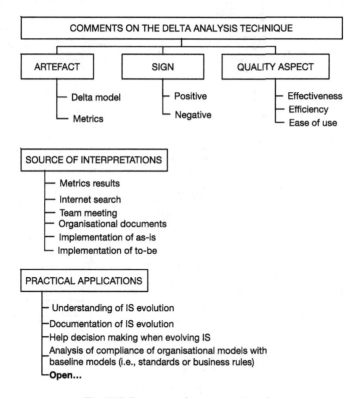

**Fig. 117.** Taxonomy for ortogonal tagging

Both explicit and orthogonal taxonomies are suitable for making the analysis of the recording. We highlight that the orthogonal taxonomy offers powerful facilities for creating queries for further analysis; nevertheless, for each comment it is necessary to add at least three tags (one for each cluster, see). Despite explicit tags are limited for querying, the possibility to make mistakes while tagging is reduced since the researchers just need to use one tag for each comment. We decided then to use explicit tagging and reduce the threat on making mistakes while tagging the focus group recording. Fig. 119 presents a screenshot during the explicit tagging of the recording using NVivo software.

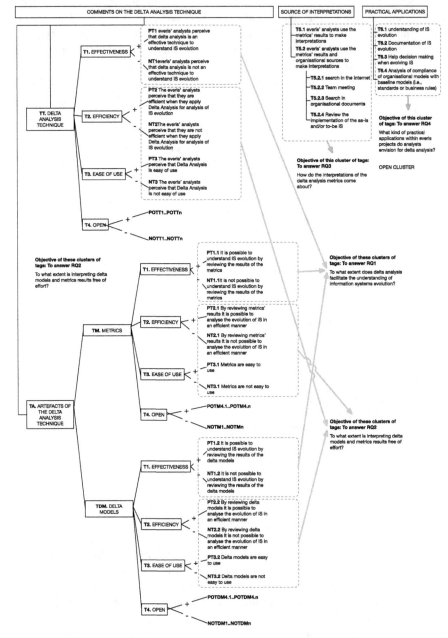

**Fig. 118.** Taxonomy for explicit tagging

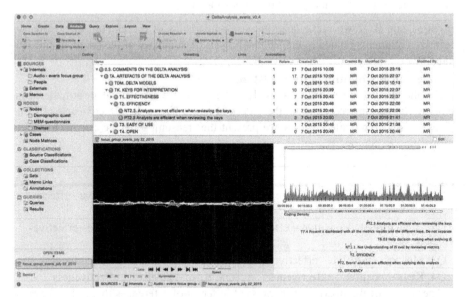

**Fig. 119.** Explicit tagging of the recording in NVivo

For the MEM and demographic questionnaires, we follow an orthogonal strategy of tagging since the amount of information is significantly less than the focus group's recording. We create tags for questions and answers. For this purpose, we also use NVivo. Fig. 120 presents the demographic questionnaires processed by using NVivo and an orthogonal tagging strategy.

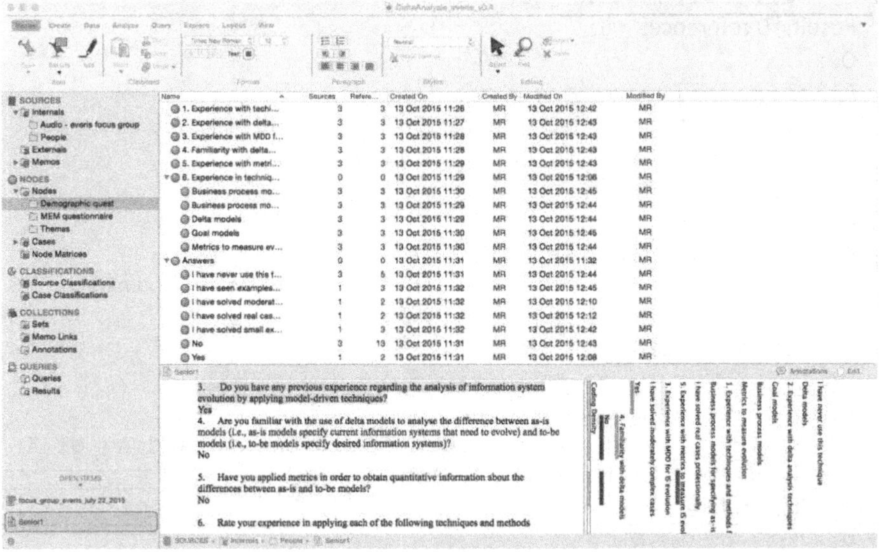

**Fig. 120.** Screenshot with the demographic questionnaire processed in NVivo

To complement the qualitative data gathered from the focus group session, the everis' analyst filled up the 5-point scale MEM questionnaire.

For RQ1 and RQ2 we make quantitative comparisons of the amount of positive vs negative comments related to the Delta Analysis. A summary of the results is presented below:

**Understanding of information systems**

For the analysis of how Delta Analysis helps on the analysis of information systems, we tagged the recording in the pieces of audio where the effectiveness of Delta Analysis was commented. Below we present the reasoning for the queries to gather information to contrast $H_{11}$ and $H_{12}$.

| $H_{11}$ | $H_{12}$ |
|---|---|
| Q1. Delta Analysis – positive – effectiveness | Q5. Delta Analysis – negative– effectiveness |
| Q2. Delta models – positive – effectiveness | Q6. Delta models – negative– effectiveness |
| Q3. Metrics – positive – effectiveness | Q7. Metrics – negative– effectiveness |
| Q4. Keys – positive – effectiveness | Q8. Keys – positive – effectiveness |

The results of the queries are expressed in terms of references that point out comments tagged in the recording with the characteristics of the query. The results are presented in the following:

**H**
$_{11}$

Q1:
```
All the following are true
    Coded at all these nodes: PT1. Delta analysis is an
    effective technique
```
Results: 0 references

Q2:
```
All the following are true
    Coded at all these nodes: PT1.2 Understanding of IS
    evol by reviewing      delta models
```
Results: 0 references

Q3:
```
All the following are true
    Coded at all these nodes: PT1.1 Understanding of IS
    evol by reviewing      metrics
```
Results: 2 references

Q4:
```
All the following are true
    Coded at all these nodes: PT1.3 Understanding of IS
    evol by reviewing      the keys
```
Results: 7 references

**H**
$_{12}$

Q5:
```
All the following are true
    Coded at all these nodes: NT1. Delta analysis is
    not an effective technique
```
Results: 0 references

Q6:
```
    All the following are true
    Coded at all these nodes: NT1.2 Not understanding
    of IS evol by reviewing delta models
```
Results: 0 references

Q7:
```
    All the following are true
    Coded at all these nodes: NT1.1 Not understanding
    of IS evol by reviewing metrics
```
Results: 2 references

Q8:
```
    All the following are true
    Coded at all these nodes: NT1.3 Not understanding
    of IS evol by reviewing the keys
```
Results: 0 references

**Table 20.** Summary of the results for effectiveness

|  | A : NT1.2 Not undestanding of IS evol by reviewing delta models | B : PT1.2 Undestanding of IS evol by reviewing delta models | C : NT1.3. Not understanding of IS evol by reviewing he keys | D : PT1.3. Understanding of IS evol by reviewing the keys | E : NT1.1. Not Understanding of IS evol by reviewing metrics | F : PT1.1. Understanding of IS evol by reviewing metrics | G : NT1. Delta analysis is not an effective technique | H : PT1. Delta analsys is an effective technique |
|---|---|---|---|---|---|---|---|---|
| 1 : TDM. DELTA MODELS | 0 | 0 | 0 | 0 | 0 |  | 0 | 0 |
| 2 : TK. KEYS FOR INTERPRETATION | 0 | 0 | 0 | 7 | 0 | 0 | 0 | 0 |
| 3 : TM. METRICS | 0 | 0 | 0 | 0 | 2 | 2 | 0 | 0 |
| 4 : TT. DELTA ANALYSIS | 0 | 0 | 0 | 0 | 0 | 0 | 0 | 0 |

We have 9 references that support $H_{11}$ and 2 references that support $H_{12}$. Some of the comments of the analyst to support $H_{11}$ are:

*"I feel that the dashboard with all the data is more useful than present numeric data". "I see the dashboard as a possible advisor to know how the evolution should be performed".* We perceived that everis' analysts are more open to review Delta Analysis results by using delta models or the dashboard than review numerical results from the metrics.

For $H_{12}$, we got the following comment: *"the metric enrichment with the analysis for each element (context information) is usable, otherwise, it is not usable".* In this sense, the analysts perceive that the metrics (specially the metric enrichment) should involve contextual information in order to make it significant. Indeed, during the focus group this need was demonstrated several times. The introduction of contextual information is a very important need that we have already identified with the metrics for the situational impact category (see Metrics for situational impact category in page 134). For this, we plan to gather contextual information from the everis situation in order to apply the metrics for situational impact category.

Since is not an objective of this action research experience to achieve statistical significance, we cannot accept or reject $H_{11}$; but *we have strong evidence that demonstrates Delta Analysis facilitates understanding of IS evolution.*

### Interpreting delta models and metrics results free of effort

To analyse if interpreting delta models and metrics results is free of effort for the everis' analysts, we capture the comments on the audio recording regarding the efficiency and ease of use. The reasoning of the queries to apply in order to analyse $H_{21}$ and $H_{22}$ are:

| $H_{21}$ | $H_{22}$ |
|---|---|
| Q9. Delta Analysis – positive – efficiency | Q17. Delta Analysis – negative– efficiency |
| Q10. Delta models – positive – efficiency | Q18. Delta models – negative– efficiency |
| Q11. Metrics – positive – efficiency | Q19. Metrics – negative– efficiency |
| Q12. Keys – positive – efficiency | Q20. Keys – positive – efficiency |
| Q13. Delta Analysis – positive – ease of use | Q21. Delta Analysis – negative– ease of use |
| Q14. Delta models – positive – ease of use | Q22. Delta models – negative– ease of use |
| Q15. Metrics – positive – ease of use | Q23. Metrics – negative– ease of use |
| Q16. Keys – positive – ease of use | Q24. Keys – positive – ease of use |

By using the former queries to analyse the explicit tagging that we have established in the recording, the results of the queries are.

**H$_{21}$**

**Q9:**

```
All the following are true
    Coded at all these nodes: PT2. Everis' analysts are
    efficient when applying delta analysis
```

**Results: 3 references**

**Q10:**

```
All the following are true
    Coded at all these nodes: PT2.2 Analysts are effi-
cient when reviewing delta models
```

Results: 0 references

Q11:

```
All the following are true
    Coded at all these nodes: PT2.1 Analysts are effi-
    cient when reviewing the metrics
```

Results: 1 references

Q12:

```
All the following are true
    Coded at all these nodes: PT2.3 Analysts are effi-
    cient when reviewing the keys
```

Results: 3 references

Q13:

```
All the following are true
    Coded at all these nodes: PT3. Delta analysis is
    easy to use
```

Results: 0 references

Q14:

```
All the following are true
    Coded at all these nodes: PT3.2 Delta models are
    easy to use
```

Results: 0 references

Q15:

```
All the following are true
    Coded at all these nodes: PT3.1 Metrics are easy to
    use
```

Results: 0 references

Q16:

```
All the following are true
    Coded at all these nodes: PT3.3 Keys are easy to
    use
```

Results: 1 references

$H_{22}$

Q17:

```
All the following are true
    Coded at all these nodes: NT2. Everis' analysts are
    not efficient when applying delta analysis
```

Results: 0 references

Q18:

```
All the following are true
    Coded at all these nodes: NT2.2 Analysts are not
    efficient when reviewing delta models
```

Results: 0 references

Q19:

```
All the following are true
    Coded at all these nodes: NT2.1 Analysts are not
    efficient when reviewing the metrics
```

Results: 1 references

Q20:

```
All the following are true
    Coded at all these nodes: NT2.3 Analysts are not
    efficient when reviewing the keys
```

Results: 1 references

Q21:

```
All the following are true
    Coded at all these nodes: NT3. Delta analysis is
    not easy to use
```

Results: 0 references

Q22:

```
All the following are true
    Coded at all these nodes: NT3.2 Delta models are
    not easy to use
```

Results: 0 references

Q23:

```
All the following are true
    Coded at all these nodes: NT3.1 Metrics are not
    easy to use
```

Results: 0 references

Q24:

```
All the following are true
    Coded at all these nodes: NT3.3 Keys are not easy
    to use
```

Results: 0 references

**Table 21.** Summary of the results for efficiency

|  | A : NT2.2 Analysts are not efficient when reviewing delta models | B : PT2.2 Analysts are efficient when reviewing delta models | C : NT2.3. Analysts are not efficient when reviewing the keys | D : PT2.3 Analysts are efficient when reviewing the keys | E : NT2.1. Analysts are not efficient when reviewing the metrics | F : PT2.1. Analysts are efficient when reviewing the metrics | G : NT2. Everis' analysts are not efficient when applying delta analysis | H : PT2. Everis analysts are efficient when applying delta analysis |
|---|---|---|---|---|---|---|---|---|
| 1 : TDM. DELTA MODELS | 0 | 0 | 0 | 0 | 0 | 0 | 0 | 0 |
| 2 : TK. KEYS FOR INTERPRETATION | 0 | 0 | 1 | 3 | 0 | 0 | 0 | 0 |
| 3 : TM. METRICS | 0 | 0 | 0 | 0 | 1 | 1 | 0 | 0 |
| 4 : TT. DELTA ANALYSIS | 0 | 0 | 0 | 0 | 0 | 0 | 0 | 3 |

**Table 22.** Summary of the results for easy of use

|  | A : NT3.2 Delta models are not easy to use | B : PT3.2 Delta models are easy to use | C : NT3.3 Keys are not easy to use | D : PT3.3 Keys are easy to use | E : NT3.1 Metrics are not easy to use | F : PT3.1. Metrics are easy o use | G : NT3. Delta analysis is not easy to use | H : PT3. Delta analysis is easy to use |
|---|---|---|---|---|---|---|---|---|
| 1 : TDM. DELTA MODELS | 0 | 0 | 0 | 0 | 0 | 0 | 0 | 0 |
| 2 : TK. KEYS FOR INTERPRETATION | 0 | 0 | 0 | 1 | 0 | 0 | 0 | 0 |
| 3 : TM. METRICS | 0 | 0 | 0 | 0 | 0 | 0 | 0 | 0 |
| 4 : TT. DELTA ANALYSIS | 0 | 0 | 0 | 0 | 0 | 0 | 0 | 0 |

As a result, we got 8 positive comments to support $H_{21}$. Among the comments we want to discuss the following:

*"It is evident that there are not changes in the IS core. The persistency metric let me to analyse if the core is persistent or not".* The everis' analysts perceived that they are more efficient in the identification of changes when using metrics results.

*"The dashboard is simple enough to have all the metrics results together to make analysis and interpretations on the evolution".* They feel that the dashboard with keys for interpretation and metrics results are easy to use.

On the other hand, they were motivated about the Delta Analysis and they wanted to have more functionality. In this sense, we got 2 negative comments to support $H_{22}$:

*"May be it is valuable to analyse what kind of parameters of the dashboard should be modified in order to achieve an optimal delta. Modify persistency and enrichment until to achieve an ideal state".* The analysts were waiting that the dashboard presents suggestions about an "optimal" evolution of their system. In this part of the discussion, we explained to them that we have designed a repository for interpretations, which collects interpretations and experiences on the usage of Delta Analysis. The idea with the repository is to generalise the results and make suggestions when evolving information systems.

In the context of an action research experience, we cannot reject or do not reject $H_{21}$; but we have strong evidence showing that analysts interpret delta models and metrics results free of effort.

### Source of metrics and delta models interpretations

Mostly, the everis' analysts performed the interpretations about the PMO and RM based on the metrics results. Although, during the moments when the delta models and a summary of the metrics were presented; the everis' analysts used other kind of sources for interpretation.

During the analysis of the delta models of the PMO, the everis' analysts started to discuss among them. We have identified the following process during the interpretation of results:

**Fig. 121.** Interpretation process of the delta models and metrics results for the PMO case

On the other hand, for the registration module we got almost the same behaviour. In this particular situation, the everis' analysts decided also to analyse the to-be implementation to contrast the results. The interpretation process is presented in the following:

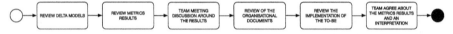

**Fig. 122.** Interpretation process of the delta models and metrics results for the RM case

We have discovered then that the everis' analysts needed to have a meeting and discuss the results in order to make an interpretation on the results that sound reasonable for them. Specifically for the PMO case the everis' analysts got attracted to consult organisational documentation in order to discover the reasons of the evolution. In this concrete case, they were shocked about the fact that the PMO case was not reduced some how. Later on, they agree that it was ok since the CDD method just influenced the inclusion of contextual elements, not the reduction or existing processes.

For the RM case the situation developed different. The everis' analyst met, reviewed organisational documentation together with the implementation of the *to-be* information system. Thanks to the Delta Analysis they were aware that several modification were performed and delta model complement the information regarding the evolution of the RM.

**Envisioned practical applications**

During the focus group session we motivate the analysts to express their envisioned practical applications for Delta Analysis. Based on our experience and evidence from the literature, we establish some possible applications that everis analysts could envision. We have the first list of applications into account in order to facilitate their detection during the focus group. In addition, we capture the emerged applications that the everis' analysts expressed during the exercise. A summary of the references to the different applications are presented in Table 22.0

**Table 23.** Summary of the envisioned practical applications

| | A : T6.01 Understanding of IS evol | B : T6.02 documentation of IS evol | C : T6.03 Help decision making when evolving IS | D : T6.04 Analysis of compliance | E : T6.05 Monitor evolution and adaptation processes | F : T6.06 Analysis of changes and improvements | G : T6.07 Previous analysis before evolution of IS | H : T6.08 Migrations of IS | I : T6.09 Comparing changes after implementations | J : T6.10 To justify changes and understand evolution |
|---|---|---|---|---|---|---|---|---|---|---|
| 1 : 0.5. PRACTICAL APPLICATIONS | 0 | 0 | 1 | 0 | 1 | 1 | 1 | 2 | 1 | 1 |

Mainly during the discussion about envisioned practical applications, the everis' analyst highlighted the importance of the applicability of Delta Analysis in software migration projects. They comment the following: *"Delta Analysis helps on the justification of changes in migration projects. It would be very good to use it in order to explain to our clients about changes"*. On the other hand, they express that *"Delta analysis can be very practical as a previous analysis before to evolve an information system"*.

The gathered envisioned applications let us abroad the possible situations where the Delta Analysis can be used. From the point of view of the TraceME method, the envisioned practical applications open the window to new situational scenarios where the method can be exploited.

### 6.3.2 Discussion

The technical action research in everis have let us several lessons learned regarding the put in practice of the Delta Analysis and future improvements. Mainly we want to highlight the following:

**The use of models is vital for the Delta Analysis technique and the TraceME method in general**. The techniques and guidelines of TraceME are designed for it application in conceptual models. Nevertheless, the senior consultant that was in the focus group session expressed: *"It is a handicap that the Delta Analysis is model-based, industry needs to adopt the MDD paradigm. Delta Analysis is a nice technique"*. Around this comment we discussed with the everis' analysts that the use of models is a precondition of the Delta Analysis. As a result, they concluded with the following: *"Normally no functional requirements are specified by means of models, and I think this is a mistake, everything should be modelled"*. Also, during the discussion around the envisioned practical application, the need of model-based techniques arose and they realised the benefits of these kind of techniques produced in academy.

**Metrics should be combined with contextual information from the case**. Several comments during the focus group make evident the need to exploit the metrics for situational impact category. In this case, it is important to achieve a commitment between industry and academy. Industry needs to be willing to be open to provide contextual information (economic information, human resources, risks analysis, etc.) in order to let academics to model that information and also measure it. From the academy, it is necessary to find the way to elicit contextual information in the way that it is possible use it for measurement purposes. For example, with the metrics for situational impact category we provide a design where contextual-dependent information can be used in order to give meaningful information about the metrics. We need to gather contextual information from the PMO and RM cases and test the metrics for situational impact category. We envision that rich information will be obtained in order to conclude about the evolution.

**The dashboard helps on the interpretation of metrics results**. During the focus group we discovered that the everis' analysts were more talk-active when the dashboard and keys for interpretation where presented. We conclude then that the metrics results are easily interpreted when they are presented all together. In addition, the keys for interpretation helped the everis' analysts to rethink about the evolution process in the sense to confirm actions and evaluate other possibilities. For the implementation of Delta Analysis, we plan to put the metrics and keys for interpretation all together to broaden the range of possible interpretations. In addition, the keys for interpretation should be editable in to facilitate their adaptation to the usage case.

### 6.4    Validation of the ca2oom integration framework: an experiment for sensitive analysis

In order to facilitate the application of the *ca2oom* integration framework, we implemented GREAT (GREAT Process Modeller in short). GREAT is an open source tool with reengineering capabilities to support information systems evolution (further details are explained in the Chapter 7). GREAT includes a plug-in for automated transformation of Communication Analysis models into OO-Method object models. The automated transformation engine implements the rules presented in [7].

We tested the feasibility of the transformation rules by means of laboratory demonstrations (a.k.a., lab-demo) [138]. As we used Communication Analysis models with good quality regarding completeness and structure, the resulting OO-Method object model has good quality too. But, what happen if the Communication Analysis model is incomplete? What happen if the Communication Analysis model has syntactic or semantic mistakes? What happen if the Communication Analysis models does not have the structure and information that the transformation engine requires to transform it into OO-Method object models?

The former ideas shape our research goal for designing an experiment for sensitivity analysis. This experiment has been designed according to Wohlin et al. [151] reported according to the [152].

### *Research goal*

By following the Goal/Question/Metric template [154], the research goal of our study is *to analyse Communication Analysis models and their impact in resulting OO-Method object models when the ca2oom integration framework is applied, with the purpose of evaluation with respect to the sensitivity of the ca2oom integration frame-*

*work from the perspective of the researchers[16] in the context of a last-year master
course at the Universitat Politècnica de València*

### 6.4.1 Experimental design

The subjects of the experiment are 11 students of the information systems engineering
course at the Universitat Politècnica de València. The experiment was performed
from April to June of 2013. In order to characterise the population, we performed a
demographic questionnaire. We found that the 55% of the subjects have experience
with Communication Analysis modelling; and the 91% have experience with the OO-
Method. In addition, some of them have experience applying conceptual modelling
and requirements engineering in industry. The master course was updated in order to
incorporate the experimental set up as part of the course assignments. For example,
we provided training in Communication Analysis to make the group of subjects more
uniform regarding to their background before to start the experimental tasks. The
subjects received grades for the achievement of each assignment. The grades kept
them motivated in order to participate actively in the activities prepared for the
course.

Properly speaking, we have performed a quasi-experiment because the subjects have
not been sampled randomly across the population [158], but this is typical in experiments with students. The experiment also can be classified in terms of the number of
subjects and objects involved in the study [167]. This experiment context is a Multi-
test within object study due to it examines the *ca2oom* integration framework across a
group of subjects.

### *Research questions*

**RQ1.** What are the subjects' perceptions when they are applying the ca2oom integration framework? To answer this question we measure the perceived usefulness, perceived ease of use and their intention to use the *ca2oom* integration framework in the
future.

**RQ2.** How sensible is the ca2oom integration framework when subjects are transforming CA models into OO-Method object models? To answer this question, the
subjects transform CA models and perform several iterations until achieve an improved CA model that allow the creation of an object model that corresponds with an
indicated requirements specification. We evaluate the completeness (semantic correctness and comprehensibility), semantic validity and syntactic correctness of the
first transformation and the last one. As a result, we compare the performance of the
subjects on their firs iteration and the last one, when the CA and the OOM models
have been improved.

### *Variables*

---

[16] The researchers of this experiment are Marcela Ruiz, Sergio España and Óscar Pastor.

We have adapted the method evaluation model [155] to structure the variables of this experiment (see Fig. 123). In addition, we applied the conceptual model quality framework by Lindland et al. [168] for the evaluation of the CA and OOM models.

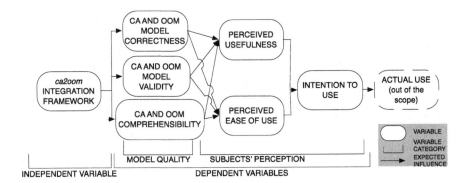

**Fig. 123.** Variables for the sensitivity analysis

### Independent variable

The independent variable **ca2oom integration framework** refers to the strategy to obtain OOM models from CA models. For this variable, we evaluate two values that correspond to the first transformation of the CA model and the last transformation (when several improvements on the CA model have been performed to obtain an OOM model that corresponds with the required information system). The objective is to gather information regarding with the sensitivity of the tool when a first transformation is performed and after certain iterations:

- **First transformation.** Subjects apply the ca2oom integration framework to obtain OOM models from CA models.
- **Last transformation.** After the first transformation exercise, the subjects modify the CA model and apply the ca2oom integration framework several times in order to obtain an OOM model that specifies the required information system.

### Dependent variables

The dependent variables are expected to be influenced by the independent variable. In the following we give the details of the dependent variables:

- **CA and OOM model correctness** (a.k.a., syntactic quality) is the degree to which the model adheres to the CA language rules. Syntactic errors and deviations from the rules decrease syntactic quality. There is only one syntactic quality goal: syntactic correctness. The extent to which the statements (a.k.a. elements) of the model are according to the syntax. A model is correct if all the statements adhere to the language rules.
- **CA and OOM model validity** (a.k.a., semantic quality) is the degree to which the model represents the problem domain. The more similar model and the domain. There are two semantic quality goals: feasible validity and feasible completeness.

- <u>Feasible validity</u>: The extent to which the statements of the model are correct and relevant to the problem domain. Invalid statements are those that do not pertain to the problem or express something incorrectly. A model has achieved feasible validity when there is no invalid statement in the model, such that the additional benefit to the conceptual model from removing the invalid statement exceeds the drawbacks of removing it.
- <u>Feasible completeness</u>: The extent to which the model includes the relevant and correct statements about the problem domain. If there is a relevant statement about the domain that is not included in the model, then the model is incomplete. A model has achieved feasible completeness when there is no relevant statement about the domain, not yet included in the model, such that the additional benefit to the conceptual model from including the relevant statement exceeds the drawbacks of including it.

- **CA and OOM model comprehensibility** (a.k.a., pragmatic quality) is the degree to which the model is correctly interpreted by its audience. The less misunderstanding, the better the pragmatic quality. There is only one pragmatic quality goal: feasible comprehension.

  - <u>Feasible comprehension</u>: The extent to which the model is understood by the people who read it; that is, the extent to which the model allows you (the reviewer) to understand it. Several aspects influence comprehension; for instance, the layout of model elements, the relevance of the names of model elements, the way the model is structured, the explanatory comments it contains.

- **Perceived usefulness:** The degree to which the subject considers that the ca2oom integration framework is effective in achieving its intended objectives. This variable is measured using a 5-point Likert scale format to obtain users' perception.
- **Perceived ease of use**: The degree to which a subject considers that using the ca2oom integration framework is free of effort. This variable is measured using a 5-point Likert scale format to obtain users' perception.
- **Intention to use:** This variable will be measured using a 5-point Likert scale format to obtain users' perception.

In order to keep the equality treatment to the subjects, they evaluate CA and OOM models when they obtain the first transformation and the last one. To do this, we design three sessions for the experimental task. In the first session the subjects specify the CA model by using GREAT. In the second session the subjects execute the transformation engine of GREAT in order to obtain the OOM models. If models are obtained, the subjects evaluate the CA and OOM models. To do this, they evaluate the models of one CA model and one OOM model of two different mates in order to avoid biased judgment. For the third session, the subjects perform several iterations until to achieve a stable version of the OOM model that corresponds with the information system specified for the task. Afterwards they evaluate a CA and OOM model for the last transformation of two different mates.

According to this design, we take two measurements on the same subject, one model evaluation for the first transformation and one model evaluation for the last

transformation. The subjects' perceptions are measured once after the model evaluation of the last transformation (by using the MEM questionnaire). In addition, we
explore the subjects' perceptions in a focus group session.

**The case for the experimental task**

The domain of the case for the experimental task is the *Expense Report*. The Expense
Report Management System is a tool that helps the process of expense reports to be
followed. Using this tool, it is easy to follow the Expense Reports life cycle, from its
creation until it is paid to the employee. Employees give in their expense reports when
all tickets relating to business travel or a business lunch have been collected. The
actors related to this case are: Account manager, company manager, personnel clerk,
employee, department manager and accountant.

### 6.4.2    Experimental procedure

We design a set of task to carry out the experiment according to the design described
above (see design in Fig. 124). During the training sessions the subjects solved some
exercises and they received feedback on their performance. For the session 1, the
subjects specified the CA models for the expense report case. Later, they received the
training in the GREAT tool in order to specify CA models and how to use the transformation engine. To do this, they followed some training exercises.

For the session 2, the subjects performed the transformation process step by step
by using GREAT. They obtained the models and give them to the researchers. The
subjects later evaluate this first transformation of the CA to OOM models. Because
each subject should not evaluate his/her own model, we distribute the CA and OOM
models among the subjects. To randomly allocate the models, we used the webpage
http://www.random.org/. The assignation of models is presented in Table 24.

**Table 24.** Assignment of models per subject

|              | First transformation | | Last transformation | |
| --- | --- | --- | --- | --- |
| **SUBJECT CODE** | **CA** | **OOM** | **CA** | **OOM** |
| S001 | CA002 | OOM009 | CA011 | OOM005 |
| S002 | CA010 | OOM007 | CA009 | OOM003 |
| S003 | CA011 | OOM002 | CA007 | OOM006 |
| S004 | CA009 | OOM006 | CA001 | OOM011 |
| S005 | CA003 | OOM001 | CA008 | OOM010 |
| S006 | CA004 | OOM003 | CA010 | OOM009 |
| S007 | CA001 | OOM010 | CA006 | OOM008 |
| S008 | CA005 | OOM011 | CA003 | OOM002 |
| S009 | CA006 | OOM008 | CA002 | OOM004 |
| S010 | CA007 | OOM004 | CA005 | OOM001 |
| S011 | CA008 | OOM005 | CA004 | OOM007 |

To perform the evaluations, the subjects were provided with templates in the format
of 7-point likert scales. Thus, each subject evaluates for both CA and OOM models
the correctness, validity, completeness and comprehensibility. Some snapshots of the
evaluation templates are presented in Fig. 125.

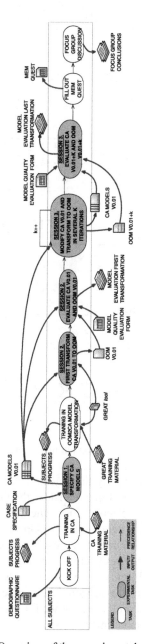

**Fig. 124.** Overview of the experimental procedure

Rate the model quality according to the following criteria.

The values of the 7-point scale correspond to:

1 = Extremely low quality
2 = Very low quality
3 = Low quality
4 = Medium quality
5 = High quality
6 = Very high quality
7 = Extremely high quality

| | 1 | 2 | 3 | 4 | 5 | 6 | 7 |
|---|---|---|---|---|---|---|---|
| Syntactic quality: Syntactic correctness | ◯ | ◯ | ◯ | ◯ | ◯ | ◯ | ◯ |
| Justify your answer: | | | | | | | |

| | 1 | 2 | 3 | 4 | 5 | 6 | 7 |
|---|---|---|---|---|---|---|---|
| Semantic quality: Feasible validity | ◯ | ◯ | ◯ | ◯ | ◯ | ◯ | ◯ |
| Justify your answer: | | | | | | | |

| | 1 | 2 | 3 | 4 | 5 | 6 | 7 |
|---|---|---|---|---|---|---|---|
| Semantic quality: Feasible completeness | ◯ | ◯ | ◯ | ◯ | ◯ | ◯ | ◯ |
| Justify your answer: | | | | | | | |

| | 1 | 2 | 3 | 4 | 5 | 6 | 7 |
|---|---|---|---|---|---|---|---|
| Pragmatic quality: Feasible comprehension | ◯ | ◯ | ◯ | ◯ | ◯ | ◯ | ◯ |
| Justify your answer: | | | | | | | |

**Fig. 125.** Snapshots of the evaluation templates for the CA and OOM models

For the session 3, the subjects modify the CA models execute the transformation engine of GREAT several times until they consider the OOM model corresponds with the requirements for the expense report case. The subjects were provided with templates to register transformation iterations, what kind of problems they found and the actions performed in the CA model. When each subject achieved the last iteration, they delivered the models to the researchers for allocate them to their corresponding reviewers. Afterwards, the subjects evaluate the models that were assigned as a result of the random allocation. After the session 3, the subjects filled out the MEM questionnaire. Finally, in the focus group session we presented a summary of the sessions and preliminary results of the experimental task.

### *Analysis of results*

In this section, we summarise the collected data and we analyse the results.

Because of the objective of this sensitivity analysis is to discover how sensitive is the
*ca2oom* integration framework according to the input CA models, we decide to perform a qualitative and quantitative analysis without the desire to make generalisations. In this way, we are not in the search of statistical significance. Thus, we analyse
the mean of the collected data when the subjects evaluated the models for the first and
last transformation sessions. We compare the mean for the three conceived variables
in for the first and last transformation. Thus, we conclude how important is the quality
of the input CA model for the *ca2oom* integration framework. To process the collected data we use descriptive statistics.

On the other hand, the collected data from the filled MEM questionnaires to discover subjects' perceptions [155], all data was compiled and aggregated to know the
mean of the results.

For the data analysis we used the values of the 11 subjects. Below we present the
statistical analysis for both CA and OOM model evaluations in the first and last iteration with the result of the evaluations (see Fig. 127). Fig. 126 presents the descriptive
statistics for the results of the model evaluation.

**Descriptive Statistics**

| | N | Minimum | Maximum | Sum | Mean | Std. Deviation |
|---|---|---|---|---|---|---|
| CA_correct_F | 11 | 5,0000 | 7,0000 | 66,0000 | 6,000000 | ,8944272 |
| CA_valid_F | 11 | 3,0000 | 7,0000 | 57,0000 | 5,181818 | 1,1677484 |
| CA_complet_F | 11 | 2,0000 | 7,0000 | 55,0000 | 5,000000 | 1,5491933 |
| CA_compreh_F | 11 | 1,0000 | 7,0000 | 54,0000 | 4,909091 | 1,7580981 |
| OOM_correct_F | 11 | 3,0000 | 7,0000 | 66,0000 | 6,000000 | 1,4142136 |
| OOM_valid_F | 11 | 1,0000 | 5,0000 | 35,0000 | 3,181818 | 1,2504545 |
| OOM_complet_F | 11 | 1,0000 | 6,0000 | 40,0000 | 3,636364 | 1,5015144 |
| OOM_compreh_F | 11 | 2,0000 | 7,0000 | 53,0000 | 4,818182 | 1,7215215 |
| CA_correct_L | 10 | 3,00 | 7,00 | 61,00 | 6,1000 | 1,44914 |
| CA_valid_L | 11 | 2,00 | 7,00 | 55,00 | 5,0000 | 1,54919 |
| CA_complet_L | 10 | 2,00 | 7,00 | 50,00 | 5,0000 | 1,69967 |
| CA_compreh_L | 11 | 3,00 | 7,00 | 58,00 | 5,2727 | 1,48936 |
| OOM_correct_L | 11 | 4,00 | 7,00 | 71,00 | 6,4545 | ,93420 |
| OOM_valid_L | 11 | 4,00 | 7,00 | 58,00 | 5,2727 | ,90453 |
| OOM_complet_L | 11 | 3,00 | 7,00 | 55,00 | 5,0000 | 1,18322 |
| OOM_compreh_L | 11 | 4,00 | 7,00 | 68,00 | 6,1818 | ,98165 |
| Valid N (listwise) | 9 | | | | | |

**Fig. 126.** Descriptive statistics for the fist (F) and last (L) transformation of the CA models

**Case Summaries^a**

| | | | CA_correct | CA_valid | CA_complet | CA_compreh | OOM_correct | OOM_valid | OOM_complet | OOM_compreh |
|---|---|---|---|---|---|---|---|---|---|---|
| Transf | First | 1 | 7,0000 | 4,0000 | 6,0000 | 6,0000 | 6,0000 | 1,0000 | 6,0000 | 7,0000 |
| | | 2 | 7,0000 | 5,0000 | 4,0000 | 7,0000 | 4,0000 | 4,0000 | 4,0000 | 6,0000 |
| | | 3 | 5,0000 | 7,0000 | 7,0000 | 1,0000 | 7,0000 | 3,0000 | 4,0000 | 7,0000 |
| | | 4 | 5,0000 | 6,0000 | 5,0000 | 6,0000 | 7,0000 | 5,0000 | 6,0000 | 4,0000 |
| | | 5 | 6,0000 | 5,0000 | 6,0000 | 4,0000 | 7,0000 | 2,0000 | 2,0000 | 2,0000 |
| | | 6 | 5,0000 | 6,0000 | 6,0000 | 4,0000 | 7,0000 | 3,0000 | 1,0000 | 7,0000 |
| | | 7 | 7,0000 | 5,0000 | 6,0000 | 5,0000 | 5,0000 | 5,0000 | 4,0000 | 4,0000 |
| | | 8 | 6,0000 | 6,0000 | 4,0000 | 6,0000 | 6,0000 | 3,0000 | 3,0000 | 3,0000 |
| | | 9 | 5,0000 | 4,0000 | 2,0000 | 4,0000 | 7,0000 | 4,0000 | 3,0000 | 5,0000 |
| | | 10 | 7,0000 | 6,0000 | 6,0000 | 7,0000 | 7,0000 | 3,0000 | 3,0000 | 4,0000 |
| | | 11 | 6,0000 | 3,0000 | 3,0000 | 4,0000 | 3,0000 | 2,0000 | 4,0000 | 4,0000 |
| | Total | N | 11 | 11 | 11 | 11 | 11 | 11 | 11 | 11 |
| | | Mean | 6,000000 | 5,181818 | 5,000000 | 4,909091 | 6,000000 | 3,181818 | 3,636364 | 4,818182 |
| | | Median | 6,000000 | 5,000000 | 6,000000 | 5,000000 | 7,000000 | 3,000000 | 4,000000 | 4,000000 |
| | | Std. Deviation | ,8944272 | 1,1677484 | 1,5491933 | 1,7580981 | 1,4142136 | 1,2504545 | 1,5015144 | 1,7215215 |
| | Last | 1 | 4,0000 | 2,0000 | 3,0000 | 5,0000 | 7,0000 | 7,0000 | 7,0000 | 7,0000 |
| | | 2 | 3,0000 | 4,0000 | 5,0000 | 5,0000 | 7,0000 | 6,0000 | 5,0000 | 6,0000 |
| | | 3 | | 6,0000 | 4,0000 | 5,0000 | 4,0000 | 6,0000 | 5,0000 | 6,0000 |
| | | 4 | 7,0000 | 4,0000 | | 4,0000 | 6,0000 | 5,0000 | 5,0000 | 5,0000 |
| | | 5 | 6,0000 | 4,0000 | 6,0000 | 4,0000 | 7,0000 | 4,0000 | 4,0000 | 4,0000 |
| | | 6 | 7,0000 | 5,0000 | 7,0000 | 3,0000 | 6,0000 | 5,0000 | 5,0000 | 7,0000 |
| | | 7 | 6,0000 | 6,0000 | 6,0000 | 7,0000 | 7,0000 | 4,0000 | 4,0000 | 6,0000 |
| | | 8 | 7,0000 | 4,0000 | 7,0000 | 7,0000 | 7,0000 | 5,0000 | 5,0000 | 6,0000 |
| | | 9 | 7,0000 | 7,0000 | 6,0000 | 7,0000 | 6,0000 | 5,0000 | 3,0000 | 7,0000 |
| | | 10 | 7,0000 | 7,0000 | 2,0000 | 4,0000 | 7,0000 | 6,0000 | 7,0000 | 7,0000 |
| | | 11 | 7,0000 | 6,0000 | 4,0000 | 7,0000 | 7,0000 | 5,0000 | 5,0000 | 7,0000 |
| | Total | N | 10 | 11 | 10 | 11 | 11 | 11 | 11 | 11 |
| | | Mean | 6,100000 | 5,000000 | 5,000000 | 5,272727 | 6,454545 | 5,272727 | 5,000000 | 6,181818 |
| | | Median | 7,000000 | 5,000000 | 5,500000 | 5,000000 | 7,000000 | 5,000000 | 5,000000 | 6,000000 |
| | | Std. Deviation | 1,4491377 | 1,5491933 | 1,6996732 | 1,4893562 | ,9341987 | ,9045340 | 1,1832160 | ,9816498 |
| Total | | N | 21 | 22 | 21 | 22 | 22 | 22 | 22 | 22 |
| | | Mean | 6,047619 | 5,090909 | 5,000000 | 5,090909 | 6,227273 | 4,227273 | 4,318182 | 5,500000 |
| | | Median | 6,000000 | 5,000000 | 6,000000 | 5,000000 | 7,000000 | 4,500000 | 4,000000 | 6,000000 |
| | | Std. Deviation | 1,1608700 | 1,3419634 | 1,5811388 | 1,6008656 | 1,1925091 | 1,5097088 | 1,4924050 | 1,5352989 |

a. Limited to first 100 cases.

**Fig. 127.** Statistical analysis for the CA and OOM model evaluations agregated by first and last transformation

## CA and OOM model correctness

The results of the descriptive statistics show an average CA model correctness of 6 points (86%) for the first transformation and 6.1 points (87%) for the last transformation. On the other hand, for the OOM models, the descriptive statistics show an average of 6 points (86%) for the first transformation and 6,45 points (92%) for the last transformation.

The results are very interesting from the point of view on how the syntactic correctness of CA models are not directly related with the syntactic correctness of resulting OOM models. The difference from the first and last transformation of the CA models is just 1%. It means that the subjects applied the CA language rules in the correct way. Nevertheless, the model correctness of the OOM models was improved in 6% because of the improvement of the other quality factors.

By reviewing the iterations templates where the subjects registered the changes performed in CA models and the obtained OOM models, we discover that the most of the problems related with correctness are related with the ordering process of communicative events. Despite the CA model were specified in a correct way and the syntax were used properly, the order of the communicative events were not properly specified. The subjects assumed that this issue impact the correctness of the OOM

models because the relationships among classes were not properly generated. The
subjects' perceived that the creation of classes without relationships is a correctness
mistake. Just OOM agent classes can be generated without any relationship.

In this point we want to highlight that the automatic transformation ensures the
correctness of CA and OOM models. The modelling tool to specify CA models implements a set of constraints that ensures the properly use of the modeller. On the
other hand, currently the tool does not implement a support in order to check if all the
classes have at least one relationship attribute.

### CA and OOM model validity

Regarding with the validity, we analyse that the results of the descriptive statistics are
not favourable for the CA models. The results show an average CA model validity of
5,18 points (74%) for the first transformation and 5 points (71%) for the last transformation. For the OOM models, the descriptive statistics show an average of 3,18
points (45%) for the first transformation and 5,27 points (75%) for the last transformation.

The results present that the validity of CA models was deteriorated. We reviewed
the iteration templates to analyse deeply modifications performed on the CA models.
We discovered that the subjects found invalid elements in the CA model regarding to
the domain. As it was the last transformation, they judge severely the mistakes performed. The CA models did not achieve a correct alignment with the domain of the
expense report, for that reason, the evaluation seems to be harder than in the first
transformation.

Moreover, the validity of the OOM models was improved. For the last transformation,
the most of the subjects gave meaningful names to the message structures; thus the
classes of the OOM model inherit more information related to the domain. On the
other hand, the subjects valued the creation of relationships and attributes positively
to represent the properly the domain.

The results of the descriptive statistics show an average CA model completeness of
5 points (71)% for the first and the last transformation. For the OOM models, the
descriptive statistics show an average of3,64 points (52%) for the first transformation
and 5 points (71%) for the last transformation.

The results regarding completeness highlight some drawbacks about GREAT. Despite
the model was complete, the modelling tool demanded to include in the message
structures several information that the subjects ignored for their first time. Despite
they were trained in the use of GREAT, we discover that the specification of message
structure is not intuitive and demands extra-work from the users. In addition, we discovered that several data that was already specified in the modelling tool was not
traceable with the information at the moment to specify the message structures. To
type twice the same information is a huge problem that derives in completeness problems that are not related to the CA models. CA models were complete as the results
shown, the problem was the replication of information.

When the subjects replied the information in the message structures, they obtained
OOM models more complete than in the first iteration.

**CA and OOM model comprehensibility**

The results of the descriptive statistics show an average CA model comprehensibility of 4,91 points (70%) for the first transformation and 5,27 points (75%) for the last transformation. For the OOM models, the descriptive statistics show an average of 4,82 points (69%) for the first transformation and 6,18 points (88%) for the last transformation.

These results demonstrate how sensible is the tool regarding to validity and correctness. When the subjects aligned the CA models with the domain, the obtained OOM models were easy to understand and read.

## *Subject perceptions*

Subjects' perceptions about the *ca2oom* integration framework were collected by means of a MEM questionnaire [155], containing 5-point Likert scale questions. The questionnaire presents several questions that are related to the variables to evaluate: perceived usefulness, perceived ease of use, and intention to use the *ca2oom* integration framework. The results of the questionnaires and the statistical analysis is summarised in Fig. 128.

**Descriptive Statistics**

|  | N | Minimum | Maximum | Sum | Mean | Std. Deviation |
|---|---|---|---|---|---|---|
| PEOU | 6 | 3,33 | 5,00 | 24,67 | 4,1111 | ,66388 |
| PU | 6 | 3,38 | 4,63 | 23,75 | 3,9583 | ,43060 |
| ITU | 6 | 3,00 | 4,00 | 20,00 | 3,3333 | ,51640 |
| Valid N (listwise) | 6 |  |  |  |  |  |

**Fig. 128.** Descriptive statistics for the subjects' perceptions analysis

In average, the subjects perceive that the ca2oom integration framework is ease of use (PEOU) (4,1 points). On the other hand, the average obtained for the perceived usefulness (PU)

## *Focus group session*

We performed a focus group session to gather more qualitative information regarding the *ca2oom* integration framework. Our objective is to discover the subjects' perceptions based on the experimental experience. Thus, we want to distinguish perceptions related to the *ca2oom* integration framework from perceptions related to GREAT (the tool to support the *ca2oom* integration framework).

The focus group session was performed in a comfortable room with all the facilities to perform a meeting. Some snacks and beverage were also provided to the subjects in order to provoke a relaxed environment for discussion. First, the researchers warmed up the environment by summarising all the activities performed during the experimental tasks. In addition, some preliminary analyses about the model evaluation were presented. Afterward, the subjects were provided with 6 post-its –three to specify perceived *ca2oom* integration framework advantages and three for the negative ones. We give some minutes to the subjects to let them reconsider all the activities during the course. When all of them filled out the post-it, they selected the main advantage and main disadvantage to expose it to their mates. To do this, we performed a discussion in the whiteboard and we started an initial classification of the post-it. Fig. 129 presents the whiteboard after the focus group discussion. The label "METODO" (in Spanish) refers to the *ca2oom* integration framework with two columns for advantages (VENTAJAS) and disadvantages (DESVENTAJAS). In the same way, the label "HERRAMIENTA" stands for the post-its related to GREAT with the two columns for advantages and disadvantages.

**Fig. 129.** Witheboard after the focus group session

As a result, we gathered 22 post-its. We performed a second classification of the post-its in order to analyse the information. To do this, we followed a clustering approach for classifying the information [160]. The clustering is presented in the

**Table 25.** Summary of the *ca2oom* advantages post-it clustering

| Clusters | | |
|---|---|---|
| Id | Num | Description |
| A1 | 1 | Facilitates model verification and validation |
| A2 | 1 | Increase efficiency |
| A3 | 2 | Facilitates the communication among analyst for design of information sys- |

|     |   | tems                                |
|-----|---|-------------------------------------|
| A4  | 1 | Keeps the traceability among models |
| A5  | 2 | Ensures model semantic validity     |

**Table 26.** Summary of the *ca2oom* disadvantages post-it clustering

| Clusters | | |
|----------|-----|----------------------------------------|
| Id | Num | Description |
| D1 | 1 | The OOM depends on the quality of the CA |

**Table 27.** Summary of the GREAT advantages post-it clustering

| Clusters | | |
|----------|-----|------------------------------------|
| Id | Num | Description |
| G1 | 3 | Improves the users' efficiency |
| G2 | 2 | Ensures model syntactic correctness |
| G3 | 1 | Ensures model semantic validity |

**Table 28.** Summary of the GREAT disadvantages post-it clustering

| Clusters | | |
|----------|-----|-------------------------------------------|
| Id | Num | Description |
| T1 | 1 | Sensible to errors in the CA model |
| T2 | 2 | The layout of the model difficult to keep |
| T3 | 4 | Usability problems |

As is evident in the number of post-its filled-out by the subjects, they accepted the ca2oom integration framework positively. Although, we discovered the tool impacted their perceptions and performance during the experimental tasks. The modelling tool ensured that syntactic errors are not introduced in the CA models. In this way, the transformation engine does not have problems to generate OOM models. However, the tool has certain properties that were no synchronised with the modeller and the subjects were obligated to introduce information that is obvious or already specified. This is a usability problem that further impacted their evaluations about completeness, correctness and comprehension.

As a conclusion of the focus group, we agreed that it is important to enforce the support for the GREAT modeller.

### *Discussions on the threats to validity*

In this section we discuss the potential threats on the validity of the experiment based on the list proposed by [169]. We are going to analyse how valid the experimental experience in respect of conclusion validity, internal validity, construct validity and external validity.

## Conclusion validity

To ensure that the conclusions made as a result of the collected data are correct, we applied statistical tools. We used SPSS 20 for obtaining the descriptive statistical analysis [170].

Regarding to the reliability of measures, we recognise that this experiment has a big threat because the most of the measures are related to perceptions and also they depend on the subjects' background and training. We validated the instruments before to use them during the experimental tasks. We assume the role of the subjects in order to foresee possible problems or mistakes in the instruments.

On the other hand, to reduce this threat we designed various strategies to collect data like the MEM questionnaire, the evaluation templates, the focus group, and subjects' evolution. We make the final conclusions by triangulating all the information sources.

We recognise a threat regarding to the reliability of treatment implementation. The subjects evaluated different CA models that were different and none of them has the same level of quality. To minimise the threat, the subjects were trained in CA modelling. Thus, we can assume that the models have the same level of quality. In addition, we propose to evaluate the models for the first and last transformation. For the last transformation the subjects evaluated homogeneous models because they worked in order to generate a OOM model traceable with the case specification.

Concerning to the random heterogeneity of subjects, we checked with the demographic questionnaire that the subjects were homogeneous according to their background.

## Internal validity

We recognise a threat regarding to the maturation of the subjects. For the evaluation of the last transformation, the subjects were more experienced in Communication Analysis, the OO-Method and how to evaluate model quality. We saw in the results that the subjects were more aware about the errors in the CA and OOM models and their evaluations were close to 2 (bad punctuation) if they did not reviewed what their were expecting. To minimise this threat, we randomise the models among the subjects to promote a blind evaluation. In this way, they evaluated different CA and OOM models (CA and OOM model evaluated does not correspond to the same author). Despite they recognised that models belong to first or last transformation, we reduced the biased because of the possibility to review their own model or models belong to the same author.

The researchers evaluated the instruments in order to perform the experimental tasks. There are some threats related to the selection of the subjects. The subjects are students of a last year master course of the University. All of the students participated as subjects of the study, thus we did not perform a deep study about the perfect population for this experiment. To minimise this threat, we performed a demographic questionnaire to know the background of the subjects and how homogeneous they are. As the subjects were part of the course, they were motivated to participate because they gain grades thanks to their performance during the experimental tasks.

**Construct validity**

Evaluation apprehension threats are present in this experiment. Some of the subjects could be afraid of the evaluation of it models. In addition, during the focus group session, there is a threat that the subjects feel afraid to share their perceptions in front of their professors and mates. To mitigate this threat, the evaluation of the models is blind. Thus, when a subject is evaluating a model, it is not possible to know who is it author. On the other hand, for the focus group session, we mitigated the apprehension threats by providing a confortable environment to let the subjects to express themselves with calm and relax.

The evaluation model templates, the MEM and the focus group post-its provide information about the perception of the subjects. To have different sources of information reduces the impact of apprehension threats in the experiment.

**External validity**

For the external validity, we recognise three threats related to interaction of selection and treatment, interaction of setting and treatment and interaction of history and treatment. For the first two treatments, we minimise the threat by identifying the subjects and report about their background and role in the society. Thus, based on this results it is possible to know if their outcomes can be generalised for a similar population. Nevertheless, this experiment was performed in an academic environment and the case that they analysed is not industry-oriented. For these reasons, we do not generalise the results of this experiment for real cases. However, the results of this sensitivity analysis motivate us to perform industry experiences with GREAT in industry. In this line, in 2014 we performed a proof of concept exercise in order to test GREAT in industrial environment. In the next sections, we discuss the outcomes.

For the interaction of history and treatment threat, we designed the experiment closer to the reality. First, the subjects specified the CA models (requirements specification) and then the specification of OOM models (design specification). The most of the software engineering projects follow these steps in this order.

### 6.4.3    Conclusions and lessons learnt

We have performed a sensitivity analysis in order to find evidence about how sensitive is the *ca2oom* integration framework. To do this, we trained a group of a last year master students (who are the subjects of the experiment) in order to use the *ca2oom* integration framework.

The experiment was designed according with the schedule of the course and we adapted the material to keep the original objectives. We prepared the instruments and tested before to apply them in the experimental tasks. The subjects received grades for their accomplishment during the experimental tasks and their participation in all the activities of the course. The grades kept them motivated to participate.

Despite results' generalisation is not our objective, we have evidence that the *ca2oom* integration framework has some sensitive points that are related to the framework itself and the too support (GREAT). Mainly, we found that the ca2oom integration framework is sensible to the quality of the CA models in respect to the semantic quality (feasible validity and feasible completeness) and pragmatic quality (feasible comprehension). On the other hand, the modelling tool ensures the syntactic quality because it keeps control on how the modelling elements in the CA and OOM models are applied. Although, some syntactic errors were detected when the subjects ordered the communicative events to establish the precedences. This task is relegated to GREAT's users, thus, if errors are introduced in the ordering process it will impact the generation of the OOM models.

Various improvements were collected in order to improve the use of GREAT because it has a strong impact on the application of the *ca2oom* integration framework. Consaequently, we discover that the most of the issues to check in great are related to the usability of the tool and assurance of syntactic validity.

On the other hand, the impact of the semantic quality and pragmatic quality of CA models on the OOM models cannot be controlled by GREAT. We envision that a good training on the usage of the tool and the ca2oom integration framework will minimise the problems regarding the mentioned quality issues.

## 6.5 Validation of the evolCA procedure: A feasibility analysis

To validate the feasibility of the *evolCA* procedure, we have performed a laboratory demonstration. First, we created the main steps of the *evolCA* procedure based on the ontological alignment between the CA and *i\** metamodels. Together with the steps of the *evolCA* procedure, we specified a set of guidelines. The *evolCA* procedure v0.05 (conception of the evolution procedure) was evaluated in several iterations until to achive the *evolCA* procedure v1.0, which is presented in the Section 4.5.

### 6.5.1 Design and procedure

The author of this book, her advisors (Sergio España and Óscar Pastor), Dolors Costal and Xavier Franch from the Universitat Politècnica de Catalunya, performed the laboratory demonstration (a.k.a, lab-demo); we (from now on, the researchers) are all collaborating for the design of the GoBIS framework and the exploitation of usage scenarios. For supporting the evolution scenario in GoBIS, we have created the *evolCA* procedure v1.0 to evolve CA models based on *i\** models. We have performed various iterations of the version during January and October of 2015.

The case selected was the Super Stationery Co. case [138]. We established a controlled environment to perform the evolution of the CA models from an *as-is* to a *to-be* state. My means of a running example we illustrates the application of the procedure and its feasibility.

Fig. 130 presents the iteration $k$ for the lab-demo. The inputs for the *evolCA* procedure are the $CA_{AS-IS}$ model (CA model to evolve), the $i^*_{AS-IS}$ that corresponds with the $CA_{AS-IS}$ model (optional), and the $i^*_{TO-BE}$ that specifies the goals of the *to-be* information system. The output of the *evolCA* procedure is a certain $CA_{TO-BE}$ model.

After the application of the *evolCA* procedure, the researchers review the obtained CA$_{TO-BE}$ model and add the necessary adjustments to the *evolCA* procedure if necessary. If changes are performed in the *evolCA* procedure, then the *evolCA* procedure V0.K+1 is issued.

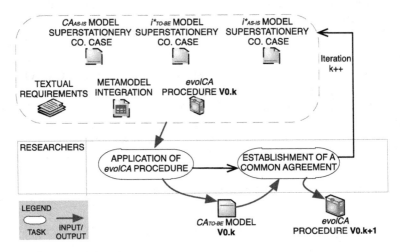

**Fig. 130.** Iteration *k* of the lab-demo aplying the *evolCA* procedure *V0.k*

### 6.5.2    Conclusions and lessons learnt

By means of the lab-demo we tested the feasibility of the *evolCA* procedure v1.0 published in this book. After the first version of the *evolCA* procedure, several improvements have been added mainly: support for explicit specification of vertical traceability relationships, and the alignment between the GoBIS metamodel and the Delta Analysis metamodel in order to support horizontal traceability relationships among CA$_{AS-IS}$ and CA$_{TO-BE}$ models. The lab-demo is detailed in the section 4.5 as the Super-Stationery Co. case is used as a running example to specify the steps of the *evolCA* procedure.

### 6.6    Summary

In this section, we have reported four empirical software engineering experiences in order to validate the TraceME method. We evaluated the four method chunks: the *iStar2ca* guidelines, the *ca2oom* integration framework, the *evolCA* procedure, and the Delta Analysis technique. We have performed laboratory demonstrations, controlled experiments, sensitivity analyses, and technical action research experiences. The four empirical evaluation experiences included a focus group session with the subjects in order to gather their perceptions on the TraceME chunks.

In 2013, we performed a sensitivity analysis to validate the *ca2oom* integration framework. The subjects were a group of last year master students of the course information system engineering at the Universitat Politècnica de València. As a result of this sensitivity analysis, we found evidence that motivate us to improve the support tool for the framework, the GREAT Process Modeller. Relative to the *ca2oom* integration framework, we found that the syntactic correctness is mainly ensured by GREAT. Nevertheless GREAT's users should do the ordering of communicative event diagrams, which makes GREAT sensible to errors. We found that the semantic and pragmatic quality of CA models influence semantic and pragmatic quality of OOM models. The *ca2oom* integration framework is sensible to the lack of quality of input CA models.

In addition, we won a contest in the Universitat Politècnica de València that let us gain budget to perform a proof of concept of GREAT. GREAT have improved their usability and sensitivity against bad quality models given as input. Currently we are using GREAT in a case study with SIVSA (http://www.sivsa.com/site/) as part of a national project. SIVSA is a software development group that offer solutions for hospital management. They are using GREAT for specifying the business process model regarding the evolution of a software system for small hospitals. Also they are using the transformation engine of GREAT for obtaining object models (OO-Method object models). As part of the case study, SIVSA will use also the Delta Analysis in order to evaluate the evolution of their information system. The usability experiments performed during 2010 [68], lab-demos, lately the sensitivity analysis and proof of concept project contributed to the maturation of the *ca2oom* integration framework and its tool support, GREAT.

In 2014 we performed a controlled experiment to validate the *iStar2ca* guidelines with a last year master students of the information systems engineering course at the Universitat Politècnica de València. The main objective of the experiment was to compare the performance and perceptions of the subjects when they were applying the *iStar2ca* guidelines or their own criteria when analysing information systems. As a result of the experiment, we found evidence (statistical significance) that demonstrate how subjects have better performance when applying the *iStar2ca* guidelines vs. subjects' criteria. In addition, the subjects' perceptions about the *iStar2ca* guidelines were very positive in contrast with the subjects' criteria.

As a result of the experiment, we issued the iStar2ca guidelines 2.0 that includes additional guidelines emerged from subjects' experience.

In 2015 we performed a laboratory-demonstration in order to evaluate the feasibility of the *evolCA* procedure. We performed various iterations reviewing the versions of the *evolCA* procedure until we achieved a stable version V1.0.

The GoBIS framework is the core for the *iStar2ca* guidelines (top-down usage scenario) and the *evolCA* procedure (evolution scenario). Further empirical evaluations are planed for the *evolCA* procedure and its combined use with the *iStar2ca* guidelines.

In 2015 we conducted an action research experience in everis Spain. everis is a Spanish consulting company. We applied the Delta Analysis together with the everis' analysts in order to analyse the evolution of two information systems that everis have implemented. As a result of the action research experience we got various inputs in order to know a) the acceptance of Delta Analysis in industry and b) preferences of industrial users to solve their needs when analysing information system evolution and c) improvements for the Delta Analysis technique. The perceptions of the everis' analysts about Delta Analysis are very positive and they are willing to use it in their future projects. The main handicap is the use of models, but they are aware about the importance to use model-based techniques for analysis, design and implementation of information systems.

In this book, we do not report the validation of the TraceME method as a whole. We are aware about the need to discover how and when a method engineer would apply the TraceME method. In the Chapter 5 we describe different situations where the TraceME method can be applied and we detailed each TraceME chunk in order to facilitate it usage. In addition, we have validated each method chunk. Despite of the former, real world evidence about the acceptance of the method are needed. The validation of TraceME is a fascinating project that is out of scope of the research presented in this book.

To conclude, we want to highlight the importance to make experimentation in software engineering. TraceME is a method that was conceived in an academic environment. It has been growing thanks to the insights from practitioners and industrial stakeholders. We want to highlight the importance to follow a research method when performing experiments: analyse, design, evaluate, and execute experiments. It is vital to think in advance about the possible threats on the validity and be open to re-design experimental plans in order to ensure the quality of the conclusions to be given. Scientific results should base on evidence, if there are not evidence to support assumptions; we are not talking in terms of science.

# Chapter 7     Tool support

> *"When you translate a dream into reality, it's never a full implementation. It is easier to dream than to do"* - Shai Agassi

## 7.1     Introduction

In this chapter we summarise the three prototypes that we build to support TraceME. First we present the GREAT Process Modeller. It supports the *ca2oom* integration framework. GREAT offers modelling environments for Communication Analysis models and automatic transformation engines to obtain the object models of OO-Method.

We develop a plug-in to support the GoBIS framework; the *iStar2ca* guidelines and the *evolCA* procedure are designed based on this framework. This prototype offers combined modelling for the *i\** language and Communication Analysis models. Thus, when applying the *iStar2ca* guidelines or the *evolCA* procedure, the prototype helps on the modelling tasks and traceability specifications.

In addition, we develop a prototype for the Delta Analysis technique. The prototype supports automatic specification of delta models and metrics applications.

All the prototypes implement the metamodels conceived for each TraceME chunk. The prototypes follow a model-driven architecture making them easy to configure and adapt. We use Eclipse technologies as they are extended in academy for model-driven methods and techniques. Also, Eclipse offers a plug-in design that is convenient due to the fragmented nature of TraceME.

The development of these prototypes is our attempt to realise the implementation of TraceME. We believe that by providing tool support for the method is feasible to implement TraceME in real world contexts.

## 7.2     The GREAT Process Modeller

It is a platform for business process modelling and information system' requirements specification focused to support software production and maintenance of excellence. Software crisis manifests in hard to manage projects, wasting time and money, and low-quality software, which does not satisfy customer requirements and is expensive to maintain.

The tool is **global**, covering the whole software development process (from system analysis and requirements specifications to code production and maintenance). It supports **reengineering** projects helping them in the adaptation of existing software assets to new environment needs. In addition, it supports agile development through

© Springer International Publishing AG, part of Springer Nature 2018
M. Ruiz: TraceME, LNBIP 312, pp. 271–277, 2018.
https://doi.org/10.1007/978-3-319-89716-5_7

**automated transformations** inside a model-driven method for software development.

Business architects, Software analysts, and all software development/maintenance concerned parties interested in the production and maintenance of quality software are the expected users of the tool.

**Fig. 131.** Presentation of the GREAT Process Modeller in Eclipse

**Tool method**

In this tool, we implement the *ca2oom* integration framework. The platform enables the agile analyses of business processes and let analysts and interviews' participants focus in the business activities, which brings new information to business, abstracting details that do not contribute to product development. It also shortens the development, or reengineering, time applying model transformation technologies that automate part of the system design. More details about the tool are given in [68].

This is achieved by the Communication Analysis method, which is comprised of several modelling techniques, namely *Communicative Event Diagrams*, *Message Structures* and *Event Specification Templates*, and a transformation engine. Transformations help in the process of changing the specification perspective of information system' requirements for the intended audience. The perspective is changed from:

   a)  the requirements specification perspective, for users that better perform focusing on the business activities and interactions to:
   b)  the system specification perspective (UML has been selected for the purpose), for users related to its development.

Thus, the methodo contributes to a better approach of software products specifications in which the most critical users (analysts, business architects, business modellers, etc) are able to specify the systems requirements at an appropiate perspective, and obtain the related UML specifcations automatically.

## Communicative Fvent Diagram modelling technique

The *Communicative Event Diagram* is a business process modelling technique that adopts a communicational perspective by focusing on communicative interactions when describing the organizational work practice, instead of focusing on physical activities[17]; at this abstraction level, we refer to business activities as communicative events.

## Message Structures modelling technique

*Message Structures* is a technique based on structured text that allows specifying the messages associated to communicative events.

## Event Specification Templates technique

*Event Specification Templates* are a means to organise the requirements concerning a communicative event.

## Transformation engine

Once the system requirements have been defined throughout the previous modelling techniques, the transformation engine switches the specification perspective to UML diagrams. The engine is sustained on several metamodels (Cametamodel[18], ecore, uml, tracer, todo) that provide the ability to automatically obtain UML diagrams from the modelled specifications, for example, using ATL[19] transformations.

The *Cametamodel* metamodel specifies the required and available entities for the definition of *Communicative Event* Diagrams, Message *Structures* and *Event Specification Templates*.

## 7.3 Plug-in for the GoBIS framework

Technological support for the GoBIS framework is necessary to carry out future case studies and facilitate industrial adoption. Although existing tools allow creating separate *i\** and CA models, we aim to support the combined modelling (See Fig. 132 with the combined modelling for the SuperStationery Co; the CA model in the right and the *i\** model in the left). The CE SALE 1 is aligned with the task PLACE ORDER.

---

[17] Physical activities such as "A warehouse worker piles up the boxes" where the client which may be relevant enough to model them, but always at a lower level of abstraction, using stepwise refinement mechanisms

[18] Cametamodel stands for CA (Communication Analysis) metamodel

[19] ATLAS Transformation Language

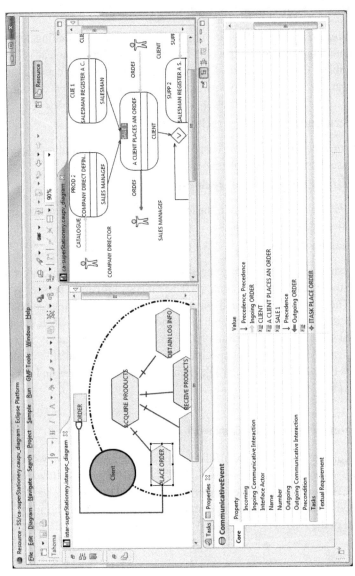

**Fig. 132.** Screenshot of the prototype: combined modelling of the *i*\* and CA for the Super-Stationery Co.

This prototype is created for the GoBIS framework. Currently it gives support to the *iStar2ca* guidelines and the *ca2oom* integration framework. Accordingly, analyst that apply the former mentioned method chunks, use this prototype in order to ensure the combined modelling of *i*\* and CA while keeping the traceability between both modelling languages.

We chose Eclipse (http://www.eclipse.org) as the technological platform. We used Eclipse Modelling Framework (http://www.eclipse.org/modeling/emf) and Graphical

Modelling Framework (GMF, http://www.eclipse.org/modeling/gmp) to implement the metamodels and modelling tools for each method. We have followed a Model-Driven Architecture (MDA) [104] approach to develop a tool for both methods. This way, method and language specifications of *i** and CA correspond to the Computation-Independent Model layer of MDA. The abstract syntax of both methods are represented by means of Platform-Independent Metamodels (PIMm), which correspond to the Platform-Independent Model layer of MDA. According to these PIMm, we have specified the Platform-Specific Metamodels (PSMm) that are compliant with Eclipse. This PSMm correspond to the Platform-Specific Model layer of MDA. Finally, we defined the concrete syntax of both languages (graphical and textual appearance). The implemented tools correspond to the Code Model layer of MDA.

Previous works present a PSMm for CA models that are compliant with GMF [68]. We adapted it based on the result of the metamodel integration in Section 4.3.2. With respect to *i**, there are several metamodels available. We analysed the PIMm presented in [129] and we opted to maintain most of its concepts, although it required some adaptations to account for the metamodel integration presented in Section 4.3.2 and to make it GMF-compliant. To design the PSM metamodel for *i**, we analysed three tool-oriented metamodels: the OpenOme metamodel [148], the metamodel presented by Giachetti [5], and the unified metamodel for *i** [171]. As a result, a combined modelling prototype is obtained with support for traceability link specification between CA and *i** modelling elements. See [126] for further information, screenshots, and technical details about the prototype.

The developed prototype helps the application of the *iStar2ca* guidelines (see Section 6) in the sense that after the manual application of the *iStar2ca* guidelines, the prototype makes traceability link specification possible among the modelling elements of *i** and CA. From a practitioner perspective, the prototype facilitates the analysis of explicit traceability links among modelling elements.

## 7.4 Plug-in the Delta Analysis technique

The specification of delta models and metrics could be a heavy task if no tool support is provided. We have performed an analysis of current tools to support model comparison and delta model specification. All the details about the design and development of the plug-in for delta analysis is available in the MSc thesis of Julio Sandobalín [172].

We build an Eclipse plug-in to offer a support to the analysis of the models comparison in evolution scenarios. The result of models comparison we derive delta models by making an instance of delta metamodel. A delta model has information about of the models comparison and with the help of delta operators (EQUAL, MODIFIED, ADDED, DELETED) specifies the kind of change between the elements of each model. Each element of a delta model has information about the traceability of evolution that suffered a system during reengineering. In this prototype, we implements horizontal traceability relationships among compared models.

To measure delta models, we implement the metrics to get a numerical value, which is used to quantify changes over the resulting model in the evolution process.

We have adapted EMF Compare[20] in order to make comparisons and obtain delta models. In Fig. 133 we present a snapshot of the tool after the comparison of two models. For this case, an evolution scenario is analysed; thus the pivot model is an *as-is* model and the satellite model is a *to-be*. The delta model is presented in the middle of *as-is* and *to-be* models with the name of *difference*. One basic metric was applied to know the equal elements, additions, modifications and simplifications. The results of the metrics are presented at the bottom of the snapshot.

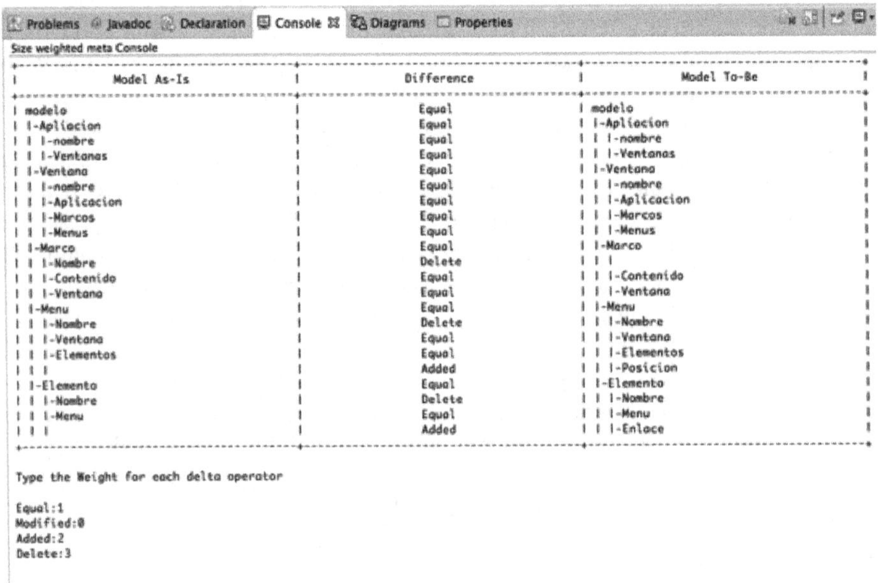

**Fig. 133.** Snapshot of the application of the tool: delta model generation and metrics results

## 7.5 Summary

The implementations of the prototypes let us to bring the gap between academy and industry. In MDD is very important to provide tool support in order to promote the application of methods and tools. For TraceME, we developed three prototypes: the GREAT Process Modeller, the plug-in for the GoBIS framework, and the plug-in for the Delta Analysis technique.

We applied Eclipse technologies since they have been applied successfully for supporting MDD methods and techniques. GREAT Process Modeller was used for analysing its sensitivity in a controlled group. The results present strong and weak points of the tool and the method, also end-users perceptions.

---

[20] http://www.obeo.fr/pages/acceleo-pro-compare/en

Further developments should be performed around these prototypes to make them more stable and usable. Currently, with these tools we evaluate that it is possible to realise the implementation of TraceME in real world conditions. The provision of tools for the TraceME chunks ensures the future execution of the engineering cycle to bring TraceME to industry.

# Chapter 8    Conclusions and open challenges

> *"The scientific man does not aim at an immediate result. He does not expect that his advanced ideas will be readily taken up... His duty is to lay the foundation for those who are to come, and point the way"* - Nikola Tesla

This book presents TraceME: a Traceability-based method for conceptual Model Evolution. Its general purpose is to support the evolution of information systems. By providing a set of four TraceME chunks, TraceME is situational-oriented. In this way, TraceME can be adapted to support different evolution projects just assembling the TraceME chunks. We provide how to use each method chunk and how to assemble them. Because of the development of this research project, various contributions can be highlighted. These contributions are the evidence about the achievement of the research goals, as well as the answers of the established research questions.

## 8.1    Wrap up: main contributions

The main contributions of this book are presented below:

**C1.** Establishment of the fundamentals for TraceME and information systems evolution in general (chapter 3)

We contributed with a theoretical framework to establish a common knowledge about information systems evolution and TraceME. In this chapter we defined the most important concepts to understand the method. In addition, some concepts were further defined in chapters 4 and 5. These concepts are related to the design of TraceME and TraceME chunks.

**C2.** Development of TraceME to support conceptual model evolution (chapter 4 and 5)

In this chapter we described a method engineering effort in order to design TraceME. For the specification of TraceME, we apply method-engineering techniques in order to describe the method, present the assembling strategies, describe each method chunk, and present how to use the method. For the design of each TraceME chunk we performed a hard method-engineering work since integration strategies were applied. Each TraceME chunk design is described in the chapter 4, also how we made decisions and the results. A summary describing the design is presented below:

We assume the *i\** language, the OO-Method and the Communication Analysis as methods chunks already available in TraceME. To provide forward strategies, we took the *i\** language, the OO-Method and the Communication Analysis method to create the *iStar2ca* guidelines chunk and the *ca2oom* integration chunk. To create the

M. Ruiz: TraceME, LNBIP 312, pp. 279–282, 2018.
https://doi.org/10.1007/978-3-319-89716-5_8

former method chunks we applied ontological integration strategies to formally define the guidelines and integration frameworks. For the *evolCA* procedure, we also used ontological integration strategies.

The Delta Analysis technique is method-independent. Thus it was no necessary to apply integrations strategies. Nevertheless its design is funded in related works and knowledge from relevant solutions in model management and traceability.

We want to clarify an important point for the chunks *iStar2ca* guidelines, *ca2oom* integration framework and *evolCA* procedure. Method engineering techniques provides facilities to make integrations "on the fly". It means that for TraceME, it would be possible just to provide the *i\** language, the Communication Analysis method and the OO-Method. Later, the integration strategies can be executed each time if needed. Nevertheless, we decided to make the effort of execute the integration strategies and provide new chunks. Our reasoning is based on the idea of "lightweight". If we provide a method easy to use, it would be easy to implement in the future.

**C3**. Empirical evidence about the feasibility of TraceME and stakeholders' perceptions (chapter 6)

Various laboratory demonstrations have been performed for each method chunk of TraceME. In a controlled laboratory environment, we tested each TraceME chunk and we evaluate it feasibility before to apply them in empirical tasks.

We performed a controlled experiment to validate the *iStar2ca* guidelines. The results were very positive for the chunk in the sense of subjects' performance and perceptions.

We performed a sensitivity validation of the *ca2oom* integration framework. In this evaluation, the subjects used GREAT in order to use the integration framework to model business process with Communication Analysis and further automatically obtain OO-Method object models. The results of the sensitivity analysis have shown that the integration framework is sensible to the Communication Analysis models given as input. Despite the modelling tool detects syntactic errors; the semantic is the responsibility of the analyst in charge to use the framework. A case study was further performed in SIVSA Spain, where analyst used GREAT for evolution by replacement strategies. They directly used the GREAT tool for obtaining the object models of a *to-be* system.

We performed a laboratory demonstration for the *evolCA* procedure to demonstrate it feasibility.

We had an action research experience with the Delta Analysis technique. We brought the Delta Analysis to everis Spain, a consulting company. We applied the Delta Analysis in order to review the evolution of an information system. The perceptions about the delta analysis are very positive. The delta analysis helped to the everis' stakeholders to rethink the evolution process and justify their decisions during the evolution project.

**C4.** Prototypes that implement the TraceME chunks increasing the opportunities to transfer TraceME to industry (chapter 7)

GREAT process modeller is a tool resulting of the work during this research project. It implements the *ca2oom* integration framework as well as the plug-in for the

GoBIS framework. This plug-in supports the *iStar2ca* guidelines and the *evolCA* procedure.

A plug-in for the Delta Analysis has been developed in order to support the delta model specification and metrics application.

We all learnt during the development of this research. We expanded our perspectives about the development of information systems by introducing evolution solutions. We made a step further by accepting that information systems development seldom start from scratch. As a result, we tackled new challenges and embraced new goals that took us to this current state. The PROS Research Centre is now offering solutions for forward and evolution software development while keeping the formalisms of the model-driven development paradigm and model-based engineering.

In summary, this book contributes with new knowledge and artefacts to the requirements engineering field and model-driven development. The evidence based on the empirical validations and tool development; point out the road map to bring this method to industrial settings.

## 8.2 Open challenges

We have a strong commitment to achieve the goals of this research project. This research project is far from perfect and various tasks need to be performed. Moreover, we conducted the design science cycle for this research successfully. The results obtained for each task of the research method let us to achieve our main research goals and to answer the established knowledge questions. We aspire to perform the complete engineering cycle (by including the implementation phase to bring TraceME to the market). We acknowledge that in order to bring TraceME to industry, several design and empirical cycles should be performed. We are pursuing this goal and we are willing (and happy) to continue working on this fascinating research project.

We envision some challenges in the research line of conceptual model evolution and traceability. We plan a set of short and long-term projects for our research agenda.

### *Short term projects*
- Technical action research experiences should be performed with two method chunks (the *iStar2ca* guidelines and *ca2oom* integration framework). Our experience with the technical action research for the Delta Analysis technique teach us how important is to involve end users in the design cycle. Several challenges should be confronted, for example, the company should provide their goals and business process specifications by using the *i\** language and Communication Analysis method. In this point, our role as main researchers is very important to give to know the modelling method (if necessary) and support all the implementation process for the *iStar2ca* guidelines and *ca2oom* integration framework.
- Delta Analysis technique needs to be applied in various evolution engineering projects to increase the interpretations repository. With a certain amount of information in the interpretations repository, Delta Analysis technique would provide

automatic interpretations and suggestions about the evolution process to analysts. We think this method chunk is very attractive and industry can take it advantages when evolving information systems.

- For TraceME we develop a tool, the GREAT Process Modeller. GREAT implements the *ca2oom* integration framework for Communication Analysis and OO-Method. Also it involves a plug-in that support the GoBIS framework, this plug-in facilitates the combined modelling for *i** language and Communication Analysis models. The support for GoBIS allows the implementation of the *iStar2ca* guidelines and the *evolCA* procedure. In this line, it is necessary to provide a wizard that guides the GREAT's user when applying the *iStar2ca* guidelines as well as the *evolCA* procedure.

- A prototype for the Delta Analysis technique was developed supporting the automatic generation of delta models and metrics application. In this line of work various adjustments are necessary: a) it is necessary to extend the solutions of the tool. Currently it is possible to compare object models. We want to offer tool support to make comparisons of any kind of model; b) it is important to offer a graphical representation of delta models, it would facilitate the analysis and further interpretations; c) the interpretations repository should be supported in the tool, in this way, users of the tool can register all their interpretations to make it grow. This line of work is vital to bring Delta Analysis to industry and perform various empirical evaluations before its implementation. In addition, it is necessary to involve the plug-in for the Delta Analysis in GREAT.

- It is necessary to develop a plug-in for TraceME. In this sense, we want to develop a tool to manage evolution projects, chunks assembling, and their application. This plug-in would be part of the solutions offered by GREAT.

### *Long-term projects*
- Increase the evolution solutions of TraceME. For example, methodological evolution is a very interesting and attractive method chunk to involve in TraceME. Methodological evolution is a huge challenge to confront.

- Involve reverse engineering solutions. Certain information systems evolution projects do not have model specifications. TraceME is model-oriented, thus it is necessary to offer solutions for evolution projects without model specifications.

- Perform controlled experiments to evaluate the sensitivity of TraceME and stakeholders' perceptions. Controlled experiments are the precursor of case studies.

- Perform a case study with TraceME. To reduce the gap between TraceME and industry, it is important to perform a case study and learn about the experience. We are confident that after a case study experience it would be possible to implement TraceME in real world scenarios.

# References

1. Koskinen, J., *Software Maintenance Costs.* 2003, Information Technology Research Institute, ELTIS-project, University of Jyväskylä: JyväsKylä, Finland.
2. Pastor, O., *Diseño y Desarrollo de un Entorno de Producción Automática de Software basado en el Modelo Orientado a Objetos*, in *Departamento de Sistemas Informáticos y Computación (DSIC).* 1992, Universitat Politècnica de València: Valencia.
3. Panach, I., *Incorporación de mecanismos de usabilidad en un entorno de producción de software dirigido por modelos* , in *Departamento de Sistemas Informáticos y Computación (DSIC).* 2010, Universitat Politècnica de València: Valencia.
4. Valverde, F., *OOWS 2.0: Un método de ingenería web dirigido por modelos para la producción de aplicaciones web 2.0*, in *Departamento de Sistemas Informáticos y Computación (DSIC).* 2010, Universitat Politècnica de València: Valencia.
5. Giachetti, G., *Supporting Automatic Interoperability in Model Driven Development Processes*, in *Departamento de Sistemas Informáticos y Computación (DSIC).* 2011, Universitat Politècnica de València: Valencia, Spain.
6. de la Vara, J.L., *Business Process-Based Requirements Specification and Object-Oriented Conceptual Modelling of Information Systems*, in *Departamento de Sistemas Informáticos y Computación (DSIC).* 2011, Universitat Poliècnica de València: Valencia, Spain.
7. España, S., *Methodological integration of Communication Analysis into a Model-Driven software development framework*, in *Departamento de Sistemas Informáticos y Computación (DSIC).* 2011, Universitat Politècnica de València: Valencia.
8. Cervera, M., *A Model-Driven Approach for the Design, Implementation, and Execution of Software Development Methods*, in *Departamento de Sistemas Informáticos y Computación.* 2015, Universitat Politècnica de València: Valencia, Spain.
9. Whittle, J., J. Hutchinson, and M. Rouncefield, *The State of Practice in Model-Driven Engineering.* IEEE Software, 2014. **31**: p. 79-85.
10. Hutchinson, J., M. Rouncefield, and J. Whittle, *Model-driven engineering practices in industry*, in *nternational Conference on Software Engineering (ICSE 2011).* 2011. p. 633 - 642.
11. Panach, I., et al., *In search of evidence for model-driven development claims: An experiment on quality, effort, productivity and satisfaction.* Information and Software Technology, 2015. **62**: p. 164-186.
12. Selic, B., *The pragmatics of Model-Driven Development.* IEEE Software, 2003: p. 19-25.
13. OMG. *Architecture-Driven Modernization (ADM).* 2012; Available from: http://adm.omg.org/.
14. Grau, G., X. Franch, and N. Maiden, *A Goal-Based Round-Trip Method for System Development*, in *Requirements Engineering For Software Quality (REFSQ 2005).* 2005: Essen, Germany.
15. Olivé, A., *Conceptual Schema-Centric Development: A grand Challenge for Information Systems Research*, in *17th International Conference on Advanced Information Systems Engineering (CAiSE 2005).* 2005: Porto, Portugal.

16. Ramesh, B., *Towards Reference Models for Requirements Traceability.* IEEE Transactions on Software Engineering, 2001. **27**(1): p. 58-92.

17. Pohl, K., *Process-Centered Requirements Engineering*, in *Advanced software development series.* 1996, Wiley & Sons

18. Ramesh, B., et al., *Implementing requirements traceability. A case study.* Annals of Software Engineering, 1997. **3**: p. 397-415.

19. Winkler, S. and J.v. Pilgrim, *A survey of traceability in requirements engineering and model-driven development.* Software Systems and Models, 2009: p. 529-565.

20. Alexander, I., *Towards automatic traceability in industrial practice*, in *1st International Workshop on Traceability in Emerging Forms of Software Engineering (TEFSE '02.* 2002.

21. Wieringa, R., *Design Science Methodology for Information Systems and Software Engineering.* 2014: Springer-Verlag Berlin Heidelberg.

22. Martin, M.J.C., *Managing Innovation and Entrepreneurship in Technology-Based Firms*, ed. I.T.O.E. MANAGEMENT. Vol. 43. 1996.

23. Finkelstein, A., *Requirements and Relationships: A Foreword*, in *Software and Systems Traceability*, J. Cleland-Huang, O. Gotel, and A. Zisman, Editors. 2012, Springer, London.

24. Ramesh, B., et al., *Implementing requirements traceability: a case study*, in *Requirements Engineering (RE'95).* 1995. p. 89-35.

25. Mäder, P. and O. Gotel, *Ready-to-Use Traceability on Evolving Projects*, in *Software and Systems Traceability*, J. Cleland-Huang, O. Gotel, and A. Zisman, Editors. 2012, Springer London.

26. Cleland-Huang, J., C. Chang, and G. Yujia, *Supporting Event based traceability thorugh High level recognition of change events*, in *26th Annual International Computer Software and Applications Conference (COMPSAC'02).* 2002.

27. Engels, G., et al., *Consistency-Preserving Model Evolution through Transformations*, in *Fifth International Conference on the Unified Modeling Language – The Language and its Applications (UML 2002).* 2002.

28. Engels, G., R. Heckel, and J. Küster, *Rule-based specification of behavioral consistency based on the UML meta-model*, in *4th International Conference UML 2001 - The Unified Modeling Language. Modeling Languages, Concepts, and Tools.* 2001, Springer: Toronto, Canada. p. 272-287.

29. Engels, G., et al., *A methodology for specifying and analyzing consistency of object-oriented behavioral models*, in *8th European software engineering conference held jointly with 9th ACM SIGSOFT international symposium on Foundations of software engineering.* 2001. p. 186-195.

30. Hnatkowska, B., Z. Huzar, and L. Tuzinkiewicz, *Refinement of UML collaborations.* International Journal of Applied Mathematics and Computer Sciences, 2006. **16**(1): p. 155-164.

31. Mens, T., R. Van Der Straeten, and J. Simmonds, *A Framework for Managing Consistency of Evolving UML Models*, in *Software Evolution with UML and XML.* 2005, IGI Global, 2005. p. 1-30.

32. Cleland-Huang, J., *Traceability in agile projects*, in *Software and Systems Traceability.* 2002. p. 265-275.

33. Mens, T. and S. Demeyer, *Future Trends in Software Evolution Metrics*, in *IWPSE'02.* 2002: Vienna, Austria. p. 83-86.

34. Gall, H., K. Hajek, and M. Jazayeri, *Detection of Logical Coupling Based on Product Release History*, in *International Conference on Software Maintenace.* 1998. p. 190-198.

35. Lehman, M., *Programs, cities, students: Limits to growth?* 1974, Imperial College of Science and Technology: London, UK.

36. Lehman, M., et al., *Metrics and Laws of Software Evolution - The Nineties View*, in *4th international symposium on Software Metrics*. 1997: Albuquerque, New Mexico. p. 20-32.
37. Fernandez-Ramil, J. and M. Lehman, *Metrics of software evolution as effort predictors - a case study*, in *International Conference on Software Maintenance*. 2000: San Jose, CA. p. 163-172.
38. Lehman, M. and J. Fernandez-Ramil, *Software Evolution*, in *Software evolution and feedback*, N. Madhavji, J. Fernandez-Ramil, and D. Perry, Editors. 2006, Wiley.
39. Omote, H., et al. *Software Evolution Support Using Traceability Link between UML diagrams*. in *Sixth Joint Conference on Knowledge-Based Software Engineering*. 2004. Protvino, Russia: IOS, Press.
40. Didonet Del Fabro, M., et al., *AMW: A Generic Model Weaver*, in *Premières Journées sur l'Ingénierie Dirigée par les Modèles (IDM'05)*. 2005: París, France.
41. Jablonski, S., B. Volz, and S. Dornstauder, *Evolution of Business Process Models and Languages*, in *2nd International Conference on Business Process and Services Computing (BPSC)*. 2009: Leipzig, Germany.
42. Rahn, E. and P.A. Bernstein, *A survey of approaches to automatic schema matching.* VLDB 2001. **10**: p. 334-350.
43. Madhavan, J., P.A. Bernstein, and E. Rahn, *Generic Schema Matching with Cupid*, in *27 th International Conference on Very Large Data Bases (VLDB 2001)*. 2001: Roma, Italy.
44. Bernstein, P.A., A.Y. Halevy, and R.A. Pottinger, *A Vision for Management of Complex Models.* ACM SIGMOND, 2000. **29**(4): p. 55-63.
45. Bernstein, P.A. *Applying Model Management to Classical Meta Data Problems.* in *First Biennial Conference on Innovative Data Systems Research (CIDR 2003)*. 2003. Asilomar.
46. Bernstein, P.A. *Applying Model Management to Classical Meta Data Problems.* in *First Biennial Conference on Innovative Data Systems Research*. 2003. Asilomar, CA.
47. Andersson, B., et al., *Towards a formal definition of goal-oriented business process patterns.* Business Process Management Journal, 2005. **11**(6): p. 650-662.
48. Guizzardi, R.S.S., et al., *Bridging the Gap between Goals, Agents and Business Processes*, in *Fourth International i\* Workshop*. 2010: Hammamet, Tunisia.
49. Cardoso, E., et al., *A Method for Eliciting Goals for Business Process Models based on Non-Functional Requirements Catalogues.* International Journal of Information System Modeling and Design (IJISMD), 2011. **2**(2).
50. Soffer, P. and Y. Wand, *On the notion of soft-goals in business process modeling.* Business Process Management Journal, 2005. **11**(6): p. 663-679.
51. Kueng, P. and P. Kawalek, *Goal-based business process models: creation and evaluation.* Business Process Management Journal, 1997. **3**(1): p. 17-38.
52. Kavakli, V. and P. Loucopoulos, *Goal-driven business process analysis application in electricity deregulation.* Information Systems, 1999. **24**(3): p. 187-207.
53. Leonardi, M.C. and R. Giandini, *Una estrategia de integración de Modelos de Objetivos con Análisis Comunicacional* in *16th Workshop on Requirements Engineering*. 2013: Montevideo, Uruguay.
54. Yu, E. and J. Mylopoulos, *From E-R to "A-R" - Modelling strategic actor relationships for business process reengineering*, in *Proceedings of the 13th International Conference on the Entity-Relationship Approach*. 1994, Springer-Verlag: Manchester. p. 548-565.
55. Yu, E., *Modelling Strategic Relationships for Process Reengineering*, in *Department of Computer Science*. 1995, University of Toronto.
56. Koliadis, G. and A. Ghose, *Relating business process models to goal-oriented requirements models in KAOS*, in *Advances in Knowledge Acquisition and Management*, A. Hoffmann, et al., Editors. 2006, Springer: Berlin. p. 25-39.

57. Morrison, E.D., et al., *Strategic alignment of business processes*, in *7th International Workshop on Engineering Service-Oriented Applications.* 2011: Paphos, Cyprus.

58. Lapouchnian, A., Y. Yu, and J. Mylopoulos, *Requirements-driven design and configuration management of business processes*, in *5th international conference on Business process management BPM'07*, Springer, Editor. 2007. p. 246-261.

59. Ghose, A., et al., *Goal-Driven Business Process Derivation*, in *9th International Conference on Service Oriented Computing, ICSOC 2011.* 2011, Springer: Paphos, Cyprus. p. 467-476.

60. Kazhamiakin, R., M. Pistore, and M. Roveri, *A framework for integrating business processes and business requirements*, in *Enterprise Distributed Object Computing Conference EDOC'04.* 2004, IEEE. p. 9-20.

61. Ulrich, F., *Multi-perspective enterprise modeling: foundational concepts, prospects and future research challenges.* Software and Systems Modeling, 2012. **13**(3): p. 941-962.

62. Salinesi, C., A. Etien, and I. Zoukar, *A Systematic Approach to Express IS Evolution Requirements Using Gap Modelling and Similarity Modelling Techniques*, in *16th International Conference, CAiSE 2004*, A. Persson and J. Stirna, Editors. 2004: Riga, Latvia. p. 339-352.

63. Rolland, C., C. Salinesi, and A. Etien, *Eliciting gaps in requirements change.* Requirements Engineering, 2004. **9**: p. 1-15.

64. Etien, A. and C. Rolland, *Measuring the fitness relationship.* Requirements Engineering, 2005. **10**: p. 184-197.

65. Ruiz, M., *A model-driven framework to integrate Communication Analysis and OO-Method*, in *Departamento de Sistemas Informáticos y Computación (DSIC).* 2011, Universitat Politècnica de València: València.

66. España, S., A. González, and Ó. Pastor, *Communication Analysis: a requirements engineering method for information systems*, in *21st International Conference on Advanced Information Systems (CAiSE'09).* 2009, Springer LNCS 5565: Amsterdam, The Netherlands. p. 530-545.

67. Pastor, O. and J.C. Molina, *Model-Driven Architecture in practice: a software production environment based on conceptual modeling.* 2007, New York: Springer. 302.

68. Ruiz, M., *A model-driven framework to integrate Communication Analysis and OO-Method*, in *Departamento de Sistemas Informáticos y Computación (DSIC).* 2011, Universitat Politècnica de València: Valencia.

69. OMG, h.w.o.o.m. *MDA - The archiecture of choice for a changing world.* Consulted on July of 2015; Available from: http://www.omg.org/mda/.

70. Pastor, O., S. España, and A. Gonzalez, *An Ontological-Based Approach to Analyze Software Production Methods*, in *United Information Systems Conference (UNISCON 2008)*, R.K.e. al, Editor. 2008, Springer-Verlag: Klagenfurt, Austria. p. 258-270.

71. Ruiz, M., et al., *Análisis de Comunicaciones como un enfoque de requisitos para el desarrollo dirigido por modelos*, in *VII Taller sobre Desarrollo de Software Dirigido por Modelos (DSDM 2010), Jornadas de Ingeniería de Software y Bases de Datos (JISBD)* O. Avila-García, et al., Editors. 2010: Valencia, España. p. 70-77.

72. Embley, D.W., S.W. Liddle, and O. Pastor, *Conceptual-model programming: a manifesto*, in *Handbook Of Conceptual Modeling*, D.W. Embley and B. Thalheim, Editors. 2011, Springer. p. 3-16.

73. OMG. *MDA Guide Version 1.0.1.* 2003 [cited 2008 12-2010]; Available from: http://www.omg.org/docs/omg/03-06-01.pdf.

74. Morgan, T., *Business rules and information systems - Aligning IT with business goals.* 2002: Addison-Wesley.

75. Olivé, A., *Conceptual Schema-Centric Development: a grand challenge for information systems research*, in *16th Conference on Advanced Information Systems Engineering*, Ó. Pastor and J.F.e. Cunha, Editors. 2005, Lecture Notes in Computer Science vol 3520, Springer-Verlag: Porto, Portugal. p. 1-15.

76. Loniewski, G., E. Insfran, and S. Abrahão, *A systematic review of the use of requirements engineering techniques in model-driven development*, in *Model driven engineering languages and systems*, D. Petriu, N. Rouquette, and Ø. Haugen, Editors. 2010, Springer. p. 213-227.

77. Pastor, Ó., et al., *The OO-method approach for information systems modeling: from object-oriented conceptual modeling to automated programming*. Information Systems, 2001. **26**(7): p. 507-534.

78. Langefors, B., *Theoretical analysis of information systems (4th ed)*. 1977, Lund, Sweden: Studentlitteratur.

79. González, A., S. España, and Ó. Pastor, *Unity criteria for Business Process Modelling: A theoretical argumentation for a Software Engineering recurrent problem.*, in *Third International Conference on Research Challenges in Information Science (RCIS 2009)*. 2009, IEEE: Fes, Morocco. p. 173-182.

80. España, S., et al., *Evaluating the completeness and granularity of functional requirements specifications: a controlled experiment*, in *17th IEEE International Requirements Engineering Conference (RE'09)*. 2009, IEEE: Atlanta, Georgia, USA. p. 161-170.

81. González, A., et al., *Message Structures: a modelling technique for information systems analysis and design*, in *14th Workshop on Requirements Engineering (WER 2011)*, M. Lencastre and H. Estrada, Editors. 2011: Rio de Janeiro, Brazil, extended version in English and Spanish available at http://arxiv.org/abs/1101.5341.

82. González, A., *Algunas consideraciones sobre el uso de la abstracción en el análisis de los sistemas de información de gestión (PhD thesis) Some considerations on the use of abstraction in management information systems analysis (in Spanish)*, in *Departamento de Sistemas Informáticos y Computación*. 2004, Universidad Politécnica de Valencia: Valencia.

83. Ruiz, M., et al., *Análisis de Comunicaciones como un enfoque de requisitos para el desarrollo dirigido por modelos*, in *VII Taller sobre Desarrollo de Software Dirigido por Modelos (DSDM 2010), Jornadas de Ingeniería de Software y Bases de Datos (JISBD)* O. Avila-García, et al., Editors. 2010: Valencia, España. p. 70-77.

84. Panach, I., et al., *Dealing with usability in model transformation technologies*, in *27th International Conference on Conceptual Modeling (ER 2008)*, Q. Li, et al., Editors. 2008: Barcelona, Spain. p. 498-511.

85. Valverde, F. and O. Pastor, *Facing the technological challenges of Web 2.0: a RIA model-driven engineering approach*, in *10th International Conference on Web Information Systems Engineering (WISE 2009)*. 2009: Poznan, Poland. p. 131-144.

86. Aquino, N., J. Vanderdonckt, and O. Pastor, *Transformation templates: adding flexibility to model-driven engineering of user interfaces*, in *25th ACM Symposium on Applied Computing (SAC 2010)*, S.Y. Shin, et al., Editors. 2010: Sierre, Switzerland. p. 1195-1202.

87. González, A., et al., *Systematic derivation of class diagrams from communication-oriented business process models*, in *12th Working Conference on Business Process Modeling, Development, and Support (BPMDS'11)*, T.A. Halpin, et al., Editors. 2011, Springer LNBIP: London, United Kingdom. p. 246-260.

88. España, S., et al., *Systematic derivation of state machines from communication-oriented business process models*, in *IEEE Fifth International Conference on Research Challenges*

*in Information Science (RCIS 2011)*. 2011, IEEE: Guadeloupe - French West Indies, France.

89. Cardoso, E., et al., *A method for eliciting goals for business process models based on non-functional requirements catalogues*. International Journal of Information System Modeling and Design, 2011. **2**(2): p. 1-18.

90. Kazman, R., S.G. Woods, and J.S. Carrière, *Requirements for Integrating Software Architecture and Reengineering Models: CORUM II*, in *Working Conference on Reverse Engineering (WCRE 1998)*. 1998.

91. Sánchez Cuadrado, J., et al., *Parametrización de las transformaciones horizontales en el modelo de herradura*, in *Jornadas de Ingeniería de Software y Bases de Datos (JISBD'12)*. 2012: Almería, Spain.

92. Kavakli, E. and P. Loucopoulos, *Goal Driven Requirements Engineering: Evaluation of Current Methods*, in *Exploring Modelling Methods for Systems Analysis and Design (EMMSAD 2003)*. 2003: Klagenfurt/ Austria.

93. Etien, A. and C. Salinesi. *Managing requirements in a co-evolution context*. in *Requirements Engineering (RE 2005)*. 2005. Paris, France.

94. Herrmann, A., A. Wallnöfer, and B. Paech, *Specifying changes only - a case study on delta requirements*, in *REFSQ 2009*. 2009, Springer-Verlag: Essen, Germany. p. 45-58.

95. Salinesi, C., A. Etien, and I. Zoukar, *A systematic approach to express IS evolution requirements using gap modelling and symilarity modelling techniques*, in *International Conference on Advanced Information Systems Engineering (CAiSE'05)*. 2005: Porto, Portugal.

96. Etien, A. and C. Rolland, *Measuring the fitness relationship*. Requirements Engineering Journal, 2005(10): p. 184-197.

97. Falkenberg, E., et al., *FRISCO: A framework of information system concepts*. 1998: IFIP WG 8.1.

98. Guizzardi, G., *On a unified foundational ontology and some applications of it in business modeling*, in *Ontologies and business systems analysis*, M. Rosemann and P. Green, Editors. 2005, IDEA Publisher.

99. Guizzardi, G. and G. Wagner, *A Unified Foundational Ontology and some Applications of it in Business Modeling*, in *CAiSE Workshops 2004*. 2004. p. 129-143.

100. Nuseibeh, B. and S. Easterbrook, *Requirements engineering: a roadmap*, in *Conference on The Future of Software Engineering (ICSE'00)*. 2000: New York, USA.

101. Mylopoulos, J., *Conceptual Modelin and Telos*, in *Conceptual Modeling, Databases, and CASE*. 1992, Wiley. p. 49-68.

102. den Haan, J., *The Enterprise Architect, Building an agile enterprise*, in *MDE - Model Driven Engineering - reference guide*, J.d. Haan, Editor. 2009.

103. Gotel, O. and A. Finkelstein. *An analysis of the requirements traceability problem*. in *International Conference on Requirements Engineering*. 1994. Colorado Springs.

104. OMG, *MDA Guide*, in *How is MDA used?* 2003, OMG. p. 1-62.

105. Goldkuhl, G., M. Lind, and U. Seigerroth, *Method integration: the need for a learning perspective*. Software IEE Proceedings, 1998. **145**(4): p. 113-118.

106. Hammer, M. and J. Champy, *Reengineering the Corporation: A Manifesto for Business Revolution*. 1993, New York.

107. Arnold, R.S., *Software Reengineering*. 1992: IEEE Press.

108. Chikofsky, E.J. and J.H. Cross II, *Reverse Engineering and Design Recovery: A Taxonomy*. IEEE Software, 1990. **7**(1).

109. Mayer, R.J. and P.S. Dewitte, *Delivering Results: Evolving BPR from art to engineering*, in *Business Process Engineering: Advancing the State of the Art*, D.J. Elzinga, T.R. Gulledge, and C.-Y. Lee, Editors. 1998.

110. Muthu, S., L. Whitman, and H.S. Cheraghi. *Business Process Reengineering: A Consolidated Methodology*. in *The 4th Annual International Conference of Industrian Engineering Theory, Applications and Practice*. 1999.

111. Bruneliere, H., et al. *MoDisco: a generic and extensible framework for model driven reverse engineering*. in *IEEE/ACM international conference on Automated software engineering (ASE'10)*. 2010. ACM.

112. González, A., et al., *Message Structures a modelling technique for information systems analysis and design*, in *XIV Workshop on Requirements Engineering (WER'11)*, M. Lencastre, H. Estrada Esquivel, and E. Figueiredo, Editors. 2011: Rio de Janeiro - Brasil. p. 407-418.

113. Gonzalez, A., S. España, and O. Pastor, *Unity criteria for business process modelling: A theoretical argumentation for a software engineering recurrent problem.*, in *Third International Conference on Research Challenges in Information Science (RCIS 2009)*. 2009, IEEE: Fes, Morocco. p. 173-182.

114. Hammer, M. and J. Champy, *Reengineering the corporation: a manifesto for business revolution (revised)*. 2003, New York: HarperCollins.

115. Henderson, J.C. and N. Venkatraman, *Strategic alignment: leveraging information Technology for transforming organizations*. IBM Syst. J., 1999. **38**(2-3): p. 472-484.

116. Zikra, I., J. Stirna, and J. Zdravkovic, *Bringing enterprise modeling closer to model-driven development*, in *The Practice of Enterprise Modeling*, P. Johannesson, J. Krogstie, and A.L. Opdahl, Editors. 2011, Springer LNBIP. p. 268-282.

117. Guizzardi, R., Nunes, Ariane, *A Method to Align Goals and Business Processes*, in *34th International Conference, ER 2015*, P. Johannesson, et al., Editors. 2015: Stockholm, Sweden. p. 79-93.

118. Cardoso, E.C.S., R.S.S. Guizzardi, and J.P.A. Almeida, *Aligning goal analysis and business process modelling: a case study in health care*. International Journal of Business Process Integration and Management, 2011. **5**(2): p. 144-158.

119. Wieringa, R., *Design science as nested problem solving*, in *4th International Conference on Design Science Research in Information Systems and Technology*. 2009, ACM: Philadelphia, Pennsylvania. p. 1-12.

120. Ralyté, J. and C. Rolland, *An assembly process model for method engineering*, in *13th International Conference, CAiSE 2001*, K. Dittrich, A. Geppert, and M. Norrie, Editors. 2001: Interlaken, Switzerland. p. 267-283.

121. Guizzardi, R.S.S. and G. Guizzardi, *Applying the UFO Ontology to Design an Agent-Oriented Engineering Language*, in *14th East European Conference, ADBIS 2010*. 2010: Novi Sad, Serbia. p. 190-203.

122. Guizzardi, R.S.S., *Agent-oriented Constructivist Knowledge Management*. 2006, University of Twente: The Netherlands.

123. Bresciani, P., et al., *Tropos: An Agent-Oriented Software Development Methodology*. Autonomous Agents and Multi-Agent Systems 2004. **8**(3): p. 203-236.

124. Wagner, G., *The Agent–Object-Relationship metamodel: towards a unified view of state and behavior*. Information Systems, 2003. **28**(5): p. 475-504.

125. España, S., *Methodological integration of Communication Analysis into a model-driven software development framework*, in *Research Centre in Software Production Methods (ProS)*. 2011, Universitat Politècnica de València: Spain.

126. Costal, D., et al., *Integration of i\* and Communication Analysis*. 2013, GESSI - Universitat Politècnica de Catalunya (UPC) & PROS - Universitat Politècnica de València (UPV).

127. Ruiz, M., et al., *Integrating the Goal and Business Process Perspectives in Information System Analysis*, in *26th International Conference on Advanced Information Systems Engineering (CAiSE 2014)*. 2014, Springer: Thessaloniki, Greece. p. 332-346.

128. Opdahl, A., B. Henderson-Sellers, and F. Barbier, *An Ontological Evaluation of the OML Metamodel*, in *IFIP TC8/WG8.1 International Conference on Information System Concepts: An Integrated Discipline Emerging (ISCO-4)*. 1999. p. 217-232.

129. Lopez, L., X. Franch, and J. Marco, *Making Explicit Some Implicit i\* Language Decisions*, in *30th International Conference on Conceptual Modeling (ER 2011)*. 2011: Brussels, Belgium. p. 62-77.

130. Alexander, C., S. Shikawa, and M. Silverstein, *A Pattern Language: Towns, Buildings, Construction*. 1997: Oxford University Press.

131. Gamma, E., et al., *Design Patterns. Elements of Reusable Object-Oriented Software*. 1994.

132. Pfiser, F., et al., *A Design Pattern Meta Model for Systems Engineering*, in *18th International Federation of Automatic Control (IFAC 2011)*. 2011. p. 11967-11972.

133. Jouault, F. *Loosely Coupled Traceability for ATL*. in *In Proceedings of the European Conference on Model Driven Architecture (ECMDA) workshop on traceability*. 2005.

134. OMG. *Unified Modeling Language v1.5*. 2003 [cited 2005 12-2005]; Available from: http://www.omg.org/cgi-bin/doc?formal/03-03-01.

135. España, S., et al., *Rules for the manual derivation of the Conceptual Model*, in *ProS-TR-2011-10*. 2011, ProS Research Centre, Universitat Poliècnica de València: València, Spain. p. 38.

136. España, S., in *Departamento de Sistemas Iformáticos y Computación (DSIC)*. 2011, Universitat Politècnica de València: Valencia.

137. España, S., *Methodological integration of Communbication Analysis into a Model-Driven software development framework*, in *Departamento de Sistemas Iformáticos y Computación (DSIC)*. 2011, Universitat Politècnica de València: Valencia.

138. España, S., et al., *Integration of Communication Analysis and the OO-Method: Manual derivation of the conceptual model. The SuperStationery Co. lab demo*, in *ProS-TR-2011-01*. 2011.

139. Budinsky, F., et al., *Eclipse Modeling Framework: A Developer's Guide*. 2003: Addison-Wesley Professional. 720.

140. van der Aalst, W.M.P., *Business alignment: using process mining as a tool for Delta analysis and conformance testing*. Requirements Engineering, 2005. **10**(3): p. 198-211.

141. Clarke, D., M. Helvensteijn, and I. Schaefer, *Abstract delta modeling*, in *Generative Programming and Component Engineering (GPCE'10)*. 2010: Eindhoven, The Netherlands.

142. van der Aalst, W.M.P. and T. Basten, *Identifying Commonalities and Differences in Object Life Cycles Using Behavioral Inheritance*, in *Applications and Theory of Petri Nets*, J.-M. Colom and M. Koutny, Editors. 2001, Springer Berlin Heidelberg. p. 32-52.

143. van der Aalst, W.M.P., *Exterminating the Dynamic Change Bug: A Concrete Approach to Support Workflow Change*. Information Systems Frontiers, 2001. **3**(3): p. 297-317.

144. OMG. *Object Management Group - Business Process Model and Notation*. Consulted on May, 2015; Available from: http://www.bpmn.org.

145. OMG. *Object Management Group - Unified Modelling Language*. Consulted on May, 2015; Available from: http://www.uml.org.

146. Herrmann, A., A. Wallnöfer, and B. Paech, *Specifying Changes Only - A Case Study on Delta Requirements*, in *Requirements Engineering For Software Quality (REFSQ 2009)*. 2009, Springer: Essen, Germany. p. 45-58.

147. Horkoff, J. and E. Yu, *Analyzing Goal Models - Different Approaches and how to choose among them*, in *SAC'11*. 2011, ACM: TaiChung, Taiwan.

148. OpenOme. *OpenOME, an open-source requirements engineering tool*. Available from: https://se.cs.toronto.edu/trac/ome/.

149. 149. España, S., et al., *Communication Analysis modelling techniques*. 2012.

150. OpenOme. Available from: https://se.cs.toronto.edu/trac/ome/wiki.

151. Wohlin, C., et al., *Experimentation in Software Engineering*. 2004: Springer.

152. Jedlitschka, A. and D. Pfahl, *Reporting guidelines for controlled experiments in software engineering*, in *4th International Symposium on Empirical Software Engineering*. 2005, IEEE: Queensland, Australia

153. Juristo, N. and A. Moreno, *Basics of Software Engineering Experimentation*. 2001: Springer.

154. Basili, V.R., G. Caldiera, and H.D. Rombach, *Goal Question Metric Paradigm*, in *Encyclopedia of Software Engineering* 1994.

155. Moody, D.L., *The Method Evaluation Model: A Theoretical Model for Validating Information Systems Design Methods*, in *The 11th European Conference on Information Systems, ECIS 2003*. 2003: Naples, Italy.

156. Lindland, O.I., G. Sindre, and A. Solvberg, *Understanding quality in conceptual modeling*. IEEE Software, 1994. **11**(2): p. 42-49.

157. Ruiz, M., et al. *Validation of the iStar2ca guidelines: variables, hypotheses, instrumentation and statistical results*. 2015; Available from: http://upcommons.upc.edu/handle/2117/27746.

158. Robson, C., *Real World Research: A Resource for Social Scientists and Practitioners-Researchers*. 2 ed. 2002: Blackwell, Oxford/Madden.

159. Ruiz, M., et al., *Appendix: Gobis - An integrated framework to analyse the Goal and Business process perspectives in Information Systems*, in *Appendix*. 2014, PROS - Universitat Politècnica de València (UPV) & GESSI - Universitat Politècnica de Catalunya (UPC).

160. Miles, M.B. and A.M. Huberman, *Qualitative Data Analysis*. 2 ed. 1994: SAGE publications.

161. Runeson, P., *Using students as experiment subjects - an analysis on graduate and freshmen student data*, in *7th International Conference on Empirical Assessment & Evaluation in Software Engineering (EASE)*. 2003, Keele University: Staffordshire, UK. p. 95-102.

162. Wieringa, R. and A. Morali, *Technical Action Research as a Validation Method in Information Systems Design Science*, in *DESRIST 2012*. 2012. p. 220 - 238.

163. Card, S., A. Newell, and T. Moran, *The Psychology of Human-Computer Interaction*. 1983.

164. Stirna, J., et al., *Capability Driven Development - An approach to Support Evolving Organizations*, in *Practices on the Enterprise Modelling PoEM 2012*. 2012.

165. Orne, M., *Demand characteristics and the concept of quasi-controls*. Artifact in behavioral research, New York: Academic Press, 1969.

166. Rosenhan, D., *The conditions and concept of evaluation apprehension*. Artifact in behavioral research. New York: Academic Press, 1969.

167. Basili, V.R., *Evolving and packaging reading technologies*. Journal of systems and software, 1997. **38**(1): p. 3-12.

168. Lindland, O., G. Sindre, and A. Solvber, *Understanding quality in conceptual modeling.* Software IEE Proceedings, 1994. **11**(2): p. 42-49.
169. Cook, T. and D. Campbell, *Quasi-experimentation - Design and Analysis Issues for Field settings.* 1979, Boston, USA: Houghton Mifflin Company.
170. IBM. *SPSS Statistics 20.* Available from: http://www-01.ibm.com/software/analytics/spss/products/statistics/index.html.
171. Santos, E., et al., *Towards a unified metamodel for i\**, in *Second International Conference on Research Challenges in Information Science (RCIS 2008).* 2008.
172. Sandobalín, J., *Un soporte a la evolución de modelos conceptuales en escenarios de evolución,* in *Departamento de Sistemas Informáticos y Computación.* 2014, Universitat Politècnica de València: Valencia, Spain.

Printed in the United States
By Bookmasters